Selling For Dummies, 2nd Edition

Qualifying Your Prospective Clients

When you first meet with prospective clients, you need to qualify them, to see whether your product or service meets your client's needs. To help you remember to focus on your client's needs, remember this creatively spelled acronym — NEADS:

N: What does your prospect have *now?*

E: What does your prospect *enjoy* most about what she has now?

A: What would your prospect *alter* or change about what she has now?

D: Who is the final *decision-maker?*

S: How can you help the prospect find the best *solution* for her needs?

Getting Referrals

The last step in the selling cycle is to get referrals from your prospective clients — whether they ended up closing the sale with you or not. Here's how to do it:

1. **Help the client bring to mind group(s) of people she knows and will probably run into in the near future.**
2. **Write the referrals' names on a 3-x-5 card.**
3. **Ask qualifying questions to find out whether the referrals would really be interested in the product or service you sell.**
4. **Ask for the addresses of the referrals.**
5. **If your client doesn't know the addresses (which she probably won't off the top of her head), turn to a phonebook.**
6. **Ask the client to call and set up the appointment.**
7. **If the client shows hesitation or refuses to call, ask if you can use her name when you call the referral.**

Meeting Prospects for the First Time

When you meet prospective clients — or anyone, for that matter — for the first time, your goal is for your prospects to like and trust you. You can accomplish that by completing the following steps, in this order:

1. **Smile, deep and wide.**
2. **Make eye contact.**
3. **Offer a greeting.**
4. **Shake hands.**
5. **Offer your name and get the prospect's name.**

Remember: Long-term relationships begin in the first ten seconds.

Words to Avoid

Here are words to replace in your selling vocabulary. The word on the left has negative connotations for most people, so replace it with the word on the right, which has positive connotations.

Instead of . . .	Use
Commission	Fee for service
Cost or price	Total amount or investment
Monthly payment	Monthly investment
Contract	Agreement or paperwork
Buy	Own
Sell	Help them acquire or get them involved
Sign	Okay, endorse, approve, or authorize

P9-CEH-233

For Dummies: Bestselling Book Series for Beginners

Selling For Dummies, 2nd Edition

Cheat Sheet

Handling Objections from Your Prospects

An important step in the selling cycle is listening to and responding to your prospect's concerns and objections. Here are the steps to take:

1. **Hear the prospect out.**

   Don't be quick to address every phrase your prospect utters. Give him time; encourage him to tell you the whole story behind his concern. If you don't get the whole story, you won't know what to do or say to change his mind.

2. **Feed the objection back.**

   By rephrasing what your prospect's concerns are, you're in effect asking for even more information. You want to be sure that he's aired it all so that no other concerns crop up after you've handled this one.

3. **Question the objection.**

   This step is where subtlety and tact come into play. Be sure to find out what feeling is behind that objection and reassure your prospect that your product or service is right for him.

4. **Answer the objection.**

   When you're confident that you have the whole story behind his concern, you can answer that concern with confidence.

5. **Confirm the answer.**

   You can confirm your answers simply by completing your answer with a statement such as, "That answers your concern, doesn't it, Bob?" If you don't complete this step, the prospect very likely will raise that objection again.

6. **Change gears with "By the way. . . ."**

   By the way are three of the most useful words in any attempt to persuade or convince another person. Use these words to change gears — to move on to the next topic. Don't just keep talking. Take a conscious, purposeful step back into your presentation.

For Dummies: Bestselling Book Series for Beginners

by Tom Hopkins

Wiley Publishing, Inc.

Selling For Dummies® 2nd Edition

Published by
Wiley Publishing, Inc.
111 River Street
Hoboken, NJ 07030
www.wiley.com

Copyright © 2001 by Wiley Publishing, Inc., Indianapolis, Indiana

Published by Wiley Publishing, Inc., Indianapolis, Indiana

Published simultaneously in Canada

For general information on our other products and services or to obtain technical support, please contact our Customer Care Department within the U.S. at 800-762-2974, outside the U.S. at 317-572-3993, or fax 317-572-4002.

Wiley also publishes its books in a variety of electronic formats. Some content that appears in print may not be available in electronic books.

Library of Congress Cataloging-in-Publication Data:

Library of Congress Control Number: 2001089327

ISBN: 0-7645-5363-1

Printed in the United States of America

15 14 13 12 11 10

2B/RV/QU/QU/IN

About the Author

Tom Hopkins is the epitome of sales success. A millionaire by the time he reached the age of 27, Hopkins now is Chairman of Tom Hopkins International, one of the largest sales-training organizations in the world.

Thirty years ago, Tom Hopkins considered himself a failure. He had dropped out of college after 90 days, and for the next 18 months he carried steel on construction sites to make a living. Believing that there had to be a better way to earn a living, he went into sales — and ran into the worst period of his life. For six months, Hopkins earned an average of $42 a month and slid deeper into debt and despair. Pulling together his last few dollars, he invested in a five-day sales training seminar that turned his life around. In the next six months, Hopkins sold more than $1 million worth of $25,000 homes. At age 21, he won the Los Angeles Sales and Marketing Institute's coveted SAMMY Award and began setting records in sales performance that still stand today.

Because of his unique ability to share his enthusiasm for the profession of selling and the successful selling techniques he developed, Hopkins began giving seminars in 1974. Training as many as 10,000 salespeople a month, he quickly became known as the world's leading sales trainer. Today, he presents approximately 75 seminars a year to over 100,000 people throughout the world.

Tom was a pioneer in producing high-quality audio and video programs for those who could not attend the seminars or who wanted further reinforcement after the seminars. Recognized as the most effective sales-training programs ever produced, they are continually updated and are now being utilized by more than 1 million people.

Tom Hopkins has also written nine other books, including *Sales Prospecting For Dummies* and *Sales Closing For Dummies,* as well as the best-selling *How to Master the Art of Selling,* which has sold over 1.3 million copies in 8 languages and 27 countries.

Hopkins is a member of the National Speakers Association and one of a select few to receive its Council of Peers Award for Excellence. He is often the keynote speaker for annual conventions and is a frequent guest on television and radio talk shows.

Dedication

This book is dedicated to all my teachers and my students. Some of you have been both to me. Thank you for your loyalty and for sharing your successes with me. You are the reason why my life has been so filled with love, laughter, and abundance.

Author's Acknowledgments

I must acknowledge my wonderful wife, Debbie, who has brought so much joy into my life. I'm grateful for your patience and understanding when my life's work takes me away. I'm also grateful for your valuable input into my teaching, and particularly in this book.

I thank Judy Slack of Tom Hopkins International for writing and managing all my material for so long. I also thank Laura Oien, my company President, and Spence Price, CFO. You all work hard to make my life easy, allowing me to do what I do best — teach.

I thank John Kilcullen, CEO of Hungry Minds, Inc., for his enthusiasm for the book and for putting together a team of wonderful, excited people who are dedicated to making *Selling For Dummies* a continued winner for all its readers.

Thanks go to Jill Alexander, Acquisitions Editor, and Nancee Reeves, Production Project Coordinator, for getting this ball rolling and keeping us all on schedule.

Special thanks go to Michael Norton, our Technical Editor. Michael helps people every day to continue to expand the concepts of how we can benefit more and more from the use of the Internet and other technology that is developing all around us.

Last, but certainly not least, I thank Elizabeth Kuball for her countless hours spent reviewing the book's content to ensure that it provided the best information in the most acceptable manner for the reader.

Publisher's Acknowledgments

We're proud of this book; please send us your comments through our online registration form located at www.dummies.com/register.

Some of the people who helped bring this book to market include the following:

Acquisitions, Editorial, and Media Development

Project Editor: Elizabeth Netedu Kuball

Acquisitions Editor: Jill Alexander

Acquisitions Coordinator: Erin Connell

Technical Editor: Michael Norton

Editorial Manager: Pamela Mourouzis

Editorial Administrator: Michelle Hacker

Editorial Assistant: Carol Strickland

Cover Photo: © Bruce Ayres/Stone

Production

Project Coordinator: Nancee Reeves

Layout and Graphics: Jill Piscitelli, Bette Schulte, Erin Zeltner

Proofreaders: John Greenough, Susan Moritz, TECHBOOKS Production Services

Indexer: TECHBOOKS Production Services

Publishing and Editorial for Consumer Dummies

    Diane Graves Steele, Vice President and Publisher, Consumer Dummies
    Joyce Pepple, Acquisitions Director, Consumer Dummies
    Kristin A. Cocks, Product Development Director, Consumer Dummies
    Michael Spring, Vice President and Publisher, Travel
    Brice Gosnell, Associate Publisher, Travel
    Suzanne Jannetta, Editorial Director, Travel

Publishing for Technology Dummies

    Richard Swadley, Vice President and Executive Group Publisher
    Andy Cummings, Vice President and Publisher

Composition Services

    Gerry Fahey, Vice President of Production Services
    Debbie Stailey, Director of Composition Services

Contents at a Glance

Cartoons at a Glance

By Rich Tennant

Table of Contents

Part IV: Growing Your Business 237

Chapter 14: Following Up and Keeping in Touch 239

Chapter 15: Using the Internet to Make More Sales 255

Chapter 16: Planning Your Time Efficiently 263

Introduction

Welcome to *Selling For Dummies.* In this book, I cover more than selling products and services to businesses and consumers. This book is really about people skills. After all, knowing how to get along well with others is a vital skill — one everyone needs to develop as early as possible in life.

To be successful in sales, you must be able to cooperate, have good listening skills, and be willing to put others' needs before your own. With selling skills in your arsenal, you'll have more happiness and contentment in *all* areas of your life, not just in your selling career (although your selling will certainly benefit, too).

About This Book

Selling For Dummies can help you get more happiness and contentment out of your life right now by helping you gain more respect, more money, more recognition for the job you do, more agreement from your friends and family, more control in negotiations, and of course, more sales. Above all, this book is a reference tool. So you don't have to read it from beginning to end. Instead, you can turn to the part of the book that gives you the information you need when you need it. And you can keep coming back to the book over and over throughout your selling career.

As the original dummy in sales, I'm the perfect person to write this book. I started my selling career in real estate at age 19. Real estate may have been a great career choice, but at the time I owned neither a suit nor a car. All I had was a band uniform and a motorcycle. And believe me, selling real estate on a motorcycle wasn't easy; I had to tell the prospective buyers to follow me to the properties and hope they didn't get lost along the way. When they finally came to their senses and realized that this kid couldn't possibly be for real, they'd keep going straight when I'd make a turn. To make things even worse, wearing a woolen band uniform in Southern California's summer heat didn't allow me to present the coolest image, either.

But I stuck it out, because I knew there was big money to be made in the selling business — if I could just find out what the successful people were doing that I wasn't. I learned it all the hard way, through trial and error. Early in my career, a professional, experienced salesperson told me I had to learn how to *close,* meaning, "to close the sale." I responded, "I don't have many clothes." See why I only averaged $42 a month in my first six months selling real estate?

Needless to say, I've come a long way since then, and it thrills me to no end to give you the chance to benefit from the mistakes I made, as well as from the subsequent success I've had. Yes, I've had successes. I achieved my goal of becoming a millionaire by the age of 30, beating my own deadline by nearly three years! At age 27, I was one of the most successful real estate agents in the whole country — a guy who started without a decent suit or a vehicle with four wheels! That just goes to show you that it doesn't matter how much of a dummy you are on this subject when you start — with this book by your side, serving as a reference for all the selling situations you encounter, you'll master the selling, persuasion, and people skills you need to really shine.

Who Needs to Read This Book

I wrote *Selling For Dummies* not only for traditional salespeople who want to discover more about their careers, but also for all people who can use selling skills to change or improve their lives. This book is for you

- ✔ Whether you're beginning a selling career, or you're just looking to brush up your skills.
- ✔ Whether you're unemployed and want a job, or you're employed and want a promotion.
- ✔ Whether you're a teen wanting to impress adults, or you're an adult wanting to succeed at negotiation.
- ✔ Whether you're a teacher searching for better ways to get through to your students, or you're a parent wanting to communicate more effectively with your children.
- ✔ Whether you have an idea that can help others, or you want to improve your personal relationships.

In other words, this book is for *everyone.* People who have attended my seminars tell me about how they used a strategy or technique to get agreement from family members on an important decision. They've told me about using a questioning technique to get their spouses or children to agree to do something they previously tried to put off. And some have used the skills to sell themselves into better jobs. Other students have been able to ask for, and to receive, better service simply because their confidence has skyrocketed. As an added bonus, when my students apply the skills and strategies to personal relationships, many find that those relationships became more rewarding.

How to Use This Book

In this book, I lay out the basics of any selling situation in a series of steps. I give an overview of those steps in Chapter 2, and I devote Part III of the book to covering them in greater detail. You can go through these steps in sequence or you can skim the Table of Contents and locate a title or heading that strikes you as interesting. Read that section first. Then go on to another area that you think will benefit you the most. Keep a pen or highlighter in hand and make notes if you want. Dog-ear the pages. Use this book in whichever way serves you best — after all, it's yours. (*Note:* If you borrowed this book from a friend or from a library, you may want to think twice before making notes in the margins. But you'll probably find that you need to go out and buy your own copy so that you can really use this book to your advantage, as a reference.)

As you get into the material, you'll read about real-life examples of people in various situations where they needed people skills in order to succeed. I tell you the good stories and the bad ones — and you'll remember them when you get into similar situations.

The methods, words, and phrases contained in this book are not put on paper in *Selling For Dummies* just because they sound good to the editors at Hungry Minds. They've been proven successful by me and my 2 million students around the world. If you're truly going to benefit by persuading, cajoling, convincing, or selling someone else on what you have to offer, why not pull out all the stops and master the strategies and tactics that have been proven to work for others (the ones you'll find in this book)?

How This Book Is Organized

Selling For Dummies is organized into six parts, and the parts are divided into chapters. In the following sections, I give you a quick preview of what to expect from each part, so you can turn to the part that interests you most.

Part I: The Art of Selling

In this part, you find out a little about what selling is and what it isn't. I fill you in what selling skills can do for you in all areas of your life, and I give you a quick tour through the seven steps of the selling cycle. I also let you know how important attitude is to the art of selling — letting you know how you can treat selling like a hobby, and get all the satisfaction and success out of it that you get out of the things you do for fun.

Part II: Doing Your Homework

Just as with virtually any pursuit in life, preparation is the key to success in the world of selling. In this part, I cover the steps to preparation — everything from knowing your clients to knowing your products — that will set you apart from average persuaders and help you hear more *yes*es in your life. I also devote a chapter to the ways you can use technology to your advantage in the preparation stage of the game, steering you to some great resources on the Internet that can make your selling life more successful.

Part III: The Anatomy of a Sale

In this part, I give each of the seven steps of the selling cycle its very own chapter. I pack in lots of useful information — including scripts of the right words to say and tips on which words to avoid — in each stage of the process. You'll discover how to find the people you can sell to, how to get an appointment with those people and make a good impression, how to make sure they need what you have, how to give fantastic presentations, how to address customer concerns, how to close the sale, and how to get referrals . . . so you can start the process all over again.

Part IV: Growing Your Business

If your goal is to build a long-term business or to take your career to great heights, this part is for you. This part is where you begin to separate yourself from the average salespeople to become one of the greats. Average salespeople make their presentations, win a few, lose a few, and move on. But the great ones view every presentation as an opportunity to build. So here I give you tips for staying in touch with your clients, making more sales through the help of the Internet, and managing your time wisely so that as your business grows you always have time for your clients. Great salespeople build not only businesses but also *relationships,* because relationships take them farther and bring them a lot more satisfaction in the long run.

Part V: You Can't Win 'Em All

Rejection is a part of life. So you need to expect it, accept it, and get over it. The fact that a prospect rejects your product or service doesn't mean that he has rejected you as a person. But when you're in the world of selling, where rejection is just part of the territory, your self-esteem can easily suffer. So in this part I help you imitate a duck by letting things run off your back like water. I also help you understand how best to use your time and keep focused on the big-picture goals, so the little negativities of life won't bring you down. ***Remember:*** With every no, you're that much closer to a yes.

Part VI: The Part of Tens

These short chapters are packed with quick ideas about selling and persuading that you can read anytime you have a few minutes. They're a great way to get yourself psyched for a presentation or for making calls. And they're good for pumping up your attitude and getting you excited. *Remember:* No one will ever want what you have if you're not excited about it.

Icons Used in This Book

Icons are those little pictures you see in the margins throughout this book, and they're meant to draw your attention to key points that are of help to you along the way. Here's a list of the icons I use and what they signify:

When you see this icon, you can bet that stories from my years of experience in selling and from my students' experiences are near by. And, oh, what stories I have to share. . . .

This icon highlights phrases to say to go beyond the basics and become a true champion at selling. When you see this icon, you'll find examples of exchanges between you and your prospective client, so you can see exactly how a conversation can develop if you know just what to say.

When you see this handshake in the margin, the paragraph next to it contains valuable information on getting one step closer to closing the sale.

Prospecting for clients is a lot like prospecting for gold, because clients are what selling is all about. This shovel and map highlight tips for finding the prospects who will make your selling business a success.

I once had a college professor who told us that he didn't care whether we slept in his class as long as we learned the things he highlighted with red flags — because those were the areas we'd be tested on! So instead of being the typical warning that red flags usually indicate, this icon highlights the crucial pieces of information and skills you need for selling anything. When you see this flag in the margin, take notice. Great selling tips are at hand.

Some things are so important that they bear repeating. So this icon — like a string tied around your finger — is a friendly reminder of information you'll want to commit to memory and use over the long haul.

This icon highlights things you want to avoid and common mistakes salespeople make. An important part of achieving success is simply eliminating the mistakes. And the information marked by this icon helps you do just that.

Where to Go from Here

Glance through the Table of Contents and find the part, chapter, or section that flips your switch. That's the best place to begin.

To benefit the most from the material in this book, do a little self-analysis to see where you're the weakest. I know admitting your faults is tough, even to yourself. But reading the material that covers your weaker areas will bring you the greatest amount of success.

Studies by Tom Hopkins International have shown that most traditional salespeople lack qualification skills. They waste a lot of time presenting to people who can't truly make decisions on what they're selling. If you're in traditional sales and you aren't sure whether qualification is your weakness, Chapter 9 may be a great place to start.

The most successful people in life are those who continue to grow. The fact that you're reading these words now puts you into that realm — because it isn't how much you know that counts, but how much you can discover *after* you "know it all."

Congratulations for believing in yourself, in your ability to change for the better, in your ability to improve your lifestyle, *and* in your ability to improve the lives of the people you help with this book's many tips on the art of selling. I wish you greatness!

Part I
The Art of Selling

The 5th Wave — By Rich Tennant

"FIRST HARRY SOLD BOWLING BALLS, SO HE TOOK ME BOWLING. THEN HE SOLD GOLF CLUBS, SO WE TOOK UP GOLF. NOW HE'S SELLING SURGICAL INSTRUMENTS, AND FRANKLY I HAVEN'T HAD A FULL NIGHT'S SLEEP SINCE."

In this part . . .

Here you find out what the seven steps of selling are and how to put them to work for you. I also fill you in on the importance of attitude in the world of selling — letting you know how you can treat selling with the same joy that you treat your hobbies and pastimes. Whether you're just starting out in sales or you've been at it since the beginning of time, this part offers great information to keep you upbeat and moving forward.

Chapter 1

You Don't Need a Plaid Sport Coat

Selling is everywhere around you, and most people (even those who aren't pros) do it every day, in one form or another. In fact, selling affects every waking moment of your day. So in this chapter, I let you know what exactly this thing called *selling* is, how it's done, and how you can use selling skills to make your life and your career better.

What Selling Is

In the strictest sense of the word, *selling* is the process of moving goods and services from the hands of those who produce them into the hands of those who will benefit most from their use. Selling involves persuasive skills on the part of the person doing the talking. It's supported by print, audio, and video messages that sell either the particular item or the brand name as being something the customer would want to have.

It's been said that nothing ever happens unless someone sells something to someone else. Without selling, products that have been manufactured would sit in warehouses for eternity, people working for those manufacturers would become unemployed, transportation and freight services wouldn't be needed, and we would all be living isolated little lives, striving to eke out livings from whatever bit of land we owned. Or would we even own the land if no one were there to sell it to us? Think about it.

The selling triangle

When I give seminars about mastering the fundamentals of selling, I use a triangle with equal sides, like the one below, to illustrate the three main elements of selling. On one side is product knowledge, which I cover in Chapter 5. On the other side are selling tactics and strategies, which I cover in Part III. And on the base of the triangle are attitude, enthusiasm, and goals, which I cover in Part V.

The three sides of the selling triangle are equally important. If product knowledge were all that mattered, then technical designers, manufacturers, or assemblers of products would make the best salespeople. Of course, these folks often know the product quite literally from the inside out. But until they are trained in selling skills and understand how much of a role attitude plays in sales, their sales approach is often 99 percent description of product and 1 percent relation of the product to the needs of the individual clients — and that doesn't usually result in a sale.

On the other hand, great selling skills without product knowledge and enthusiasm won't get you far either. Even if you're comfortable talking with practically anyone, and you've invested a tremendous amount of time mastering the best words for creating positive pictures in the minds of your prospects, if you don't have a clear picture in your own mind of what your product, service, or idea will do for your customers, how can you paint the right pictures in someone else's mind?

And if you're excited about selling, but you have little knowledge or experience with selling tactics and strategies, your enthusiasm will open the doors a crack. But you'll get your fingers slammed when you start pushing product (because *pushing product* isn't how you sell anything).

Remember: A professional who has failed to develop any one side of the triangle is failing to reach his full potential and letting down clients, who expect to work with a competent person. Do your best to develop all three areas of your selling life, and you'll reap the rewards.

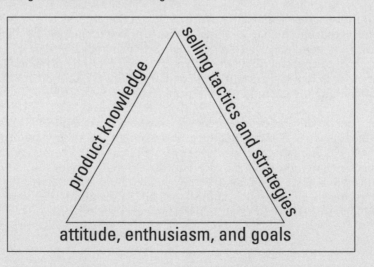

Look around you right now. You can probably spot hundreds, if not thousands, of things that were sold in order to get where they are right now. Even if you're totally naked, sitting in the woods, you had to be involved in some sort of selling process to have this book with you. If you choose to ignore material possessions, take stock of yourself internally. What do you believe? Why do you believe what you do? Did someone — like your parents or your peers — sell you a set of values as you were growing up? Did your teachers persuade you to believe, through demonstration, that 2 + 2 = 4? Or did you figure that one out on your own? Odds are, whether you're living in a material world or you've forsaken nearly all possessions, you've been involved in selling one way or another.

The preceding paragraph should have persuaded you to at least look at selling a bit differently than you have in the past. It was done, too, without pushing facts and figures on you. Good selling isn't pushing; it's gently pulling with questions and getting people to think a bit differently than they have before.

How Selling Is Done

Although the definition of selling may be fairly straightforward, the approaches to selling are virtually endless. In this section, I cover some of the main ways that products and services are sold today and give you some important tips for using them.

Telemarketing

With a telephone, salespeople have the potential to reach nearly any other person on the planet. And what you say when your prospective client answers the phone, if he answers at all, is critical. In some industries, you actually try to sell the product on the first call (referred to as a *one-time close*). In other industries, you're selling interest — enough interest that the person to whom you speak gets out of his home and down to your store or lets you come visit him in his home or place of business. Either way, you're selling what your business is all about, leaving the person on the other end with a very distinct impression of you and your company — good or bad.

Although telemarketing is still a thriving method for reaching potential clients, many telemarketers are finding it more and more difficult to reach a real person when they place their calls. If you plan to use this method of approach, be prepared to leave curiosity-building messages on voice mail or answering machines in order to make a connection with potential clients. More and more people are screening their calls with caller ID features and voice mail than ever before. So unless you have your number listed in the phone book as "Sweepstakes Winner Announcement," plan on reaching a lot of answering devices. If you make a call and hear a real person say "Hello" on the other end of the line, you almost have cause for rejoicing — and you'll have to be just as prepared for that happening.

Despite the difficulty telemarketers often have in getting through to people who are willing to listen, telemarketing has become widely accepted and recognized as a true sales profession. It requires tact, training, and the ability to articulate a message in a very brief amount of time, as well as the skill of helping others recognize you as a warm, caring individual who has their needs at heart. Many companies across many industries are quickly realizing that gifted telemarketers can help bring a product or service to market in a much more efficient and cost-effective manner than ever before.

Direct mail

Every piece of mail you receive, whether it's a letter of solicitation, a coupon, or a catalog is devised for a single purpose — to sell you something. Companies play the odds that enough people will stop long enough to look at and actually order their products before the direct mail hits the trash.

Believe it or not, a 1 percent response rate for direct mail is considered average. That means only 1 out of 100 catalogs may actually have an order placed from it. Ninety-nine of those catalogs hit the round file without ever generating a penny for the company that sent it out. Plus, each of those catalogs may cost a good bit to produce and distribute, especially if they contain a lot of full-color photos. So if that's the case, why is direct mail so prevalent? The reason is simple: When you place an order from a company, you'll probably order something else from that company in the future. You have become a customer, and good companies work very hard to keep you coming back for more.

E-Mail

Many companies are doing less telemarketing and direct-mail selling and are instead sending more e-mail solicitations. Why? Because even though direct mail allows to you get your message to the proper address, that doesn't necessarily mean it will make it into the appropriate hands. Well-intentioned secretaries, receptionists, spouses, or children often take the liberty of tossing what they deem "junk mail" addressed to the recipient. If you send your message via e-mail, however, you're more likely to get it directly to the person you want to reach.

The computer revolution — and your role in it

If you plan to have a successful career in sales, you need to become somewhat computer-savvy. Even if you're still selling something as simple as buggy whips, you need to track your client contacts in the most efficient manner possible in order to maximize your sales. You also need to have access to the phenomenal volume and quality of information available on the Internet. Not becoming familiar with the basics of computers and what they can do for you is like locking yourself outside your place of business with nothing more than a business card.

Understanding the basics of today's technology is also crucial so you can converse with clients who are in tune with it. Nothing ruins your credibility faster than pulling out your 3-x-5-inch index cards to jot down a client's contact information when she's using the latest handheld device or Internet-connected phone. Take advantage of contact management software or sales force automation (SFA), both of which allow you to maintain customer lists, prospect information, schedules, contact information, and a variety of other sales-related tasks that salespeople of days gone by used to store in shoeboxes under their desks. I hear from my students that ACT! and Goldmine are both excellent programs, although I have not had experience with them myself. Many companies, such as Siebel.com are also offering online contact management software on a subscription basis. Talk with others in your particular field to determine which software has the features you will benefit from the most. Or see if your company has made arrangements to use a certain program in-house, across the board for everyone.

So far, business e-mail appears to be deemed personal territory. Secretaries and receptionists may receive copies of e-mails, but they aren't likely to delete e-mail messages from their bosses' computers. Home e-mail, on the other hand, may not be thought of as so sacred, but it still has a good chance of being seen by the person you want to reach.

To make sure that your intended recipient receives the message you're sending, I suggest putting the recipient's name in the subject line (for example, "Personal Message for John Doe").

If you use e-mail as a way of connecting with prospective clients, you can include your message in the body of the e-mail itself or you can send it in the form of an attachment that looks like one of your ads or printed pieces or that contains a link to your Web site. Another alternative may be to include an attached PowerPoint slide presentation customized just for the potential client you're targeting.

E-mail, when used properly, is an extraordinary vehicle for getting your message out. However, you need to be aware of the laws governing the use of e-mail. Sending follow-up e-mails or proposals and presentation materials is fine, but if you're planning to use e-mail as part of a larger sales campaign (similar to the way you would use direct mail), you must first get the permission of the recipient of the message, or what is commonly referred to as an *opt-in e-mail list*. I discuss e-mail lists in more depth in Chapter 7.

The Internet

Imagine that you're a customer, and you really, really want a new widget in a razzle-dazzle raspberry color. If you want to see it right away, to be sure the color matches or complements your other widgets, what's the best solution? You can place a call to a physical widget manufacturer and wait for a salesperson to contact you and then send you a brochure or catalog. Or you can visit the manufacturer's Web site and, within a few minutes, see the actual widget in all its razzle-dazzleness. As a busy customer, what's the best use of your time? To go online and visit the Web site, of course. This way, you haven't wasted your time or the time of the salesperson if it turns out that the color wasn't what you had in mind.

Wouldn't your customers want to take advantage of the same opportunity? Yes, and if you don't offer your customers that opportunity, your competitors probably will.

Efficiency is the name of the game when it comes to technology. And you have to take advantage of every method possible to increase your efficiency while remaining easily accessible to your client base. The key is not to invest so much time in mastering the technology that you have no time remaining to do what you're paid for — and that is to sell products and services.

The Internet is like the library. You can find just about any piece of information you want there — and so can your potential customers. Not too many people will invest a lot of time trotting down to their local library to look up information. They will, however, click on over to the Internet and search for information on your product or service and those of your competition.

The people you approach to do business will likely have much more knowledge about your product or service today than they have at any other time in history. So you'd better know your product or service better than they do (see Chapter 5 for more on this important topic). Look at the same resource information that your customers see. In fact, add to your repertoire a question about where they did their research on your product. Find out where your customers are going for information, and if you have any impact on what's put there, make sure it's positive.

I'd like to buy the world a Coke . . .

You know that radio and TV commercials sell you, but you may not realize how deeply their advertising campaigns register in your mind. For example, you may not drink Coca-Cola, but I bet if you hear the music from one of its current commercials you can probably hum right along. Better yet for the advertisers, you can probably picture in your mind the million-dollar graphics display they put together with that music when you saw the ad on primetime TV last night. Even if you don't buy Coca-Cola, if someone else asked you to stop by the store and pick up a six-pack of Coke for him, how long would it take you to find it on the shelf? Not very long. And why is that? Partly because Coca-Cola has premium shelf space in most supermarkets, but mainly because you know exactly what Coca-Cola's product packaging looks like.

With the use of phenomenal technology and extremely creative art directors, some of today's TV and radio commercials are more fun to watch and listen to than the actual programs. You may not be interested in the product, but you can probably describe a company's latest commercial, if it caught your attention. Advertising is an important part of selling products and services. For more information, turn to *Advertising For Dummies*, by Gary Dahl (published by Hungry Minds, Inc.).

Person-to-person

On an average day, most sales are concluded in a face-to-face fashion. Breakfast, lunch, and dinner are purchased in person at favorite restaurants. People physically register into hotels or check in at airport counters. Retail stores abound with sales opportunities, and millions of salespeople sit across a desk, conference table, or kitchen table turning prospects into clients. Person-to-person selling is the single largest type of selling that is conducted worldwide. Because of this, much of the content in the balance of this book is aimed at person-to-person selling.

The fun part about person-to-person selling is that you can watch the prospects' body language and speak with yours. You can hand them information. Have them handle your product or experience the service firsthand. Involve all their senses. Have them taste, touch, smell, hear, and see just how cool your widget is. (I cover specific methods for doing this in Chapter 10.)

What Selling Skills Can Do for You

Selling skills can do for you what a way with words did for Cyrano de Bergerac and William Shakespeare. They can do for you what sex appeal did for Marilyn Monroe. They can do for you what powerful communication skills did for historical greats like Abraham Lincoln, Franklin D. Roosevelt, and Martin Luther King, Jr. Selling skills can make or break you in whatever endeavor you choose. They can mean the difference between getting the promotion, job, or girl or guy of your dreams, or having to settle for less.

If you're good at selling, you probably earn a satisfactory income and have rewarding personal relationships. If you're not completely satisfied with your income level or with the quality of your personal relationships, make the development of selling skills a priority and you'll reap the rewards.

Having selling skills is like having an inside track on what the next batch of winning lottery numbers will be. All you have to do is invest a bit of your time and effort to understand and apply these tried-and-true, proven-effective skills to your everyday life. Before you know it, they'll be such a natural part of you that no one, including yourself, will even recognize them as selling skills. People around you will just see you as a really nice, competent person instead of the stereotypical, cigar-chomping, back-slapping, plaid-coated, hand-mashing, used-car salesman that most people associate with selling. And, believe me, you'll then be in the class of people who make the world go 'round.

Salespeople are everywhere — even where you least expect them

The person who isn't selling isn't living. Think about that: At some point nearly every day, you're involved in a selling situation of some sort. You may call it by a different name or not even recognize it as an act of selling but, all the same, selling it is. Here's just a short list of the people who sell things, and whose "products" you buy:

✔ **Actors and actresses:** If you've ever watched a TV show, movie, or play and gotten caught up in the story, you've been a part of a selling situation. The actress has given a believable performance — she's sold you on her portrayal of a character.

✔ **Waiters and waitresses:** The wise waiter gives you choices of drinks, appetizers, meals, and desserts. He doesn't just ask to take your order. Why? Because when he employs a bit of salesmanship, he's almost guaranteed to receive a higher tip.

✔ **Doctors:** Doctors get tremendous rewards when they know — and use — selling skills. Not only is your doctor better prepared to convince you to follow her professional advice, she's also building her practice because you're so happy with her advice that you tell your friends and family how great your doctor is, thus sending her referral business.

✔ **Lawyers:** Lawyers need selling skills in every aspect of their profession. Lawyers have to sell not only to get business, but also to persuade judges and juries that their clients are in the right.

✔ **Politicians:** How does the public develop its expectations about political candidates? How do politicians get elected? They persuade the most people that, if they're elected, they can and will do the job the voters want done.

✔ **Parents:** Whether by words or example, parents constantly sell their children values and beliefs. They convince or persuade their kids on what to wear or eat, how to act, who to have as friends, how to be a friend, and thousands of other things children need to learn in order to grow into happy, well-adjusted adults.

✔ **Kids:** Few children can go into a store and resist the things shopkeepers purposefully place on the lower shelves to tempt the young. (Considerate of those shopkeepers, isn't it?) Get ready, though. You are about to observe master sellers at work. Simply notice what kids say and how they act when they try to persuade Mom or Dad to get them what they want. It's selling at its best.

✔ **Spouses-to-be:** If you get married someday, you will put forth one of the most important sales presentations of your life in persuading your significant other of the value of spending the rest of his or her life with you. And if you're already married, the trick is to keep persuading your significant other to stay with you.

✔ **Friends:** If your friends like a movie, they'll probably want to tell you about it — and sell you on going to see it yourself. Your friends may recommend a place to eat or persuade you to go to concerts or sporting events with them. All of these are examples of selling — but they're also examples of ways your friends build the relationships they have with you. The more memories you share, the closer you'll continue to be — and so it is with the art of selling.

You're not immune from selling situations in your daily life — even if you don't come into contact with professional salespeople — and you may not even be aware that selling has occurred. We had a saying in our household when my children were young: "You've got to sell to survive." If this list hasn't convinced you of that, nothing will. (And if it has, then I've sold you on my ideas.)

Chapter 2

The Seven-Step Selling Cycle

I like to think of selling as a cycle because, if it's done properly, the last step in the cycle will lead you back to the first. Your new, happy client will give you the names of other people he feels would benefit from your product or service, and then you have your next lead or prospect to work with.

I also like the fact that selling breaks down neatly into seven steps. Everyone can remember seven things, can't they? Committing to memory these seven steps is no more difficult than memorizing the seven digits in your telephone number.

The seven steps I cover here are an overview of what you'll find in the Chapters in Part III. Each step is equally valuable to you. Rarely will you be able to skip a step and still make the sale. Each step plays a critical role and, if done properly, will lead you to the next step in a natural, flowing manner.

Step #1: Prospecting

Prospecting means finding the right potential buyer for what you're selling. When considering your product or service, ask yourself, "Who would benefit most from this?" If the end user is a corporation, you need to make contacts within corporations. Usually, a purchasing agent will be assigned to make buying decisions on behalf of the company, so you need to find a way to get in touch with that person. If your end user is a family with school-aged children, you need to go where families are (for example, soccer games, grocery stores, dance classes, the park, and so on). Or acquire a list from a credible source (turn to Chapter 7 for more information) and start contacting those prospects at home.

To make an informed decision about which prospects to approach, you need to find out some information about the people or companies you've chosen as possibilities. Do some research about any prospective client company at the local library or online. This legwork is sort of a prequalification step in prospecting. You'll do even more qualification when you meet a prospective client — but why waste time on an appointment with a company or person who wouldn't have a need for your offering? Prequalifying helps you just like market research helps companies determine their best target markets. In fact, one of the best places to begin your research in finding the most likely candidates for your product or service is your company's marketing department. The marketing department has done research during the product development stage to determine what people want in the product or service you sell. Study their results and you'll get a handle on where to begin.

If your company does advertising to promote your products, you will likely receive *leads* — names of people who called or otherwise contacted the company for more information about the product. Treat any client-generated contact like gold! What better person to contact than one who has called you for information first!

Other valuable assets are your friends, relatives, and business acquaintances. Tell them what type of product or service you're selling. See what suggestions they come up with. Who knows, one of them just may know people at one of your prospect companies who would be happy to talk with you. If there's something good going on, people are always willing to share their stories with others.

A word of advice here that applies to all selling situations: Never begin any selling cycle until you've taken a few moments to put yourself in the shoes of the other person. Take yourself out of the picture and look at the entire situation through the eyes of the buyer. Mentally put yourself in their shoes and think about what would motivate *you* to invest your valuable time reading a letter about your product or taking a salesperson's call. If you can't come up with solid answers, you may not have enough information about your product to even be selling it in the first place. Or, you may not know enough about your potential audience to sell to them. If that's the case, it's back to the books for you. Study more about both areas until you're comfortable with being in that person's shoes. In other words, don't go out prospecting until you have something of value to share with your prospects — something that's worth their while to investigate and, hopefully, purchase.

You may need to take a somewhat unusual approach to get noticed by your prospects or to bring about a positive response. Some ideas my students have used include:

- ✔ **Enclosing a photograph of your warm, smiling, professional self.** If your goal is to arrange to meet with these people in their home, they'll need to make some sort of connection with you other than seeing your John Hancock on a cover letter.

- ✔ **Enclosing a tasteful comic about the situation your potential clients find themselves in without your product or service.** Your prospect will recognize the relief or benefit the product provides much sooner.

- ✔ **Adding a clever quote or anecdote to the bottom of your cover letter.** You can find books that have quotes for nearly any occasion. Check out Uinspire.com (`www.uinspire.com`) to find just the right quote online. Taking a few moments to find this kind of attention-getter can make your letter stand out from the rest.

- ✔ **Using letters in place of numbers for your telephone number, so it's easier to remember.** If your telephone number is 344-6279 and your name is Mary, you can use the alphabet on the telephone pad to ask your prospects to call 344-MARY. If your name is Agamemnon, this approach won't work for you.

These ideas may be a bit gimmicky if you're selling corporate jets, but they've worked for some of my students who were marketing everyday products and services to the average consumer. The idea is to open your creative mind to unusual ways of reaching people and capturing their attention.

To ensure that your name gets in front of the prospective client more than once, send a thank-you note the day you make your first contact with them. Thank-you notes always get read — and if the prospect hasn't had the time to review your letter and/or brochure when he receives your thank-you note, don't you think he'll go looking for your name among the stacks of other mail he's received? You'll have made a positive first impression that will very likely bring you closer to getting an appointment.

Step #2: Original Contact

You've found the people. Now you actually get to meet them. To persuade another person to give you their valuable time, you need to offer something of value in return. To gain entrance to someone's home, you need to offer a free estimate or gift in exchange for his opinion on the demonstration of your product. With a business-to-business appointment, getting an appointment may be a bit easier because you'll often be working with a purchasing agent whose job it is to meet with and gather information from people like you. If you offer anything remotely like a product her company may use, it's her duty to investigate what you have to offer.

Your goal is to make agreeing to an appointment as easy as possible. I strongly recommend giving your prospect two options with regard to dates and times. Say something like, "I have an appointment opening on Tuesday at 9:30 a.m., or would Wednesday at 3:00 p.m. be better for you?" This makes the prospect look at her calendar and consider the open blocks of time in her schedule. Whereas, if you just say, "When can we get together?" she's likely to look at how busy she is and hesitate to commit.

When you get a commitment, confirm all the details such as where the meeting will take place — and get directions if you haven't been there before. Asking for directions is often smart even if you *have* been there, just in case the street in front of the prospect's home or building is under construction and you have to take an unusual route. Also, get a commitment as to who will be present. If you sell products to consumers and you know you'll need to have the agreement of both spouses, for example, you need to confirm that they'll both be present. If you're talking with a young, single person, he may decide to have a parent or other adult present to help him make his decision.

You've passed the first hurdle and been invited to visit with a potential client. Be sure to appear at ease so your prospect is comfortable with you. After all, the number one need of people is the need to be comfortable. If you're uncomfortable, chances are good that unless you're a really good actor, your discomfort will show — and it may make your prospect uncomfortable, too.

Any tension at this point in the selling cycle will take a bit of doing on both sides to overcome. If you don't get past the tension, you can end up turning a potential win-win into a lose-lose situation. You won't make the sale, and the potential client will miss out on having your talents and fantastic product to benefit from.

First and foremost, you need to consider what you look like to your prospect. We all know the old saying, "You never get a second chance to make a good first impression." When in doubt about what to wear to an appointment, err on the side of conservatism. Skip the band uniform. You want to look your best. But also remember to be comfortable. If your new shoes are too tight or they squeak, you'll be conscious of that fact and you won't be able to put all your concentration into the visit.

In a prospective client's mind, any shabbiness in your appearance translates into shabbiness in work habits.

Think twice before you wear your favorite cologne or perfume. Subtlety is the motto here. You never know if you'll meet someone who is allergic to your added scents. If the potential client opens the window, goes into a sneezing frenzy, or just plain keels over, you went a bit heavy on the fragrance — and you probably lost the sale.

A special concern for women is the jewelry they wear to an appointment. If it's attractive, that's great. But if it could be considered distracting, like a diamond tiara, that's bad. You don't want to be remembered as "that woman we talked with who had those humongous earrings." You want them to remember your competence and professionalism.

Because this is a business situation, be prepared to shake hands, make eye contact, and build rapport. Building rapport is the getting-to-know-you stage that comes with any new contact. You must immediately begin building trust. People buy from people they like and trust. They must feel your trustworthiness as early as possible in the contact you make.

Step #3: Qualification

When you finally sit down with your prospect, you need to find out if she's qualified to be your client of choice. In selling, *qualifying* your prospects means finding out who they are, what they do, what they have, and what they need.

You don't have to take on every client who qualifies for your product or service. If Mr. Big Bucks could become your biggest client, you'll likely be investing a large amount of your time with him. If you can't stand the guy after your first meeting, consider how well you'll really serve his needs and whether someone else may be better suited to the stress this client could cause you.

If you've done your homework and looked up information about the prospect, you'll know what questions to ask. You'll eventually have to know a lot of information about the prospect, providing you get the account, so if you're truly convinced this is a good match for you, you may as well ask questions now. The more specific your questions, the more impressed your potential client will be with your expertise. Asking pertinent questions now shows that you're interested in more than just a closed sale and that you're looking into the future as a valued business partner with your client.

Your prospects will be qualifying you, too. So be aware of what you're showing them. Most clients are looking for people who are dependable, loyal, trustworthy, intelligent, competent, and even a little fun. Do your prospects see that when they look at you? If you need to communicate a trait that's difficult to see, short of wearing your Scout uniform, figure out how you can bring those images to mind in the answers you give to their questions and the information you offer in your discussion of their needs.

The goal of your qualification discussion is to determine how well suited your product or service is to their situation. Ask questions to get them talking about what they have now, how it's not fulfilling their current needs, and how much of a budget they have for making an improvement. These questions are the same whether you're selling to a business or an individual consumer.

Step #4: Presentation

Your presentation of your product, service, or idea requires the most preparation. In your preparation, practice your answers to common questions with a family member or close friend. Make a list of the benefits you think are your strongest persuaders in placing your product. Then try to figure out a way to work those points into responses to the common questions.

For example, suppose you're selling a brand-new service where busy people can dial up a number to hear all of this week's grocery sale items at their favorite store. Then they can speak into the phone the quantity they'd like of each item (whether on sale or not) and have the items delivered to their homes. Because the service is new, you don't have a track record of success to brag about. So here's where you may start:

PROSPECT: Well, it sounds like a good idea, but you haven't proven it to be successful. I'd hate to be a guinea pig and end up having to do my shopping anyway because it didn't work out.

SALESPERSON: Because this is a new service, we're paying special attention to the orders that come in. In fact, we have two people who listen to the recording of each call to confirm that your verbal request is what shows up on our shopping list. One of them will give you a quick call to let you know your list was received in good order and to arrange the best delivery time for you.

The real issue is not that the service is new, but that the client doesn't feel he would have the time to shop if the service didn't end up working out. By showing that you have backup systems in place to ensure the order is handled properly, you've answered the quality control question that triggered the prospect's "guinea pig" reference.

To demonstrate personal dependability, tell the prospective client an anecdote from another client situation or even from an outside activity. If you were an Eagle Scout as a kid, that says a lot about you, doesn't it? Even if you didn't make Eagle but were active in scouting for a number of years, that presents a positive image, one that says you stick to things and honor your commitments. Find a way to bring up those kinds of activities.

Your clients buy more than your product — they buy you.

Amazing things can happen during the rapport-establishing phase of a meeting. I know of someone who was in a meeting and noticed a small golf figurine on the prospective client's desk. She asked if the decision-maker liked to play golf — a fairly general and safe question. The guy gave her a brief answer that didn't carry the conversation too far in that direction. Then she remembered a brand-new type of golf club that her husband had talked about. She asked her prospect if he had ever heard of these new clubs and explained briefly why she was asking. Because her husband was so crazy about them, she wanted to get him a set for his upcoming birthday. It just so happened that the prospect's son was a cofounder of the company that developed and marketed those particular clubs. Suddenly, this prospective client was very interested in hearing the salesperson's husband's thoughts on the clubs, and a deeper level of rapport was established.

Step #5: Addressing Concerns

How do you handle any negative comments or qualifications that your prospect may raise during or after your presentation? Answer in simple, unemotional terms, and have recommendations in mind. For example, if your product is only available in certain colors, and none of them quite fit the décor of your prospect's office, be prepared to recommend the least offensive color suggestion. In fact, when you get around to discussing the colors, suggest something like this: "Based on your color scheme, the sunrise blue would best complement your décor." That way, you've already seen and addressed the objection before the prospect brought it up.

If you sidestep obstacles during your presentation, there's a good chance they'll come back to haunt you if you do get the sale. Find a way to bring up and elaborate on any concerns about fulfilling the needs of the buyer as early in the presentation as is appropriate. Don't let unfulfilled expectations bring your long-term relationship with a potential client to a bitter end. Cover all her concerns and make sure that she understands how those concerns will be handled — and that she's comfortable with it.

The most common concern you'll encounter in your entire selling career is the good old standby stall: "I want to think it over." When someone says he wants to think it over, that means he's interested. And if he's interested, you need to strike while the iron is hot. Find out exactly what it is he wants to think over. Again, in the majority of the cases, you'll find that it's the money involved. Surprise, surprise! Everyone wants a bargain. Unless your product or service is severely underpriced most of your potential clients will want to bargain or will hesitate to see if you'll offer to include something else just to get them to buy. I cover this in more detail in Chapters 11 and 12.

Step #6: Closing the Sale

If you've researched your prospect properly, given yourself enough valuable preparation time, and handled all the previous steps in a professional manner, you'll likely close the sale. Closing should follow naturally and smoothly after you address your prospect's concerns. But if your prospect doesn't automatically pick up a pen to approve your paperwork or write a check, don't panic. You don't have to turn into Joe Typical Salesperson and apply pressure to get what you want. Getting your prospect's business can be as simple as saying, "How soon do we start?" At this point, if you're confident about being able to give her what she needs, you should begin taking verbal ownership of your future business relationship with assumptive statements and questions.

You may also want to use analogies, quotes from famous people, or today's news to persuade people to go ahead and do it today. Use similar-situation stories about other clients who got involved with your product or service and are happy they did. Be prepared to show the potential client how she can afford this product or service if that's her area of hesitation. Often, that's just a matter of doing the math to show her how affordable the item is compared to the benefits she'll receive.

When it comes time to close, you've hopefully reduced any sales resistance this person had early on and increased her level of sales acceptance so that it's just a matter of agreeing on the details of startup or delivery dates and/or financing arrangements. I cover many methods of getting that pen to paper in Chapter 12.

Step #7: Getting Referrals

After you close the sale with your client, take a moment to ask for referrals. This can be as simple as asking, "Because you're so happy with this decision today, would you mind if I ask you for the names of other people you know who may also be interested in learning about this product?" If the client has mentioned other family members in the area, ask, "Who in your family would also enjoy the benefits of our fine lawn service?" Or, "Which of your neighbors takes the most pride in their yard?"

In a corporate situation, ask about other departments within the company who may need your same service. Then ask about other office locations that the same company has. Finally, ask about associates of the purchasing agent who may work at noncompeting companies.

Always ask for an introduction to the new party. If the client seems uncomfortable with that, at least get a quick letter of introduction that you may use when you contact the person.

If for some reason you and the prospective client find that this isn't the best time to go forward with the sale, instead of just walking out the door and saying goodbye, make the contact a part of your network of people who can help you find *more* people who may benefit from your product or service. For example, another department in your prospect's company may have people who could benefit from your product or service. Or the prospect may know of other companies needing your product. Don't ever just walk away from an opportunity to network. And immediately upon leaving the premises, drop a thank-you note in the mail to the person. This will guarantee that your discussion will stay fresh in his mind for at least a few days. During that time, the right lead for you may come his way, and if you've left a good impression with your thank-you note, he'll be more likely to give you the referral.

Chapter 3

Making Selling Your Hobby: It's All in the Attitude

*T*he main factor that separates the top five percent of us in sales from those who struggle to accomplish their goals is elementary (you thought I was going to say, "my dear Watson," didn't you?). Highly successful salespeople actually *enjoy* the crazy business of sales. To champion salespeople, selling isn't a job. Instead, champion salespeople have discovered how to turn their job (selling) into a hobby.

When champion salespeople prospect for new clients, go to appointments, have a chance to visit, and ask for sales, they are doing what they love to do. It just so happens that champions get paid very well for their hobbies. If you're struggling with your ability to sell *and* with finding the desire to make it to the top, then be glad that you and I are having this bookside chat, because I've just given you the key to excelling in sales: *Turn your job into a hobby.* Before you know it, your new hobby will be a way of life. You will live and breathe selling — all to your advantage.

The more involved you get with selling, the more selling you observe going on around you in all areas of your life. When you truly *study* selling, you see that selling pervades every communication you have with others; and, on a purely business level, you notice and compare the selling efforts of others to your own. The fun part is that people never know what you're up to. You get to make all the mental notes you want, and they get to be your teachers. The best opportunity for discovery often (if not usually) occurs in an informal, non-selling atmosphere. In other words, get used to a new sensation. In times and situations that you may not see as sales situations per se, a realization will creep right up on you and whisper, "Hey, there's selling going on here. You should be taking notes."

In this chapter, I show you the way people usually approach their hobbies and help you find a way to approach selling in the same way. I show you how you can challenge yourself throughout your lifetime to discover new things and forge new trails. And I give you an idea of what to expect along the way. Attitude and enthusiasm are a huge part of success — in sales or in life — and in this chapter I let you know about both so that you can put them to work for you.

Taking a Long, Hard Look at Your Job Satisfaction

You've probably heard the advice to "never mix business with pleasure." Whoever wrote that maxim must not have had work that was much fun to do — and the person certainly wasn't a champion salesperson. When you make selling your hobby, you blur the distinction between what you do to live and what you live to do. When you get the hang of making your work your hobby, you *always* mix business with pleasure.

When you don't enjoy what you do to earn money, you make a draining trade-off — interminably long hours for incalculably short vacations. My question to you is this: As short as life is, are those 2 fun-filled weeks every summer worth the 50 weeks of drudgery you have to go through to earn them? I certainly hope they are. After all, you're on this earth for such a short time that you may as well do something you enjoy.

If you're in sales, you can find ways to enjoy what you're already doing. If you discover and practice the communication skills that are a part of selling, your life is guaranteed to be more interesting. And anything that you're interested in has to include at least a little fun or it won't hold your interest.

Do you ever feel guilty about taking time away from your job when you have fun on vacation? If you answer "yes" to that question, you need to take a long, hard look at what you do for a living and how much satisfaction it's leaving you with. You may even want to seek professional career advice. Don't do a job just because it provides for you and your family. Consider what kind of life you're providing if every day you leave the house unhappy to go slogging again through the trenches and you can't even enjoy the little bit of vacation time you take because you're worried about what will lie in wait for you upon your return. Too many people work twice as hard the weeks before and after a vacation. If you work double time for those two weeks, you really haven't taken a vacation, have you? The company has received 52 weeks of work from you, and you may have worked 2 extra weeks without compensation.

ANECDOTE

Love the one you're with . . .

A merging of passion and profession has occurred in my life with selling. For me, selling began as a career opportunity that would fulfill a need — the need to make money. When I failed miserably at first, I knew I needed help, and I started a journey of study. I knew that some people made huge incomes in sales, so I assumed that they must have known something I'd not yet discovered.

It was at that point that I chose to turn selling into my hobby. When I started to educate myself — by watching everyday people and looking for little nuances of selling that worked for them, and by reading up on the subject — I also started making a lot of money. Believe me when I say that, at first, money was my motivation for keeping up my selling hobby. But since then I've managed to transform my job-turned-hobby into something much more: It has become a way of life. Today, I live and breathe selling. I've built my business in such a way that I enjoy what I do for a living. I don't "work" anymore, if *work* means "doing some particular thing when you'd rather be doing something else." Selling now pervades every communication I have with others, and I thoroughly enjoy my life these days.

If you're in a job you don't like in order to earn a living, stop a moment and analyze what's going on. Why don't you like what you're doing? Chances are pretty good that it's because you're not growing, achieving, or having fun. The reasons behind those feelings usually have something to do with how competent you are in your field. If you're not really any good at what you do, it's no wonder your life's no fun.

If this description fits your life, you have two ways out: You can either change what you do to something that is more fun, or you can get better at what you already do in order to make it more fun. That's the great thing about living today: You have choices. No one is going to hold a gun to your head and tell you that you have to have this career and none other. If you aren't happy with what you've got, thousands of other choices are available to you. You have no excuse for staying in a job you don't thoroughly enjoy, but it's up to you to do something about it.

Wouldn't it be much more fun to take each day and enjoy it to its fullest, looking forward to getting up every morning, bright-eyed and bushy-tailed, vibrant with anticipation for what the day will bring? Wouldn't it be better to enjoy your workdays as much as you enjoy your free time? What would your life be like if you could enjoy your job as much as you enjoy your hobbies? What kind of life would you be providing for those around you if the central element of your life was no longer drudgery but the joy that comes from self-fulfillment? It would be like going to Disneyland every day — just without your kids. And if you're willing to spend a little time figuring out how to make your job into a hobby, you can turn this dream into a reality.

Knowing What Sets Hobbies Apart from Jobs

Think about how you treat your hobbies and how you treat your job. If you're like most people, you gladly talk about your children's lives, your last ski trip, your favorite authors, your vacations to fun places, and friends you enjoy. You may show off your craftwork or even proudly invite people to the cabin you built in the woods. People always express attitudes toward hobbies positively, talking gleefully of the latest doodad they hope to invest in (soon!) to keep up to date with their passion.

What makes people successful in their hobbies? Have you ever noticed the difference in expression and animation in people when they talk about their hobbies compared to when they talk about their jobs? If you haven't noticed this up to now, test this theory yourself. Ask a few people this question and pay attention to their answers: "How do you like to spend your days?" Rarely will you hear about people's jobs. Instead, the conversation usually turns to how they spend their recreation time.

Being the best, the top of the heap, in your hobby is much easier than excelling on the job. Why? Because you have passion for your hobby. I contend that if more people looked at selling as a hobby — with energy, enthusiasm, excitement, fervor, anticipation, devotion, and sheer fun — they would be leaders in all walks of their lives. In fact, we'd be watching them on *Lifestyles of the Happy and Fulfilled*.

In the following sections, I take a closer look at the way people view their hobbies and let you know how you can harness those same traits and apply them to your selling — a path sure to bring you success.

Attitude makes the difference

Studies have proven that attitude is one of the traits that separate so-so salespeople from their highly successful colleagues. And I have to believe that this is true in life in general, not just in sales. Think about the happiest, most successful people you know. How do you usually find them? Are they depressed, negative, or even apathetic? I doubt it. They're probably upbeat, smiling, and positive about life.

Why not take the same positive, interested attitude you have toward your hobbies and transfer your passion to your ability to sell yourself, your ideas, and your products or services? Challenge yourself to read up on selling strategies. Of course, you're doing that with this book, but what will you do after that? While you're driving, will you listen to the radio, or will you inspire yourself to greater success by listening to selling skills CDs or audiocassettes?

Give yourself permission to explore some creative ways of starting conversations with others who may have a need for your product or service. Observe how the next salesperson you encounter makes you feel. What did he say or do that brought about that feeling? Challenge yourself to pay attention and you'll soon find yourself eagerly anticipating the next selling situation as much as you anticipate your next issue of *Great Gardening Tips* magazine.

Instead of turning your selling job into a hobby, why not take the hobby you love so much and figure out how to market that hobby or yourself? If you're involved in craftwork or handiwork, like woodworking or knitting, you may be able to sell the things you make. I'm not saying this change will make you a millionaire, but money isn't the only measure of success. If you could support yourself comfortably on the earnings from your hobby, I would deem you as having a successful life. Think about it! You already have the built-in enthusiasm, excitement, and knowledge of your hobby. Now all you need to do is show others why they need to feel the same way. If you do a little research, you'll find that many very successful businesspeople started out by selling their hobbies. Determine what you love to do, and then figure out a way to get paid for it. What could be better?

Success can fit many definitions — including yours

I always enjoy asking my seminar audiences for definitions of the term *success*. I've probably asked well over 3,000 people to define *success* for me over the years. I haven't kept strict records on their answers, but I'd have to guess that I have rarely gotten repeat answers. That's because success is something like a fingerprint; it's individual. Of course, many of the answers I've received have reflected a desire for monetary riches, love, and security, but few people have been able to come up with a definition of success that could be understood and agreed upon by all who hear it.

I've thought a lot about a definition of success and developed this one that I teach my students. It seems to cover most of the answers I've heard.

Success is the continuous journey toward the achievement of predetermined, worthwhile goals.

I like the phrase *continuous journey* because I don't think anyone really wants to arrive at success and be done. In fact, I don't think it's possible to reach a place called *success* and be happy there forever. Look at Olympic athletes: At very young ages, they achieve greatness, worldwide acclaim, and medals that many people say show they're successful. If that achievement were success and if after achieving success they just stopped, then what would those athletes do with the rest of their lives?

The other phrase that I like in my definition of *success* is *predetermined, worthwhile goals*. *Predetermined* shows that a choice was made, a course was set. It was something that required thorough consideration, and perhaps inspiration, to commit to. *Worthwhile* is key because I truly believe in the good of all mankind and that the majority of people in the world want to do something of worth with their lives.

Consider using this definition for yourself and lay a course for an exciting journey toward success!

Emotional involvement supplies the meaning

Another key trait that hobby enthusiasts have that many people don't have with their work is emotional involvement. If your hobby is an outdoor sport, such as mountain biking, nothing is more exciting than cresting mountain peaks at sunrise or soaring downhill so fast that you have a permanent grin on your face. It's not just a physical experience either: It's charged with emotional involvement. When you schedule a biking event, it becomes a highlight that gives you a great feeling whenever you think about it. You involve yourself in planning every detail to make the outing the best one yet. You live and breathe for the next opportunity to get out there with your mountain-biking cohorts. When you think about your biking events, you feel an emotional jolt. Mountain biking also involves a great deal of physical preparation and can be quite challenging. But if the emotional involvement is strong enough, you can hurdle those barriers with no sweat (so to speak). When you get right down to it, avid mountain bikers have become sold on their pastime because they want to experience the emotional involvement that others have shared with them.

But people often lack that emotional involvement with their jobs. Too many people who are disillusioned with their jobs become detached from what goes on in their work environment. They become disinterested observers. They don't join in the company's extracurricular activities or interact much with others.

Those who are emotionally involved with their work, however, bring enthusiasm to their jobs. And for those people, life is much more interesting and more fun. Even if you're not thrilled with what you do for a living, you must at least be pleased with living itself. Find a way to bring that pleasure into your work, and your work just may become more fun, too.

You must be able to find at least a smidgen of something you like about your job — even if it's just the cool telephone you get to use or having snazzy business cards. Maybe it's having someone other than a relative who calls you by name. Whatever it is, there must be *something* you like about what you do for a living.

Many of the salespeople I have talked with over the years love meeting new people. They are curious, interested in how other people live their lives. They seek out new ideas and opinions on topics that they previously barely knew existed. Some enjoy the challenge of the selling cycle — meeting a perfect stranger and, before too long, turning that person into a lifelong client. I think nearly everyone in sales gets off on the high of satisfying a need that someone had. It's a service attitude for most. For some, especially in the beginning, it's the knowledge that only they set the limit on how much income they earn. For those sales positions that require travel, many people enjoy meeting other travelers, seeing new sites, visiting different climates. Finding out about cultures different from their own inspires many salespeople who are involved in international business. For some, the flexibility that's often available in certain sales positions allows them to schedule valuable family time or to participate in hobbies or sporting events that occur when the rest of the world works. In some industries, entertaining clients involves attending sporting events that some salespeople wouldn't otherwise have opportunities to attend.

If you're having trouble finding even one little thing to like about your job, then I suggest that you seriously consider making a change: Either change yourself or change your job. No one should have to suffer through a job he hates. And if you are, you aren't doing yourself or your employer any good by continuing on with it.

Trading Knowledge for a Sense of Wonder

Starting the hobby of selling is pretty simple. You don't need any special tools or equipment. No large financial investment is required. And you don't have to travel far to participate.

So what do you need to do to start making selling your hobby? Pay attention to the way your children or parents communicate with you about family matters. Watch how retail clerks treat you, and notice how you feel about the store in response. Get into the habit of really *reading* billboards and newspaper ads. Which ones are talking directly to you and why? Listen carefully to radio spots; those that hold your attention the longest deserve some analysis. In general, become a student of the selling that is presented to you daily by everyone from sales and marketing experts to your friends and family.

Making learning a lifetime pursuit

Although people allow their children the privilege of ample time to learn, they often don't allow themselves as adults the same privilege. The large majority of people discontinue their conscious learning experiences in life when they complete their formal education. Hundreds of thousands of mature adults have not learned in the past 20 years half as much as they learned in their 4 years of high school or college courses.

Adults make excuses for themselves, saying that they don't have the time to take educational courses. Or they think that they can learn faster on their own. Or they assume that they don't really need to know much more than they already know. (Tune into *Jeopardy!* sometime to find out exactly how much you don't know if you fall into that last category.)

Most adults fail to continue the learning process not because of a lack of desire, but because of a perceived lack of time. They expect youngsters to spend most of their time on education, with a strong dose of fun thrown in for good measure. But somewhere along the way, as people grow into adults, that focus shifts to the responsibilities they have for financial and family matters. Their desire for achievement overwhelms them, and taking time out for education just doesn't happen.

The good news is this: Studies have shown that developing the habit of listening to educational programs in your car during commuting time can provide you just as much information as studying for a Master's degree. How hard can it be to carry some tapes or CDs around with you all the time? You probably already do it with music. But when was the last time your favorite music group taught you anything that made you more successful in life?

I offer most of the same training you'll find in this book on audiocassette, compact disc, video tapes, or DVD. How often are you in a place where you cannot listen to or watch at least one of these forms of education? I also offer some of my courses online — available 24 hours a day, 7 days a week, 365 days a year — so more and more of the standard excuses are being eliminated. You can't say it isn't convenient, can you?

Many other companies offer volumes of audio, video, and online learning programs as well. Nightingale-Conant is one that has been around the longest. CareerTrack is another good resource. Fred Pryor is another. Many bookstores carry books on tape. Publishers offer CDs or CD-ROMs with many of the books that are published today.

So, in eliminating convenience, what's left is time. Do you recall the old story about the two men cutting wood? One worked hard and steady all day. The other worked hard, too, but every now and then would stop. At the end of the day the second man had cut more wood, much to the surprise of the first. When asked how he did it, he said, "Every time I took a break, I sharpened my saw." I challenge you to set aside a specific amount of time every week, or at the very least, every month, to sharpen your saw. Register for a seminar that's coming to your area. Invest a couple hours a week in the bookstore or library to find out about the latest books that have been published on the field of selling or on your industry in particular. Put your hands on one and read! After taking in that new information, you won't be the same person you were before. You'll see the world just a little bit differently and your hobby of selling will progress even further.

From now on, challenge yourself to think of training seminars and educational events as professional necessities. Take these learning tools out of the realm of things to do "when you have the time" and put them into the category of things that you *must* do to reach the levels of success you set for yourself. Shift your perspective only that much, and you will *make* the time to continue your education — you will become a lifelong learner.

REMEMBER

Working through brain cramps

When you begin to learn anything, you can absorb only so much before you experience what I call a *brain cramp*. The best approach is to learn, practice, learn some more, and then practice some more. You can internalize only so much information at once. If you take on a whole new subject, such as selling, all at once, it will overwhelm you and you'll be so uncomfortable that you may decide to give it up. Set a goal to find out, one step at a time, what you need to know.

If you're new to sales, you'll want to concentrate on prospecting and qualifying strategies. That way you'll be spending more of your time with people who could actually want to own your product or service. If you find yourself uncomfortable with that first-meeting greeting, work just on that for a while. Write yourself a script and stick to it. Then change one word or phrase and continue to use it — refining it as you go until you find the one that breaks the ice with more new people faster.

Many novices who choose to consciously develop sales skills want instant success. I think it has something to do with being an adult and the expectation that adults must be quick studies. It's an assumption many people make: "I'm an intelligent adult. I *must* be able to figure out something as simple as this rather quickly." Well, figuring it out isn't too difficult, but the application can be tricky. Don't look at others who are more successful than you are and try to duplicate their sales techniques overnight. They are successful because they have practiced, drilled, and rehearsed the material over a long period of time. They've already experimented with the nuances of body language, voice intonation, and inflection that you're just introducing yourself to. Keep in mind that old saying, "Don't assume anything about another person until you've walked in his shoes."

If you're truly serious about your selling career, consider attending the three-day high-intensity sales seminar my company offer every August in Scottsdale, Arizona. I know it's hot there, but we want to boil the information into your brains. You will leave having mastered much of the material — ready for your very next sales call. Visit my Web site (www.tomhopkins.com) for details.

Being accepting of productive mistakes

Giving yourself permission to be a lifelong student can change your life dramatically. But students don't always do things right the first time around. So when you give yourself permission to be a student, you also give yourself the right to make mistakes. It takes some of the pressure off: You don't have to be right all the time just because you're an educated adult.

No discomfort, no progress

To get to the level of comfort and success you want in your selling, you need to step outside of your comfort zone. Your *comfort zone* is where you are today, and unless you change who and what you are today, you will never change what you are getting out of life. You can't let the desire to be comfortable rule your life until you recognize it and figure out how to use it to your advantage. You see, when you open your mind to learning something new, you're not the same old comfortable person you were even a minute before. With that realization, you make yourself *un*comfortable with the extent of your own ignorance.

But everyone wants to be comfortable more than anything else. So, even after you start your quest for growth, you set goals, do some research, and invest your time learning until you again reach a level of comfort with the knowledge you have and use in your everyday life. The trick is to find a way to make yourself *keep* growing — to make yourself just uncomfortable enough about today that you'll better yourself for tomorrow.

This striving for knowledge can become wonderfully habit-forming. It's such a kick to learn and benefit from new concepts and ideas that the highest achievers in life have become addicted to it. They wouldn't think of facing a single day without the anticipation of learning something new.

Develop a picture of the new you who will take the place of that old comfortable you. I teach my students that, at times, developing the "fake it 'til you make it" approach is extremely valuable. I don't mean this in a negative way at all. I mean for you to think about the person who already has all the traits you desire; visualize yourself as the person who uses selling skills effectively to get the raise or promotion she wants or as the person who gets great fun as a result of persuading others. When you act like that person, you'll try to say and do what she would say and do. Eventually, you begin having small successes with the material and, before you know it, you *are* that person. You'll wear the suit of success. And the more you wear it, the more comfortable it will seem.

Professional athletes use this method of visualization all the time. Basketball players develop a clear picture in their mind's eye of just how the basketball will leave their hands for a three-point shot. They picture their fingers releasing the ball and see nothing of the crowd, only the net. When they first begin visualizing this, their bodies may not be up to speed with the picture, but if they play the picture often enough, chances are good that their bodies get the hint and soon perform accordingly. And you can do the same with your selling skills if you're willing to move out of your comfort zone long enough to learn something new.

If you have the attitude and mindset of a student, you won't beat yourself up over your failures and mistakes. Instead, you'll look at your mistakes as learning experiences. As a student, you must admit that you are fallible. Until you make that admission, you won't move far off the mark you're currently standing on.

After you do admit that you can make mistakes, though, seek out others who can teach you, people who can help you grow into the person you want to become. When you open yourself up to the possibility that you don't know everything and don't have all the answers, you start a quest to discover what you don't know — and that's an important step in the learning process.

One of my favorite reminders about learning is this: You can recognize true professionals by how much they learn *after* they "know it all." If you ever assume you know all there is to know about something, or even if you accept that you know enough, you have just doomed yourself to mediocrity.

Being Prepared for the Learning Curve: Passing from Caterpillar to Butterfly

No one masters something new the first time he tries it. Of course, some people do have natural talents or skills that apply to the new experience, but mastery cannot occur on initial impact. You didn't learn to walk on your first try. And learning anything takes time and practice. This is what people refer to as a *learning curve* — the time it naturally takes for someone to progress from a complete beginner (or a caterpillar) to an expert (or a butterfly). In any learning curve, you go through four major phases or levels of competency. I cover each of them in the following sections.

Unconscious incompetence

The first level of competency is known as *unconscious incompetence*. In this most elementary phase, you find people who don't even know that they don't know what they're doing. These people are the hardest ones to help because they haven't yet recognized or won't admit they need help. In daily life, these are the people who drift into your lane on the freeway and never realize you were there. They unknowingly leave grocery carts perilously close to new cars. They tend to live rather mediocre lives because either they haven't realized there's more to be learned — more to be aware of — or they have simply resigned themselves to be whatever they are at the present moment.

In business, this may include someone who has been in sales for a little while. He knows the product and how to fill out the paperwork and thinks that's all there is to the story. He thinks that Joe Champion is so good because of his looks or his tight connections with the boss. He doesn't even know there are things such as closes, proper methods of questions, and so on.

A second type of individual falls into this category as well. It's you and me. "What?" you say, "I never do things like that." You may not *now,* but chances are pretty good that you did before you became aware. Everyone is at the unconscious incompetence level of learning whenever they first try something new. Not convinced? Watch a baby learning to walk. He doesn't know he doesn't know how to walk. He just tries it because everyone else is doing it. When he learns, by falling, that it's not as easy as it looks, he reaches for helping hands. The instant he reaches for help, he moves to the next level of competency.

Conscious incompetence

The second level is *conscious incompetence.* People abandon unconscious incompetence when they suddenly realize that they don't know what they're doing. In the wonderful world of sales, you are very likely at the conscious incompetence level right now simply because you're reading this book. You've admitted that you don't have all the answers and that you want to find out more. And how do I know such an intimate thing about you? Because you wouldn't be reading this book if you hadn't admitted that you still have something to learn about selling.

Once upon a time, a future champion salesperson froze solid in his second-grade production of *Sleeping Beauty*

For an example of acutely conscious incompetence in action, think about the first time you had to give a presentation in front of a group. It probably wasn't much fun, was it? If it was anything like *my* first time, you came out of it with strong misgivings about making public speaking your hobby.

My first public performance was in the second grade, where it was my honor to be chosen to be Prince Charming in our class presentation of Sleeping Beauty. This was pretty cool. I got to wear a neat costume and carry a sword. I was even going to get to kiss the Princess. At that point in the learning curve, I was definitely at

the unconscious incompetent level in terms of my understanding of performing.

When it was time for me to go on stage, I walked out and saw the smiling faces of dozens of parents . . . and I froze. After I stood there for a couple of consciously incompetent minutes, my merciful teacher came out and led me off the stage. Needless to say, I eliminated public speaking from my list of potential careers. The irony is that my success in sales demanded that I give at least acknowledgment speeches at awards presentations, so I later had to face my dragon in order to continue on my journey toward success.

In fact, the first time I was contacted to give a formal talk, I responded with a reflexive but polite, "No, thank you." No trophy was involved, so I had little desire to get anywhere near a podium. But my dear friend, my mentor in sales, the great sales trainer of the 1950s and 1960s, J. Douglas Edwards, urged me to use the opportunity to overcome my fear of public speaking. He stressed that the ability to speak in public is extremely valuable if you want to be a leader in any field. His words etched themselves upon my mind and I've been able to apply them to many situations in which I once was uncomfortable:

Do what you fear the most, and you will conquer your fear.

You see, I was afraid of the unknown. The fear became so big in my mind that I couldn't see around it, over it, or past it to any sort of positive ending. I couldn't predict the outcome of giving that talk, so I convinced myself that there were too many ways it could go wrong for the talk to be worth the risk. All I could think of was that frightened second-grade boy standing frozen with fear onstage. I had determined that I'd never put myself in that position again.

Doug encouraged me, though, and I reluctantly consented to give the talk. I prepared for hours. I made meticulous notes on 3-x-5 cards, and I rehearsed my speech many times over. When the day of the presentation arrived, I was so nervous that I was afraid the sweat from my hands would smear my notes. My heart raced as I walked up to the podium.

I covered my well-prepared 45 minutes of presentation material in 15 minutes, leaving me with half an hour to go and no idea what to do! So I went through it all again — and my time *still* wasn't up! Thinking fast, I said, "I can tell by the intelligence of this audience that you have some great questions, so let's hear them." Luckily, they did have great questions and I was able to answer them.

Overall, my presentation wasn't great or even good. It was awful. But I did it, and my world didn't end. The huge fear that stood between me and the platform had just gotten a little bit smaller. I realized then — just as I did when I figured out that selling was a learned skill — that effective public speaking is a skill that I could learn. I evaluated my performance and identified what about my speaking performance I could change for the better. In a way, that was the beginning of where I am today as a trainer.

I began to understand that public speaking isn't just public speaking. It is salesmanship in the format of a speech. And if there was one thing I did know how to do well, even then, it was selling. My greatest fear and weakness has become my hobby and the greatest love of my life.

But heed one word of caution here: Now that you realize that you need to discover more, take action right away! Too many potentially great careers have been stalled at this level because people don't know where to turn for help or won't expend the effort to find the right kind of help. Your lack of competency can be overwhelming if you don't take charge. Don't be like the deer you see in your headlights at night, frozen to a spot on the road. You must *move* in order to rise to the third level of competency.

Begin by reading this book, of course. Then move on to *Sales Closing For Dummies* and *Sales Prospecting For Dummies*. (The folks at Hungry Minds are trying to be as helpful as possible in providing resources for you.)

If you learn better in person, start reading the ads in the business section of your local newspaper or business journal to find out what seminars are coming to your area (including mine) and make a commitment to attend. If you prefer to listen to something while you exercise or drive, borrow tapes from a friend or the library, or invest in some yourself. Then listen to them a minimum of six times to achieve maximum retention of the material. The next trick will take you to the next level of competence — trying the strategies out in the real world.

Conscious competence

When you reach the third level, *conscious competence,* you find new challenges and new victories. By this point, your desire to improve has become strong enough to overcome the discomfort of learning something new. You're testing the waters now. You know how to do the thing you're learning, but you have to think about it, be conscious of it, in order to succeed.

You're practicing the new material you've learned. You're honing the skills with your friends and associates *before* testing new strategies on qualified clients and potentially losing them due to awkwardness with the material. You're trying new things and making adjustments — and that's good.

Just don't place too high a level of expectation on yourself and you'll do better faster. Tensing up when you try new things takes your enjoyment from the experience. The tension also clouds your judgment when you must analyze how well you did and how you can improve the next time.

Unconscious competence

At the fourth and final level of competence, *unconscious competence,* you apply all your previous knowledge without making a conscious effort to do so.

You are smack in the middle of an example of unconscious competence right now — you're reading this book. You probably aren't reading it as would someone who is just learning to read. Instead of uttering each syllable individually as you point and sound it out, hoping for eventual comprehension, you're able to cruise along and seek the content you're looking for, not even thinking about what you're doing.

As an unconscious competent salesperson, the strategies are now a natural part of your presentation. In fact, if you were to tape your presentation, you'd recognize each nuance and recall when and why you added it — because it sounded good at the time. You've kept it because it works!

A tremendous advantage of being a lifelong student is that you no longer allow yourself the luxury of seeing yourself as a victim of circumstance. You take responsibility for your successes *and* your failures, and you're more likely to be honest with yourself when it comes to evaluating those successes and failures.

Liking to Sell What Your Customers Like to Buy

As in any area of life, in the world of selling, if you have the wrong attitude, you can end up being your own worst enemy. Many people in selling situations have a challenge with their own likes and dislikes — they tend to sell only what they like and mostly to the people they like. You do need to like and believe in what you're selling. But if you're in a career sales position, you'll probably have to sell other items in the product line that may not be your favorites.

You must always keep what's right for the customer in the forefront of your mind. If you sell only what you like, you also severely limit your income and you leave yourself, at the end of the day, with plenty of things on hand that you don't like. Then what will you do?

Your job is to enthusiastically sell whatever benefits your customers, whoever they may be. During your selling career, you will have to work with some people whom you won't particularly like. (I discuss how to deal with several personality types in Chapter 7.) If you refuse to work with some people, both you and the customers lose. You lose opportunities to make sales, and the customers lose opportunities to have their needs satisfied. The people you turn down will just get their needs filled by someone else. The moral of the story: Keep your mind and your opportunities open.

Be sure not to prejudge people when you're selling to them. Whether you realize it or not, you make some sort of judgment about people the moment you lay your eyes on them. You judge them based on their physical condition, their clothing, their hairstyles, their postures. In selling situations, though, acting on preconceptions is a dangerous habit that you need to control. If you're committed to becoming a professional, force yourself to look at every customer with clear vision. Eliminate those preconceived notions before they start costing you money!

Someone else's nightmare can be your dream come true

One Saturday early in my sales career, a couple pulled up outside the real estate office I was working in. They drove a beat-up truck and their clothes suggested that they had been doing heavy labor. Another agent in my office took one look at them and said, "Tom, you can have this one." He walked away, leaving me to talk with the unkempt couple.

As it turned out, they were looking for a fixer-upper property to invest in. They had made a business out of buying run-down properties and applying their do-it-yourself abilities to turn those properties into desirable homes. They then sold the homes for a tidy profit.

I helped the couple find their next fixer-upper, and a few months later they came back to me for help in investing some of their profits into a luxurious home for themselves. Over the years, I sold the same couple many fixer-uppers — and, as icing on what turned out to be a very satisfying cake, I resold those homes when the couple finished remodeling them. Had I pre-judged these folks by their appearance, I may have been the one to walk away from what turned out to be a lucrative opportunity.

Treat your prospects with the respect you would expect to receive were you in their shoes. This may sound suspiciously similar to the Golden Rule — as well it should. Keep in mind the following tips about the kind of attitude you need to have in the world of selling, and your self-control will pay off in the long run:

- ✔ If you want others to agree with you, you must first be agreeable.
- ✔ Don't let people's outward appearances affect the way you react to them.
- ✔ Always act as though each person you contact is the most important person in your life.

If what you're offering is vitally important to you, your product, service, or idea can be a significant link for you to billions of other people who need what you have to offer.

Part II
Doing Your Homework

The 5th Wave   By Rich Tennant

SALES MANAGEMENT PICNIC

" Get names!"

In this part . . .

When you were in school, homework was what you did to prepare for class, where you really had to perform. And that's just what homework is when you apply it to selling. In this part, you'll find information on what to know about your prospective clients and your product before you try to sell. And you'll also gather some great tips for using technology to your advantage when it comes to researching.

Chapter 4

What You Don't Know about Your Clients Can Kill Your Chances of Success

Sometimes the hardest thing in starting something new is breaking through old teachings or beliefs that you once felt were acceptable for successful living. I'm sure you remember the old adages "Ignorance is bliss" or "What you don't know can't hurt you." Although living by these sayings may have worked in people's personal lives in simpler times, such maxims were *never* sage advice for people who were trying to sell or persuade others. In fact, the loss of sales and the personal career damage caused by ignorance can be so disastrous that some people give up on selling altogether.

When you look at the best of the best, the cream of the crop in the selling world, you don't see all the time those people put in behind the scenes. But that time spent behind the scenes is what selling is all about. When a pro makes selling look *natural,* you can bet that he has spent hours and hours of planning and preparation before those few minutes of face-to-face selling began.

In this chapter, I let you know some specific ways you can prepare, so you can serve your clients better — everything from researching your prospective customers before you even set up an appointment to knowing how to listen to them when you finally do meet. I also give you some great pointers on selling to people from countries and cultures other than your own. In the world of selling, preparation is key, and this chapter is a great introduction to issues you may not have considered before.

Obviously, knowing everything about everything is impossible — and when you think you know it all, you're only setting yourself up for a gigantic fall. I've long taught that the sign of a true professional is how much he can learn *after* he supposedly knows it all. The enemy of learning is knowing. And admitting that you need to find out some things is the first step to achieving anything.

Understanding Why Research Is Important

Why do you need to research your prospective clients and their businesses? So that, at the moment of truth, when you're giving a presentation or getting ready to close the sale, your lack of knowledge won't make you look bad. You do all your research simply to build for that final moment when your prospect gives you the okay to deliver your product and to start building a long-term relationship with him or his company.

For example, if you sell air-treatment systems to homes and businesses, and you find out that a particular business must manufacture its products according to exacting standards, that's important information to know. Why? Because it means that the business must have a high level of concern for cleanliness and precision. And your air cleaner can help them get there.

Adapting your message to what your clients tell you about themselves and their needs

If you doubt the validity of the premise that knowledge is power, take a look at how much information Web sites gather about the people who visit them. For example, Amazon.com doesn't just sell products. It offers you an opportunity to establish a Wish List of products that you may be interested in buying (or receiving as gifts) someday. What does Amazon do with that Wish List? It can use the products you add to that list, along with your purchases and what you look at on its site, to find out where your interests lie. If Amazon.com begins offering a new book that someone with your interests would like, it will customize the Web site so that that new book is the first thing you see when you go the Amazon.com site. Amazon is customizing its offers to your particular interests and needs. And you're the one telling Amazon what you're likely to buy.

You can take advantage of these strategies for your business, too. If your company is gathering this kind of information and making it accessible to the entire salesforce, you're off to a great start. If your company isn't gathering this information for you, you may want to establish a very detailed information sheet on your clients' interests and needs so you can lead them to purchasing more products and services from you and from others with whom you may share referred leads (with their permission).

If you discover that the company is growing, but it hasn't expanded its work site, you can probably count on the fact that its employees are working in close proximity to one another. And the closer the proximity, the greater the likelihood that germs could be spread rapidly from one employee to the next. No employer can afford to have its people taking a lot of sick time, so your air-treatment system can help.

If the business's financial reports show solid growth and explosive future plans, you know that it's poised for change and probably wide open to new ideas. Show the company that your air-treatment system is state of the art, and you'll probably get their interest.

RED FLAG

The more you know about a prospect, the more competent you will appear and the stronger you will be when you present your case.

The same principle that you use when you sell to business applies when you sell to individuals or families: The more you know about their background, the better. (Besides, what you discover can become great background material for that novel you're planning to write after you retire.) You'll warm people up faster when you talk about their hobbies, jobs, and kids than you will if you know nothing other than their address and phone number. For example, if you're still selling air-treatment systems, and you know that one of their children has allergies or asthma, that's another bullet in your arsenal of benefits when you present your product.

You may be wondering how you'd find out about that child's asthma. You can do that in one of several ways, including a brief survey-type phone call asking if anyone in the home has or has ever had allergies or other illnesses that are affected by the quality of the air in the home.

You may rent a list from a list broker that would include families in the area who purchase certain supplies related to those types of illnesses. List brokers often have enough information about a potential client that you can find out what types of pets they have, cleaning products they purchase, and whether or not they make a lot of long-distance phone calls. How do they get this information? Think about it. Have you ever filled out a survey about the products you use in order to receive free grocery coupons? Do you send in for rebates on products? If you do any of this sort of thing, those companies don't just send your coupons or rebates and toss your reply card. They store that valuable purchasing information about you in their databases for future reference.

Starting at Ground Zero: Knowing Your Clients Inside and Out

To be successful at selling, you must be constantly on the prowl for information. What type of information? Everything and anything about your product, your company, your competition, and (most importantly) your prospect. And with the Internet just a mouse-click away, you really have no excuse for not being informed. An abundance of information is available, quite literally, at your fingertips. All you need is the commitment to locate and internalize it. Never forget: Knowledge is power.

The most important thing to remember when you're selling is the benefit of being able to walk in someone else's shoes. You can't be of any help to a prospective client with what you're offering him until you truly understand what he needs and where he's coming from.

So where do you begin in your quest to walk in your prospects' shoes? Not at the shoe store. Instead, you need to do some basic research into your prospective clients, their businesses, and their goals. Start by following these tips:

- **Gather as much literature and other information as possible on a company before approaching it with your offering.** You want to be as prepared as possible before you make that first approach — that way, you're starting off on the right foot from the very beginning.

- **Visit the business's Web site.** Pay particular attention to the business's online product catalog (if there is one), and look for press releases posted on the site so you're up to date on the most recent news related to the business. Plus, always look for an "About Us" link on the Web site. The information you'll find there will give you valuable insight into the management team and their backgrounds. And who knows? You may find out that you know someone who works there or you know someone who knows someone there.

- **Get copies of the company's product brochures and/or catalogs.** Talk with one of their customer service representatives about what the company offers. If you're familiar with the products that your prospective client sells, you'll be better able to sell them *your* product.

- **Go to the library or surf the Web and look up past news articles on the business.** If you're familiar with what's been happening in the business in the past few months, you'll be able to work that information into your conversations with the people who work there. The prospect will get the sense that you've done your homework about them — so you've probably done your homework about your own products, too. And that's exactly the impression you want to make.

- **Check out the business's financial report, if it's available.** Get the names of the company president and other key people — and find out how to pronounce and spell their names. For the pronunciation, simply call the company and ask the receptionist for that information.

Leave no paperwork or link on a prospect unturned when you do your research. Your legwork will pay handsome dividends in the long run. Knowledge is power when it's properly applied. And you should *always* apply that philosophy to research that will help you sell.

ANECDOTE

The very picture of diligent research

I know of a guy — I'll call him Sam — who went so deep into his study of his competition that he got to know the personal habits of the salesman who covered the same territory he did. Because the two directly competed for the same business, Sam had a chance to research his competitor just by talking to the prospects they shared. Sam learned his competitor's name, his method of operation, and his presentation style. What was the result? Because of Sam's detailed efforts, his company was number one in the territory. Seldom does someone take the process that far, but doing so paid off big for Sam and his company.

And just how far did Sam's knowledge of his competition go? He once showed me a photograph of that competing salesman from a piece of literature put out by that salesman's company. Sam carried that photo with him every day. And he said whenever he felt like quitting early or taking a shortcut, he would pull out that photo and remind himself that this guy would be the next one to talk with the customer if Sam didn't give his prospects 100 percent of his effort every time.

Although doing your research and gathering information about your prospective client is essential, knowing when you have enough information is often difficult. In the end, it's up to you, of course. When you think you know enough to get the job done and make the sale, you've probably researched enough. If a question comes up during your presentation that you don't know the answer to, and if what you don't know may hurt your chances of closing the sale, then you don't know enough. Experience will tell you how much you need to prepare, but you're better off erring on the side of preparing too much than not preparing enough.

Working with Buyers' Different Personality Types

When you work with companies, a key concern is who the true decision-maker really is. It may be the office manager, a purchasing agent, or a department head. You can usually find out simply by asking the receptionist who is responsible for the area of business to which your products or services apply. After she tells you, ask a confirming question, such as, "So, Ms. Carter has the responsibility of authorizing purchase orders, is that right?" If Ms. Carter *does* handle the area, but she has to get approval on purchase orders from someone like the comptroller, you need to know that going in (and your question will verify that for you).

When you have the name and position of the person responsible for purchasing in your area, you need to know a little about that person's style. My research has uncovered nine basic personality types of buyers (I cover each of these in the following sections). If you recognize the personality type of the person you want to sell to, you'll be able to respond appropriately.

Your delivery style must be flexible enough to relate to all the different personality types. Never settle for having one presentation style. Having only one style severely limits the number of people you can serve. I'm not advising you to develop multiple personalities. Just remember that if you don't like the personality of the decision-maker, you can learn to like the opportunity he is offering you to do business with him.

Note: These personality types are exaggerated for the purpose of example, and they're not limited to the genders I've identified them with. They demonstrate characteristics of buyers, but the people you encounter in the real world won't fit into boxes as neatly as these examples do.

Buyer #1: Believing Bart

Believing Bart is already sold on your company or brand. He knows just what to expect from them — and he likes their reliability. He's easy to work with and, after you convince him of your personal competence, he will remain loyal to you and your product. If he's *not* convinced that you're competent, Bart won't hesitate to call your company and request another representative.

How do you appeal to this personality type? Don't short-sell the product or service just because he's already sold on its quality. You need to exhibit great product knowledge to garner his trust and belief in your ability to meet his needs. Providing dependable service and follow-up will help you close the sale and gain Bart's repeat business.

Buyer #2: Freebie Freddie

Freebie Freddie is a real wheeler-dealer, the guy who won't settle until he thinks he has the upper hand and you've agreed to give him something extra. Today's market is full of these types of buyers. If you give Freddie any extras in order to consummate the sale, he'll probably brag to and upset others who may not have received the same benefit.

So how do you handle this type? Let Freddie know that he's important and special — that he drives a hard bargain and that you admire his business savvy. If you think Freddie's business is worth giving something extra to, consult with your manager or the business owner about the best way to handle it. You may not have to give away your company's back forty to entice this guy to buy. The enticement can be as simple as sending him thank-you notes or making a few extra calls to let Freddie know how important he is.

Buyer #3: Purchasing Polly

Purchasing Polly is a distant, matter-of-fact type who carries a high level of responsibility. As with many other purchasing agents, she may have little personal contact throughout the day besides the contact she gets from the salespeople who parade through her office. She can't risk liking you too much because she may have to replace you with the competition at any time.

When you're dealing with Purchasing Polly, give a no-fluff presentation. Don't try to become too familiar. Stick to the facts and figures. She'll be grading you every step of the way. By being low-key, you'll be different from the other all-too-typical salespeople she encounters — and she'll remember you for that. Let her know that you understand how important and challenging her position can be. Send her thank-you notes. Present all figures to Polly in the most professional manner possible. And do everything in writing — she needs the certainty of documentation.

Buyer #4: Evasive Ed

Evasive Ed is your most challenging buyer. He refuses to return your phone calls, he postpones appointments or reschedules at the last minute, he likes to shop around and keeps you waiting in the meantime, and he tests your patience at every turn.

If you've found yourself up against an Evasive Ed, enlist the aid of his secretary or support staff. They may be able to tell you how to get and keep his business. If they tell you "that's just the way he is," you'll need to work on creating urgency in your presentations so he'll see the benefit of making a decision quickly and, just as important, what he'll lose if he doesn't make the decision. A good example of this would be a special reduced investment or closeout on a product where you can only offer it for a short period of time or on a first-come, first-served basis.

Buyer #5: Griping Greg

Griping Greg always has something to complain about or something negative to say. He wouldn't be your first choice for a companion if you ever got stranded on a desert island.

If you're dealing with a Griping Greg, you have to decide whether the income his business generates for you is worth all the energy he'll steal from you. If his business is not one of your bread-and-butter accounts, you may want to consider finding other clients who don't take so much out of you. ***Remember:*** No client is worth risking your mental and physical health for.

The most important thing you can do for Greg is listen and be empathetic. (Maybe he can't afford a therapist, and you're the next best thing.) To limit your exposure to Greg's negativity, only call him a few minutes before his normal lunch hour or just before the end of the day, so he won't want to talk long. If he calls you at other times and begins to cost you valuable selling time, find polite ways to get off the line.

When you first get on the line, you may want to say something like this:

> Greg! Glad you called. I'm just heading out for an appointment. What can I do for you in the next five minutes?

Stay pleasant and helpful; after all, that's why Greg gives you his business. If Greg gets to be too much to handle, the easiest and least costly thing to do may be to refer him to someone else in your organization. The person receiving this new client may not be as strongly affected by Greg's personality and may be able to get along just fine with him.

Buyer #6: Analytical Anna

Analytical Anna knows exactly what she wants — and she wants it written in blood or at least carved in stone. She nitpicks everything and needs to feel like she has complete control.

When you're dealing with Analytical Anna, be *very* organized. She appreciates — nay, she craves — organization. Handle every detail in writing. Be punctual. Double-check everything and let her see that you do. When she knows she can depend on you, she will do just that. Confirm appointments, and always reconfirm details of your meetings with her in writing. Fax Anna a recap of every meeting you have with her. Also, fax ahead to let her know what information you plan to bring to your next appointment. In other words, treat her as she treats others. Everyone wants to be around people who are just like themselves.

Disorder in any form shatters Anna's day, so don't be a source of disorder for Anna — if you want to get and keep her business.

Buyer #7: Domineering Donna

Donna is a strong-willed ball of fire who most likely has designs on a more powerful position in the company. She often hides her needs because she expects you to have done your homework — and if you have, she figures, then you already know her needs.

In talking to Donna, perhaps the most important thing you can do is to compliment her on her importance and remind her of the value of her abilities to her company. *Remember:* She likely bowls others over with her ambition for power — and most people try to avoid working with people who dominate like this. But you don't have that option. Besides, Donna can become a *positive* force for you if you have challenges with billing or want to sell your product to another department or branch of her company. If Donna believes in you and your product, she'll be your best supporter.

Buyer #8: Controlling Carl

For Controlling Carl, it's his way or the highway. He's a self-proclaimed expert. But he's also poor at delegating authority. Carl wants everyone and everything to be reported to him. He may also be rude and interrupt your presentation while he takes calls or gives directions to his secretary.

When dealing with a Controlling Carl, be extremely polite, prepared, and concise. By all means, don't make any assumptions. Let him know that you value his time. If the interruptions become too distracting, pulling out your lunch isn't the best answer. Instead, offer to reschedule your meeting off the premises — for, say, a lunch appointment — so that you can have Carl's undivided attention. Or you can, simply by asking, enlist the aid of Carl's secretary or assistant in keeping interruptions to a minimum during your appointment. Unless Carl has a rule carved in granite that he takes all calls and sees all visitors, you're likely to get the assistance you want just by making a polite request.

Buyer #9: Cynical Cindy

Cynical Cindy is the first to say, "But we've *always* done it this way." She fights change, is suspicious, and questions your every move. She's very likely part of the old guard where she works — a long-term employee.

Welcome Cindy's objections — even compliment her for being smart enough to bring them up. Impress Cindy by dropping the names of people and companies she trusts; in order for Cindy to bring down her wall of doubt, she needs to know who else uses your product or service. For you, though, Cindy's hesitancy can become the best thing about her. Why? Because if *you* have such a difficult time overcoming her objections, you'd better believe that your competition will get discouraged trying to win her over. It'll be hard for your competition to persuade her to change her loyalties when she sees the value of becoming *your* client. And loyalty like that is what you're after.

Being Aware of Unique Cultural Needs

If you're planning to do business in another country, you need to invest as much time understanding their culture as you do understanding their needs in terms of your products and services. The same rule holds true even if you do business within cultural groups different from your own in the country in which you live. Even if you're not actively doing business in another country, but you're building a Web site that may be viewed by people from many different countries or cultures, you need to be aware of words and phrases that just don't translate or may be offensive when a translation is made.

Cultural Etiquette 101: Finding the resources you need

If you need or want to find out about another culture, some wonderful resources are available to steer you in the right direction and tell you everything you need to know. Spend some time browsing through your local library or bookstore to see what's out there. Or check out the following books, all of which are very helpful:

✔ *International Business Etiquette Europe: What You Need to Know to Conduct Business Abroad with Charm and Savvy,* by Ann Marie Sabath

✔ *Kiss, Bow, or Shake Hands: How to Do Business in Sixty Countries,* by Terri Morrison, Wayne A. Conaway, and George A. Borden, Ph.D.

✔ *Multicultural Manners: New Rules of Etiquette for a Changing Society,* by Norine Dresser

Some very informative Web sites are also great sources for tips, articles, newsletters, magazines, and even personal consultants who specialize in cultural etiquette. Here are just a few I recommend:

✔ **Motria's Image and Etiquette Services** (www.motria.mb.ca/motria.html) is a consulting firm that specializes in "projecting a professional image, in proper business etiquette, and in appropriate international etiquette." This site provides great general information on nearly every country as well as culture-specific advice. It even breaks its advice down into categories, such as handling greetings, negotiating tips, conducting conversation, and using proper etiquette for dining, tipping, and transportation.

✔ **Etiquette International** (www.etiquetteintl.com) is a full-service business etiquette firm that offers one-on-one coaching sessions, presentations, and training/educational materials for its clients. At the Etiquette International Web site, you can find tip sheets on everything from making effective cocktail conversation to handling gender relations in the business world.

✔ **BusinessCulture.com** (www.businessculture.com) offers access to Worldwide Business Reports on over 100 countries, PreDeparture Reports, and Executive Business Reports. It provides a list of countries for which it does research (over 80 at last count, ranging from Argentina to Yemen), along with some expert advice about crosscultural issues. You can also conduct a search from this site for international news posted on the ABC News and BBC News Web sites. The BusinessCulture.com world travel information includes weather reports from around the world, contact information for international airports and hotels, a currency converter, and advice on how to stay healthy abroad.

✔ **Protocol Advisors** (www.protocoladvisors.com) "provides customized training in etiquette and international protocol to Fortune 500 companies." This includes helping companies in cutting edge fields to familiarize their executives, sales staff, and those who may be transferring to another country with what to expect. It's also a great source for students who may be taking courses abroad. Find out about the idiosyncrasies of the culture, as well as the do's and don'ts, so that your experience abroad is a positive one.

✔ **Protocol Professionals, Inc.** (www.protocolprofessionals.com) is "an international relations consulting firm specializing in protocol and etiquette training." This organization has worked with very high-profile groups, including the Diplomatic Corps and U.S. Ambassadors. If your involvement in another country is going to be with higher-ups, this is a great resource site.

If you're planning to sell to clients from cultures other than your own, check out any of these resources before you make your initial contact.

In 1992, I had my own experience with the impact of translation. I needed to have one of my most popular audio programs translated into Spanish. Because I don't speak Spanish, I worked with international recording star, Omar Periu, who is fluent in several languages and found a professional translator to help him with the job. In creating the translation, a couple of challenges arose. For example, one of the techniques I described on the tape is called the "Porcupine" questioning strategy (covered in Chapter 12 of this book). Because the porcupine is indigenous to North America, the visual image we created with it had no counterpart in Spanish. The closest thing the translator could come up with could have been misconstrued by the listener to be something less than, shall we say, appropriate for the business world. So, I had to teach the strategy in an entirely different manner.

In the following sections, I let you know about different cultural traditions you need to be aware of when dealing with clients. But first, here are a few general pointers from Sherri Ferris, President and CEO of Protocol Professionals, Inc. (www.protocolprofessionals.com):

- ✔ **Be patient when building trust and establishing relationships.** People from countries other than the U.S. generally need more time to build trust. Observing a greater degree of formality when becoming acquainted is important.

- ✔ **Speak more slowly than you normally do, but don't raise your voice because you think the other person can't understand you.** Volume doesn't usually increase comprehension.

- ✔ **Avoid slang, buzzwords, idioms, jargon, and lingo.** These can all be easily misunderstood by those who may not speak your language as natives would.

- ✔ **If you're using an interpreter, make sure the interpreter meets ahead of time with the people for whom he is interpreting.** This will allow the interpreter to learn the language patterns, special terminology, and numbers used by the people he's translating for, such as product identifiers or other codes specific to a company or industry. All of these details can change the whole dimension of what's being said.

- ✔ **Pay attention to nonverbal interaction cues.** The word *yes* or an affirmative nod often means, "Yes, I hear you," in Asian cultures, not, "Yes, I agree."

Culture is as much an influence on people as their personal experiences, so knowing about your clients' customs and traditions only makes sense. That way, neither you nor your client will be made to feel uncomfortable. *Remember:* Knowledge is power.

Getting names right

A person's name is the most important thing to him. You can lose everything else in life and still have a name. When a client hears you use his name correctly, he knows that you put forth the effort to get it right — and that goes a long way toward earning his respect and trust. If you forget a client's name — or mispronounce it — you'll have to work that much harder to remedy the situation and earn the client's respect in the future (if he'll even give you a second chance).

In some cultures, a person's *surname* (or last name) is given before his *proper name* (or first name). Take the time to find out which cultures place the surname first, or you may find yourself addressing Mr. Ling as Mr. Bob.

For example, Hispanic names usually include both the father's and mother's family names. The father's name comes first and should be used as the term of address. So, if you're dealing with someone by the name of Luis Mendoza Trujillo, *Luis* is his first name, *Mendoza* is his father's family name, and *Trujillo* is his mother's family name. And you should address him as Señor Mendoza.

In Germany, the preference is to be addressed by your job title as opposed to the German equivalent of Mr. or Ms. So addressing someone as Vice President Schmidt is considered appropriate. In Italy, including someone's profession when introducing or referring to him is considered more appropriate (for example, "our engineer, Mr. Puccini").

In any culture, including your own, never address someone by his first name unless he specifically asks you to do so. And never abbreviate a name unless instructed to do so. Robert is Robert, not Rob, Robbie, Bob, Bobby, or any other version.

Making appointments

Getting together with people on neutral, or at least acceptable, territory can be the most difficult aspect of selling to someone from another culture. Knowing your client's customs is critical. Be sure to not make any faux pas before you get your foot in the door.

When you're planning to sell to a client from a culture other than your own, determine the best way to approach someone for an appointment. In India, for example, mail delivery can be unreliable, so convey important messages, such as requests for meetings, by fax, telephone, or e-mail. Find out whether the country you'll be selling in requires any similar considerations.

After you've determined the best method to use to reach your client, decide which environment would be most conducive to doing business with her. Although many business people prefer formal, corporate, conference room settings, others prefer more relaxed locations (such as restaurants or clubs) for business discussions. In the Chinese culture, for example, the feng shui of the location can play an important part in how the business goes. Paying attention to details such as those may be the key to your success with Chinese clients. (For more information on feng shui, turn to *Feng Shui For Dummies,* by David Daniel Kennedy and Lin Yun, Ph.D. [published by Hungry Minds, Inc.].)

When you have an appointment, confirm all the details and do your homework on what to wear, what to bring with you, and how to give your presentation. Always be punctual, but don't expect the other person to be. In many cultures, relationships are much more important than time clocks. Value the time your client gives you, but don't count the minutes.

Presenting your business card

Having some business cards made with your contact information in the language of the recipient is a good idea. If your card is two-sided, with your language on one side and another language on the other, always present your card with the client's language facing up. Doing this will make your client most comfortable with understanding the information. Allow the client a moment to read the card before talking or moving on to the next aspect of your presentation. If you're the one in charge of having this printing done, seek out the advice of a professional, such as the protocol folks mentioned earlier in this chapter, to ensure that it's done properly. You wouldn't want your high school son or daughter to just take a chance on a literal translation in the same order that you would use it in your country.

Some countries have specific etiquette surrounding the use of business cards. For example, if you're going to Japan, take plenty of business cards and give one to every person you're introduced to. Also, academic degrees are important in Japanese culture, so if you have a Master's degree, be certain to show that on your card. Only pull out one card at a time; holding a stack of business cards in your hand is considered bad manners in Japan. *Remember:* Be sure to find out what rules apply in the culture or country you'll be visiting.

Knowing the regional manners

Even if you're doing all your business within your native country, you may need to pay attention to differences among various regions. Although you all speak the same language, you may do it with different accents or in a dialect different from the client's. For example, people in nearly every region of the U.S. have accents or certain ways of saying particular words. These accents can be charming or irritating to others, depending on their existing assumptions.

If you're from the Southern U.S. and do business with folks in the Northeast, be prepared to talk a bit faster than normal in order to keep their attention. Also, you may want to train yourself to listen more effectively, because people in that part of the country tend to talk faster than the people you're used to being around.

The opposite is true if you're a Northeasterner doing business with some Southerners — or even a city person doing business with people who live in small towns. Some people from the South and in small towns handle business in a more relaxed manner than do folks in the Northeast.

Unless your name is Meryl Streep, you probably can't do much to change your accent, but you can be aware of the speed with which you speak and you can pay attention to the speech patterns of your clients. As much as possible, try to adapt to your clients' way of conversing — that way they'll feel more comfortable and focus more on what you're saying than how you're saying it.

Warning: If you're from Seattle, be sure that you don't pick up a Tennessee twang while doing business with someone from Memphis. Although it can be easy to do, the other person may think that you're making fun of him.

In any culture, taking the time to read the card of each person who gives you one before accepting another card is wise. Do not set the cards aside quickly — that would be like dismissing the person to move on to someone else. Putting the cards in a business card case shows respect for the person who gave it to you; shoving it in your pocket or notebook does not.

Respecting personal space

All people, regardless of the country they live in, have a need for *personal space* (the distance between you and another person when you're talking to one another). Personal space is just that — personal. But in each culture, the amount of personal space people need is different from what you may be used to. For example, the British want more personal space than people from the U.S. (Next time you see a photograph of the Queen of England, pay attention to the people standing next to her. The people most likely won't be standing hip to hip.) Russians and Arabs, on the other hand, need less personal space than most Americans do.

If you want to be sure that people feel comfortable around you (a necessity in the world of selling), don't invade another person's space. If you're working with people from cultures where less personal space is required than you're used to, be sure not to back away when they step into your larger personal space. That can be construed as a sign that you are fearful or hesitant about the other person. Neither are good things to have happen with potential business clients.

Meeting and greeting new people

Some countries, particularly Arab ones, include embraces or handshakes when meeting and departing. Determine in advance whether your potential client would be more likely to welcome an embrace or a handshake. Inquiring about the person's health is a positive gesture in Arab culture. Also, when the relationship becomes closer, don't be surprised if you are given a kiss on the cheek — even from one man to another.

Don't extend your hand to shake an Arab woman's hand unless she extends hers first.

Taking time to read up on the small details of how people meet and greet one another in the country you'll be visiting can make a huge difference in how the balance of your contact time goes with each potential client.

Making presentations

In some cultures, getting down to the bottom line as soon as possible is critical. In others, you need to spend more time telling your clients about the history of your company and helping them feel comfortable with you and your product. In yet other cultures, underscoring the personal and emotional benefits of your proposal is important. In some cultures, people prefer to touch and feel samples of your product, whereas in others they may prefer to just read analyses, complete with graphs and testimonials.

When you give a presentation in another country, always be organized. Have professional-looking paperwork to explain all the details of your proposal, and bring a copy for everyone in the room. Leaving anyone out or asking for additional copies to be made is a major mistake.

In some countries, the negotiation is the best part of the game. Negotiation may include shouting orders, banging fists on tables, or simply silence. In other countries, you present and they either accept or decline and then move on with little or no chance for you to reiterate important points or give a benefit summary. So, your first shot needs to be your best shot.

You simply *cannot* prepare too much for a meeting with someone from another culture. Expect to be asked for any and every little detail about your company, product, service, and location, as well as about yourself. That way, no matter what comes up, you'll be ready.

Giving gifts

The decision-makers at most companies understand the value of appropriate gift giving and will usually establish certain parameters for gift giving by their staff. If your company doesn't have specific guidelines for you to follow, ask what they prefer. Or, better yet, suggest some appropriate parameters based on the potential value of each client to the company. If you're the sales representative who is the main source of contact with the client, you'll want to ensure that the client thinks well of you when he receives the gift. So, don't be afraid to jump in there with some solid suggestions.

The stronger your relationship with your client, the more personalized your gift should be. You wouldn't send a long-standing client whose business represents 20 percent of your sales volume a vinyl datebook. If you've done business with the client for a while, you should know what that person likes and gear your gift to his highest level of enjoyment.

Making sure gifts are truly free

Some countries require duties or other fees to be paid on shipments from outside that country. Be sure to find out whether this applies in the country you're visiting, and pay any duty in advance so the gift you're sending is truly free.

You can get this information from the nearest consulate for that country. Or you can simply order the gift from a major supplier within that country.

Beware that some cultures find the giving and receiving of gifts a personal matter, not a business matter. For example, in France, business gifts aren't given. If you're invited to a French business associate's home, however, be certain to bring flowers, chocolates, or a bottle of high-quality spirits, such as vodka or scotch. Don't bring wine, however. The French are considered by many in the world, including themselves, as wine experts. The host or hostess would have already chosen the proper wine for the meal.

In some cultures, gifts that would be considered very appropriate where you're from may be completely offensive to people in the country you're visiting. For example, in Japan or Latin America, a gift of a letter opener may imply that you are severing the relationship, because the letter opener looks like a knife. Someone from India would not appreciate a gift made of leather, because the cow is considered sacred in that country. In Japan, white is used in funeral services, so you want to make sure that you don't wrap gifts in white or send white flowers. In Germany, red roses are only given in personal relationships, never in business ones. And in many Asian cultures, singling someone out with a gift or a compliment may be considered offensive rather than polite. Just be sure to read up on the country in which you'll be selling, so that you avoid offending your clients and so everyone's attention is focused on what you're selling instead of on an unfortunate faux pas.

Be sure that the recipient doesn't construe the gift as being inappropriate. Giving a Rolex watch to a client who only purchased $500 worth of product from you is probably not a wise move — financially or for the business relationship (and this goes for gift giving in your own country as well). If the client is uncomfortable at all with the gift, he may wonder whether you're offering a bribe for future business — and that's exactly the opposite of the reaction you're going for.

Before you give a gift to a client, determine whether the recipient's company has a policy on receiving gifts. Many companies won't allow their employees to accept gifts; if you offer one, your client may be in the uncomfortable position of having to decline or return your gift. If the company doesn't allow the receiving of gifts, ask the person with whom you have the best relationship in the company what you can do. Maybe you can send a box of candy or a basket of fruit for the department to share, but not a pen-and-pencil set for the individual.

Dressing appropriately

Because your appearance is the first cue others get about how you feel about yourself and your business, take extra care in dressing for business meetings and events. When in doubt, dressing conservatively and more formally than you would if you were meeting with a client from your area is always wise.

In many countries, such as Malaysia and some Arab countries, it is considered inappropriate for women to wear slacks or shorts. Find out about this before you even begin to pack; otherwise your potential business may be over before you even get close enough to shake the client's hand.

Eating out with ease

Asians, on average, dedicate more hours to work-related activities than people from the U.S. do, which means that they include after-hours dinners as a normal part of their workday. So, if you're working with an Asian client, you may be expected to wine and dine with him as part of the meeting. If you're the one being wined and dined in his country, be prepared to reciprocate before you leave.

In some cultures, slurping, burping, and even drinking from another person's glass during dinner is perfectly acceptable; in others, it's absolutely not. When you're visiting another country, you don't necessarily have to join in on behaviors you have trouble with, but you should at least be aware of them so you don't act inappropriately shocked if your guest does so. And at the very least, know what's considered rude, and avoid those behaviors during your meals.

Be sure to understand your potential client's needs with regard to specific foods or preparation of such foods. When dining with a client, make certain you're not taking her to a restaurant whose menu will not provide appropriate foods for her. Also, consider customs the client may have, whether cultural or religious, with regard to taking a meal. You may need to allow a few moments for prayer or indulge the client in eating very slowly and consuming many courses.

Etiquette, in any country, is all about behaving in such a way that everyone feels comfortable. As that old saying goes, "When in Rome, do as the Romans do." And when you're entertaining foreign clients in your own country, do everything you can to make them feel at home.

Responding to Your Clients' Fears

In all its forms, fear is the greatest enemy you will ever encounter in persuading your clients. The toughest part of your job is helping other people admit to and overcome their fears so you can earn the opportunity to do business with them. Fear is what builds those walls of resistance that salespeople so often run into. You need to know how to climb over or break through those walls if you're going to travel the road to sales success.

I've identified eight common fears that you'll need to help your prospects overcome. When you recognize these fears as barriers to your ability to serve your prospects with excellent service, you're ready to discover how to dismantle those walls, one brick at a time, thus gaining your prospect's confidence and trust.

Your goal is to get your prospects to like you and trust you. They do that when you serve them with warmth and empathy.

Fear of salespeople

At first, every prospect is afraid of you. Why? Because you're a salesperson, and you want something from them. Plus, what you want involves some kind of a change on the prospect's part, and most people are afraid of change, at least to some degree. Even if you're selling to someone you already know — a friend, an acquaintance, or even a relative — when you meet that person in the role of a sales professional, certain fears inevitably arise. The only exception may be selling to your parents or grandparents, simply because they probably believe in you and trust you no matter *what* role you play with them. To them you come across as you should to everyone — with a natural, non-sales personality.

As a salesperson, when you meet with someone who, like most people, tries very hard to hang on to his hard-earned cash (or at least not to part with it too easily), you can safely assume a certain amount of fear is involved. Face it: Not too many people over the age of 21 walk around looking for places to spend their money. They separate themselves from their money only for products and services they believe they need. Your job is to help them recognize the need, and build the value of your product's ability to serve that need to a point where their fear now becomes a fear of what happens if they *don't* allow you to help them.

Most people, when you first encounter them, will show their fear in their body language. They may cross their arms or lean back away from you. In retail settings, they may actually take a small step backward when you approach them on the sales floor. A wise tactic to help overcome this is to warmly invite them to stand or sit beside you while you show them all the good stuff your product does or has. This way, you're looking at it together. You encourage them to put their hands on the product, push buttons, turn dials, make things light up, heat up, or move. When they get involved with the product, their fear of you lessens. After all, you're the one who introduced the prospects to the product, and look what great fun they're having now!

Fear of failure

The fear of failure is one you're likely to encounter in your clients, because virtually everyone has this fear to some degree. Why? Because everyone has made mistakes, and everyone has regrets. Whether your failure was in choosing the wrong hair color or purchasing a vehicle that wasn't right for you, you know the frustration of making a mistake. Somewhere in your psyche, you have a fear, not necessarily because of your bad decision, but because you remember that mistake as being associated with a salesperson (the hairstylist who told you that you'd look great with green hair or the car salesman who convinced you that your five kids could happily pile into a two-seater convertible).

No one wants to handle a transaction in which the customer may be dissatisfied with the result. Believe me, the grief you get from a dissatisfied customer isn't worth the fee you'll earn on the sale. Although dissatisfied customers aren't (and shouldn't be) the norm, you must go into every presentation with a sharp interest in the who, what, when, where, and why of your client's needs. When you've satisfied yourself that buying your product or service is in your client's best interest, then it's your duty as the expert to convince her that this decision is truly good for her. Take the time to talk your prospect through every aspect of her decision very carefully, giving her the time she needs to make a choice she'll be comfortable with.

Sell to your client's needs, not to your wants.

Fear of owing money

Prospects are also tremendously afraid of owing too much money — to you, to your company, to a finance company. Your fee for service is almost always a point of contention with prospective customers — and not just because they're being stubborn, but because they're legitimately afraid of owing too much money.

Most people won't attempt to negotiate with a company about its fees, but as a salesperson your clients don't see you as an institution. You're not cold, forbidding concrete walls and walkways. Instead, you're a warm, flesh-and-blood fellow human — and because of this, your clients will often try to negotiate with you. Depending on your clients' negotiation skills, they may do any or all of the following:

- ✔ **Put off making a decision, forcing you to draw them out.** I cover what to do in this situation in Chapter 11.

- ✔ **Tell you point-blank that they're concerned about the cost.** In this situation, you need to sell them on the value of the product or service you provide.

- ✔ **Voice their concerns in a roundabout way.** For example, a client may say something like, "Another company I talked with will charge a lot less."

If your client has reservations about the cost of your product or service, I recommend saying something like this:

> You know, I've learned something over the years. People look for three things when they spend money. They look for the finest quality, the best service, and, of course, the lowest investment. I've also found that no company can offer all three. They can't offer the finest quality and the best service for the lowest investment. So, for your long-term happiness, which of the three would you be most willing to give up? Fine quality? Excellent service? Or the lowest fee?

Most people say that quality and service are of the utmost concern, which overcomes their concern about the fee. Your next move is to reiterate everything you will do for them. Again, sell the value of the product you and your company provide.

If you run into a client who is truly concerned only with getting the lowest investment and you can't provide it, you may have to bow out of the picture. Do it gracefully and stay in touch. Chances are good that he'll get what he pays for and he'll eventually see the wisdom in spending more for the quality product or service that you can provide.

Fear of being lied to

Another common fear in buyers is the fear of being lied to. As a general rule, clients who are afraid of being lied to doubt everything you're saying about how much they'll benefit from your product, service, or idea.

When you face a client with this fear, a strong past track record comes into play. Having a long list of happy clients should help you calm this fear. If you're new and you don't yet have an established track record, tell your prospect you made a point of choosing her company because it has a great track record. If you're doing something entirely new with a new company, new product or service, or new concept, you have to build on the personal integrity and credentials of those involved in the project. For some products, there is a salesperson (you), a technical advisor who would review technical details of either manufacture or installation of a product, the actual installer, and the after-market customer services folks.

There is *never* any reason to lie to a customer. If you're honest with your customers and always share the truth with them, even if it's bad news, they will respect you and give you the benefit of the doubt. Honesty and integrity in every selling situation will make you a winner each and every time.

Fear of embarrassment

Many people fear being embarrassed with anyone who can possibly know about the decision if it's a bad one. Have you ever made a poor decision that was big enough that most of your friends and family members knew about it (and then kept reminding you about it)? They may have only been teasing you. However, it may have demeaned and embarrassed you. Bad decisions make you feel like a child again — insecure and powerless. Because many potential clients have this fear of being embarrassed by a bad decision, they put off making any decision at all.

If you're selling to more than one decision-maker (such as a married couple or business partners), odds are that neither person will want to risk being embarrassed in front of the other. Chances are they've disagreed about something in the past and they don't want to have that uncomfortable situation arise again.

Knowing that this fear can block your sale, your primary goal when working with clients who are afraid of being embarrassed should be to help them feel secure with you. Let them know that they're not relinquishing total power to you — you're merely acting on their behalf, providing a product or service they need.

Fear of the unknown

Fear of the unknown is another common fear in buyers. A lack of understanding of your product or service, or of its value to the prospect's company, is a reasonable cause for delaying any transaction. National name recognition will dispel some of this fear. But if you work for a local company, I recommend that you join forces with the rest of your company's sales staff to earn a great local reputation as a competent business with great products. Over the years, a great reputation saves you a bundle of time in the selling business.

Former teachers (at least the good ones) often make the best salespeople if they switch to careers in sales. Why? Because selling is all about educating people about the benefits of doing business with you. When you educate them past their fear of the unknown, they feel confident about their decision to do business with you.

Always spend a little extra time on what your product actually does and the benefits it brings when you're working with a customer who is unaware of your offering — and afraid of the unknown.

Fear of repeating past mistakes made with similar products or services

Having a bad past experience generates fear in the hearts of some potential customers. If they've used a product or service like yours before, find out what kind of experience it was for them. If they hesitate to tell you, you may assume that their past experience was bad and that you have to overcome a lot more fear than if they've never used a product or service like yours before.

Try offering the product or service on a sample or trial basis. Give the prospect the names of your satisfied customers who will give unbiased testimony as to the value of your offering. (Check with those customers first to make sure they don't mind if you have prospects contact them.)

Fear generated by others

A prospect's fear also may come from third-party information. Someone he admires or respects may have told him something negative about your company, about your type of product, or even about another representative of your company. Either way, that third party will stand between you and your prospect like a brick wall until you convince or persuade him that you can help him more than that third party can, because *you* are the expert on your product or service. You'll have to work hard to earn the prospect's trust. Enlist the aid of some of your past happy clients as references, if necessary.

Choosing Your Words Wisely

When you're getting to know your clients, you need to think about the effective power of language. Every word you utter creates a picture in the mind's eye of the listener. Do you use that power to your greatest advantage?

Every word paints a symbol or picture in your mind. When you hear a word, you picture a symbol of what that word represents. Each symbol often has emotions attached to it as well. Words — such as *spring, summer, autumn,* and *winter* — can generate positive or negative emotions in you. If you love gardening, the warm spring air brings to mind beautiful blossoms, the opportunity to get your fingers in the dirt, preparing your soil for a summer crop. If you are a hay fever sufferer, the picture painted by the word *spring* is totally different.

The same rule applies to the words you use in your contacts with customers. You don't know in advance which words about you, your product, and your company will generate positive feelings in your clients. So you need to become extra-sensitive to the way you use words if you want to have a successful sales career.

Knowing the best words to use

Many words common to sales and selling situations can generate fearful or negative images in your clients' minds. The experience of hundreds of thousands of salespeople confirms that replacing such words with more positive, pacifying words and phrases (like the ones in Table 4-1) is crucial.

Table 4-1	Words to Eliminate from Your Sales Vocabulary
Instead of . . .	*Use . . .*
Sell	*Get them involved* or *help them acquire*
Contract	*Paperwork, agreement,* or *form*
Cost or *price*	*Investment* or *amount*
Down payment	*Initial investment* or *initial amount*
Monthly payment	*Monthly investment* or *monthly amount*
Buy	*Own*
Deal	*Opportunity* or *transaction*
Objection	*Area of concern*
Problem	*Challenge*
Pitch	*Present* or *demonstrate*
Commission	*Fee for service*
Appointment	*Visit,* as in "pop by and visit"
Sign	*Approve, authorize, endorse,* or *okay*

The first terms I recommend that you remove from your vocabulary are *sell* and *sold.* Many salespeople tell prospects how many units of their product they have *sold.* Or they brag about having *sold* the same product to another customer. What are the mental images these words create? No one likes the idea of being *sold* anything. The word reminds people of high-pressure sales tactics and usually turns them off. It makes the transaction sound one-sided, as if the customer really had little say in the matter. So what can you use in place of these common words? Replace *sell* or *sold* with *helped them acquire* or *got them involved* — phrases that create softer images of a helpful sales-person and a receptive customer becoming involved together in the same process.

Another commonly used word in sales is *contract.* What images does that term bring to mind, especially when you picture yourself as a consumer? For most people, *contract* evokes negative images — something Mom and Dad have warned you about all your life. Contracts bring with them fine print, legalities, and being locked into something. Where do you go to get out of a contract? To court — not a pleasant image for most people. So I recommend that you stop using the word *contract,* unless your particular line of business requires it. Instead, use *paperwork, agreement,* or *form.* Do those words bring to mind threatening images? Maybe, but they're are a lot less threatening than the images the word *contract* evokes. And that's exactly what you're going for.

What about *cost* and *price?* When I hear those words, I see my hard-earned cash leaving my pocket. That's why I train people to substitute the words *investment* or *amount* for *cost* or *price.* When most people hear the word *investment,* they envision the positive image of getting a return on their money. For products for which the word *investment* just doesn't fit, use the word *amount* — it's been proven to be less threatening to most consumers than *cost* or *price.*

The same idea applies to the terms *down payment* and *monthly payment.* Most people envision down payments as large deposits that lock them into many smaller monthly payments for, if not an eternity, at least a few years. They see themselves receiving bills and writing checks every month — not a pleas-ant image for most people. So replace those phrases with these: *initial invest-ment* and *initial amount* or *monthly investment* and *monthly amount.* In the selling business, we call these terms *money terms,* and anyone who wants to persuade someone to part with money needs to use these terms well.

What about the word *buy?* When people hear the word *buy,* they see money leaving their pockets again. Use the term *own* instead. *Own* conjures images of what they'll get for their money, where they'll put the product in their home, showing it with pride to friends or relatives, and many other positive thoughts.

Don't ask 'em to sign when you can ask for an autograph

I know a man who helps people acquire recreational vehicles. An RV isn't a minor investment for anyone. So when the moment of truth comes, he simply turns his paperwork around and says these words: "Bill and Sue, let me make you famous for a moment and ask for your autograph." While he's saying these words, he's handing them a pen and smiling. Nice picture, isn't it?

Another term overused by salespeople is *deal.* This word brings to mind something people have always wanted but never found. Images of used-car salesmen (decked out in the plaid coat I mention in Chapter 1) are only too closely associated with the word *deal.* Top salespeople never give their clients *deals.* They offer *opportunities* or get them involved in a *transaction.*

Customers don't raise *objections* about your products or services. Instead, they express *areas of concern.* I never have *problems* with my sales. Every now and then I may, however, face some *challenges* with my transactions. I never *pitch* my product or service to my customer. Instead, I *present* or *demonstrate* my product or service — the way any self-respecting professional would.

And as an authority or expert on your product or service, you don't earn *commissions,* either. You do, however, receive *fees for service.* If a client ever asks you about your *commission* on a sale, elevate your conversation to a more appropriate level with language such as this:

> Mrs. Johnson, I'm fortunate that my company has included a fee for service in every transaction. In that way, they compensate me for the high level of service I give to each and every client, and that's what you really want, isn't it?

Another word that can potentially raise concerns in the mind of a consumer is *appointment.* Now, in the business-to-business world, this may not be as strong. However, consumers will view the appointment as interfering with their regular schedule even if the schedule shows that time as free time. Rather than equate meeting with you to an appointment with a doctor or dentist, use the softer term *visit:*

I'd love to have the opportunity to visit with you, would Wednesday evening or Thursday afternoon be better?

Better yet, offer to "pop by and visit." What mental image does that create? That you're going to pop in and pop out. That you'll only be there a short time. In the business world, a "pop by" can conjure the image of a brief handshake and exchange of information in the lobby with no sit-down, conference room involvement at all.

The last but definitely not the least important term I recommend that you replace is *sign*. If you replace nothing else in your selling vocabulary after reading this book, never again ask a customer to *sign* an agreement, form, or paperwork. What happens emotionally when people are asked to *sign* something? In most cases, a warning goes off in their heads. They become hesitant and cautious. They want to review whatever it is they're signing, scanning the page for the infamous fine print. Anytime now, they may even head for the door. It's been drilled into almost everyone from early childhood never to *sign* anything without careful consideration. And why would you want to create that emotion in anyone you were trying to *get happily involved* with your product or service? Instead of asking your clients to *sign,* ask them to *approve, authorize, endorse,* or *okay* your *paperwork, agreement,* or *form.* Any of those word pictures carries the positive associations that you want to inspire in your clients.

REMEMBER

Concentrating on what appears to be such minor details may seem foolish, but some of those details pack a hefty punch. You may consider these words minor and think that all my fussing over them is misplaced. But if you really think about it, I think you'll see what I've been hinting at all along: Language is a salesperson's *only* tool — period. The salesperson who uses language well, for the genuine benefit of other people, is a salesperson who sells, and sells, and sells. The words you use are not minor details at all. They are the very center of your profession. So, when you write down and practice your own product presentation, go through it and make sure that your words stress comfort, convenience, and ownership from your prospects' perspective. After all, satisfying your prospects' needs is what this business of selling is all about — and the words you send out to them are the only way that you, and not your competition, can earn the opportunity to satisfy those needs.

Using only the jargon your clients know

Today more than ever, your selling vocabulary matters because of the phenomenon of *trade talk,* or jargon. *Jargon* is defined as words and phrases particular to a given field of work. If you sell medical supplies to doctors, you need to know the jargon medical professionals use and use it yourself, liberally. But if you sell medical supplies to the general public, limit your use of technical terms to the bare minimum until you can determine your client's level of knowledge about the product. You don't want to alienate your customers by using acronyms or words they're not familiar with. ***Remember:*** Your goal is to make your customers feel important — and it's tough to feel important when you don't feel very smart.

When your product or service has anything to do with the Internet, knowing when to use jargon — and when to steer clear of it — is especially important. Although by now you may feel like the whole world knows about the Internet, seeking out the lowest common denominator with potential clients is always wise. That way, you won't overwhelm or confuse them with terms or acronyms specific to your field.

The human mind can assimilate information rapidly only if it understands what is being said. If you're talking to Joe Consumer about bits and bytes and he doesn't understand those terms, his mind stops at those terms and tries in vain to find an image that fits them. Many people won't stop to ask you for explanations, because they're afraid of showing their lack of knowledge and being embarrassed in the process. Others may get the gist of what you're talking about but struggle to keep up. While they're trying to keep up, they miss the next few valuable points you relay to them. In other words, you've lost them. If your subject sounds more complicated than your customer can comprehend, you risk squelching his desire to ever own or use your product or service *and* you risk losing the sale. More often than not, you lose such customers to a salesperson who uses lay terms and simple definitions.

Good things come to salespeople who take the time to find out how to speak their clients' language.

Developing your vocabulary to excel in sales

Words are readily available to anyone who wants to use them. Webster didn't reserve certain words and their meanings for the rich. Everyone has access to the same dictionary, and everyone has the same opportunity to choose the words that make their speech outstanding and memorable. Every time you need to convey a concept to someone, you have a choice of any one of thousands of words to establish your meaning. You have no excuse *not* to choose your words carefully. Because you know that your words reflect the person you are, investigate the word choices you make and the reasons you make them.

Developing your selling vocabulary isn't about mastering the words you were tested on for the SAT or GRE exams. It's about taking the time to make a list of powerful but easy-to-understand words and phrases that are specific to your product or service. Then test those words on a friend or relative — someone who is *not* a qualified prospect. If your test person doesn't have a clear understanding of the terms, prepare brief definitions of those terms in lay language (language your test person — and anyone else — can understand). The first time you use the terms with new or prospective clients, be prepared to give them the definition in lay terms if it's something vital to the transaction or if the term will recur frequently in your discussion with these customers.

You need to strike a balance between speaking the language of your clients and educating them about the terms they'll need to know if they're going to use your product or service. The key is to not make any assumptions about the terminology your clients are familiar with — and to be ready to explain any terms they don't know.

Anyone who wants to persuade others (and if you're in the selling business, that's you) should recognize and choose appropriate language. Take a look at the two following examples. Be aware of the differences in language between the two situations. Even though you can't *see* these two salespeople, pay attention to the mental picture you get of each of them and their selling styles.

Here's the situation: The manager of Continual Care Hair (CCH) has been courting an account with a major chain of salons (owned by someone named Mr. Dunn) for two months. Mr. Dunn's salons now carry the products of one of CCH's competitors, but they have agreed to hear a presentation by a CCH representative. The CCH manager needs to choose the salesperson who can consummate all the manager's hard work — making a sale and landing the account. The manager calls a meeting with each salesperson she is considering. The one who succeeds in representing the company can receive a sizable increase in earnings. Which one would you choose?

MANAGER: Now that you understand what will be expected of you, how would you give this presentation?

DAWN: I would just love the chance to tell Mr. Dunn how much better our products are than what he's using. I would go to Mr. Dunn's salon tomorrow morning. I know I can convince him to dump what he uses now and replace his stock with ours.

MANAGER: What's your next step?

DAWN: Well, after I got all the information, I would tell Mr. Dunn what we can do for him and I would try to get him on my side before the presentation to his staff so he can help me sell his stylists on the products.

MANAGER: I'm interested to hear how you would do this, Dawn.

DAWN: Well, I guess I'd tell him how much money he would save and how much more he'll make by selling our products.

Now, here's the same situation — a hopeful salesperson talking to CCH's manager — except now the salesperson is Sue:

> MANAGER: Now that you understand what will be expected of you, how will you handle this presentation?
>
> SUE: I believe the first step would be to contact Mr. Dunn and request a meeting at his convenience. Then, with your approval, I would examine your files on the salon, so I'm prepared for the presentation.
>
> MANAGER: What's your next step?
>
> SUE: I will ask Mr. Dunn to show me his salons. I will familiarize myself with Mr. Dunn's needs, his stylist's needs, and those of the salons' clientele. Then I will offer Mr. Dunn the opportunity to use Continual Care Hair products and ask his permission to present the products to his stylists.
>
> MANAGER: I'm interested to hear how you would do this, Sue.
>
> SUE: Although considering his financial benefits is important, I will encourage Mr. Dunn to examine the improved condition of hair that has been treated with Continual Care Hair products. Making hair more beautiful will give Mr. Dunn happier customers as well as increased profits. Would it be possible to take a few company models with me on the presentation?

These two conversations have created two pictures in the mind of the manager. Who will represent her company with the most success? The answer is Sue. Why? Because Sue radiated calm enthusiasm and a thoughtful manner. But the turning point in Sue's interview is her choice of the phrase *I will* instead of the indefinite terms like *I guess* or even *I would* that Dawn uses. Sue speaks as if she's already been chosen, whereas Dawn uses iffier, less-confident language. This difference is subtle but very effective. And it isn't long before the manager agrees to send models out with Sue for her presentation.

Sue is an *above average* salesperson with a powerful command of language. She creates positive word pictures with every word she utters. Here are some words you may hear an *average* salesperson deliver. Think about the pictures they create in your mind.

> SALESPERSON: All the kids in your neighborhood will love playing in your new pool.
>
> PROSPECT: I'm probably going to have trouble getting my kids out of it.
>
> SALESPERSON: When should we start digging? Would this Saturday or next Monday be better?

What's wrong with this dialogue between the salesperson and the prospect? What image comes to your mind from the salesperson's statement that "all the kids in your neighborhood will love playing in your new pool"? Loads of kids jumping, splashing, running, and yelling at the tops of their lungs comes to my mind. It's not too peaceful a scene.

Think about the word pictures you paint. Just a few careless words can destroy hours of hard work. In this case, the salesperson would do better to say, "Most of our customers tell us they enjoy spending quality time with their families in their new pools." This image is much more pleasant — and it leaves the picture more open to interpretation. So if the client would *enjoy* a bunch of kids playing in the pool, that's what she can see, but if she would prefer a more laid back atmosphere, she can see that as well.

The salesperson's next words — "When should we start digging? Would this Saturday or next Monday be better?" — carry their own negative images. With the word *digging,* the prospect may envision a huge tractor roaring through her yard digging up plants and mound after mound of dirt, making a general mess of the prospect's home — and on a weekend to boot.

The salesperson would do better to say this:

> Some people prefer to be present when we begin the first phase of their new swimming pool. Others prefer to just tell us when and then have us tell them when the pool is ready to swim in. We can begin Phase 1 Saturday or next Monday. Which would you prefer?

I can't emphasize enough how important your choice of words is to your selling career. Your words can make or break the sale without you even knowing it. In many cases, if you ask a customer why she *didn't* buy from you, she may not be able to put her finger on any one deciding moment. She "just didn't feel right" about going ahead.

Words create images, which in turn evoke emotions, so start paying careful attention not only to your prospects, but also to the effects your words have on them.

Knowing How to Listen to Your Clients

The human body has two ears and one mouth. To be good at persuading or selling, you must find out how to use those natural devices in proportion: Listen twice as much as you talk, and you'll succeed in persuading others nearly every time. When you do most of the talking,

- ✔ You aren't finding out about either your customer or your customer's needs.

- ✔ You aren't hearing buying clues or concerns.

- ✔ You may be raising concerns the prospect may not have had in the first place.

- ✔ You're shifting your prospect's attention from your offering.

- ✔ You're giving your prospect more opportunity to disagree with you, to distrust one of your statements, or both.

- ✔ You're taking center stage away from the customer.

- ✔ You aren't able to think ahead.

- ✔ You aren't able to guide the conversation.

- ✔ You aren't able to convince the other person of the best decision for him.

Most people don't think they talk too much, but if you had listened to as many sales presentations as I have over 25 years of teaching, selling, and sales management, you would have developed a keen ear for how much talking is done compared to how much is needed — and the answer all too often, is too much.

To develop your ear, try these two simple exercises:

- ✔ **Listen to a salesperson selling others or trying to sell you.** Pay attention to what his words are doing. While you're listening, ask yourself these questions:

  - • Do his words paint positive or negative mental pictures?

  - • Do his words say anything that may raise a new objection to his product or service?

  - • Are all his words necessary?

- Does he ask questions and then carefully listen to the prospect's answers?

- Does he move forward with questions, or does he get off course by talking about features and benefits the customer has not expressed a need for?

✔ **Record yourself when you're talking with a customer.** You may be shocked at how much chatter you can cut out. To detect what you need to cut, ask yourself these questions:

- What is the quality of the questions I ask?

- Am I asking information-gathering questions to help myself move forward with my sale, or am I just asking questions to fill a sound void? (Questions don't mean much unless the answers are helping you get the information you need to help you serve your customer better and keep the sale moving forward.)

Watch and listen to others and to yourself more carefully than you're used to listening in everyday conversation. Acquaint yourself with what good listening really "sounds" like. It should sound like the voice of others, not your own voice. As you discover more and more about selling well, the phrase "putting your foot in your mouth" will gain new meaning for you. After all, you can't put your foot in your mouth if it's closed. So close it, and listen more.

Chapter 5

Knowing Your Product

. . . .

In This Chapter

▶ Getting the vital statistics on your product

▶ Talking with other salespeople to find out how they sell the product

▶ Being prepared to answer any question that comes your way

. . . .

*O*ne of the best advantages of a career in selling is that good selling skills are portable. By that I mean that after you master the skills, you'll have the education you need to sell any product that interests you when you complete your product knowledge. Product knowledge is one whole side of the selling triangle I discuss in Chapter 1, which tells you that it's one-third of what you need to know to be successful.

In this chapter, I cover some specific suggestions for ways you can develop your product knowledge and be prepared for nearly any question that comes your way when you're with potential clients. By investing time in product research upfront, it'll pay off when you're ready to put your selling strategies to work.

What You Need to Know

What must you absolutely, positively, truly *know* about your product in order to sell it? Always begin with the obvious:

✔ **What the product is called.** Know the specific product name and model, as well as the product/part number so if your customers refer to it by a number, you'll know exactly what they're talking about. You also need to have a clear understanding of what it does as you're bound to run into potential clients who will refer to it as, "that type of vacuum that picks the lint off of fleas. At least I think that's what it said in the ad I saw."

✔ **Whether the product is the latest model or release.** Many of the potential clients you'll encounter will want the latest version of your product.

✔ **How it improves a previous model or version.** Be able to list the new features or options and what they can do for your customers.

✔ **How fast, powerful, or accurate it is.** Be able to offer up a comparison of the product to its competition so you can tell your customers how your product stacks up. It's better if the comparison was done by an independent study group. If it's just your word against that of the competition, you may not have much of a leg to stand on. If there's not independent study available, at least have your satisfied clients who are already using it give you a testimonial that it's better than what they had before.

✔ **How to operate it during demonstrations.** Nothing is worse than trying to demonstrate a product to a prospective customer, only to find out that you're not sure how to make it do what they've asked. Be able to operate the product as well as you operate the car you drive every day.

✔ **What colors the product comes in.** Being able to tell your customers right away whether you have a specific color available will come in handy when they want to know whether it meets their needs.

✔ **What your current inventory is for setting delivery dates.** Your client may have seen a review of your product in a magazine, even though it's not due out for two more months. You'll need to know what he's talking about, inform him of delivery delays, and see if he needs the benefits of the product sooner. If the product is currently in production, but on back-order, brag about its popularity and know the projected delivery dates.

✔ **How much of an investment the product would be.** Be sure to phrase the price of the product in terms of an *investment* as opposed to a *cost.* Also be prepared to reduce that amount to a monthly amount if your product is something that requires financing. Many purchasing agents will consider how much something will add to monthly overhead and how soon they can recover their investment.

✔ **What terms and financing are available.** If your company offers financing, consider it another product and know how it works as well as you know the product itself. Don't risk losing a sale when you've gotten all the way through to the financing stage of things.

✔ **If you work for a manufacturer, whether there are distributors who may offer the product for less.** If there are, know who these distributors are and what price they're selling the product for.

Even companies with the most basic product training should cover these topics with new salespeople before sending them out to talk with customers. Unfortunately, however, some companies provide only the bare minimum of information and you have to develop the rest on your own. With all this preparation, you should be pretty well off. However, be prepared to encounter a potential client who will ask an odd question — something out of the ordinary that you can't discern the answer to with your current knowledge. Never make up an answer! Tell the person that you'd be happy to find out the answer to that question for her and then do it — quickly — before she considers the competition's product over yours. In cases such as this, you may have to do a lot of additional information gathering in the course of researching the answers to your customers' questions. And that's okay, because you build your product knowledge as needed.

Keep in mind that if a potential client ever comes to you with valid information about your product or service that is a surprise to you, your credibility with that client will be on shaky ground. After all, you're supposed to be the expert clients come to for information or advice. If they know more than you do, why do they need *you?*

How to Get the Information You Need

How can you be sure you're armed with the product knowledge you need before you head out to make a sale? Take advantage of as many different resources as you can. If your company offers training sessions on the product, attend. If they hand out brochures and pamphlets, know them backward and forward. Talk with your customers about the product so you know what questions they have, and discuss the product with your fellow salespeople to get suggestions. And be sure to know your competition's product so you can tell your customers how your product measures up. I cover each of these resources in the following sections.

Attending training sessions and reading product literature

Your company or the manufacturer of the products you represent may hold regularly scheduled training sessions about the product. If they do, then by all means go to these training sessions. They're your best opportunity for getting the scoop about your product from reliable sources. And *always* attend these sessions with a list of questions and a notepad for writing down the answers. If the speaker doesn't answer your questions during the presentation, find a way to ask your questions before this knowledgeable person gets away.

In between training sessions, watch for e-mail or Web updates of product information from the company as well. Visit your own company's Web site every morning and watch for a product revision date, if those are posted on the site. If something has changed in the past 24 hours, you need to read it and be familiar with it as soon as possible. After all, your best new prospect may have read that information already, and you want to be able to show that your information is current.

If you get information from online news sites like CNN (www.cnn.com) or MSNBC (www.msnbc.com), take advantage of the customizing features on those sites. Many news sites will let you tell them what industry or company you need the latest news for. When you visit your customized home page on the site, links to that information will show up automatically.

Your company will probably inundate you with brochures and technical information on your product or service, even if they don't offer specific product-training sessions. Set aside a specific amount of time in your schedule to sit and read such literature — but don't just read through it the way a customer would. Study it. Read it every day for at least three weeks. By the end of that time, you'll have the information memorized and know exactly what your customers are referring to when they ask questions. Nothing is worse than having to look to a higher source when your customer asks a question that you should know the answer to.

If training sessions and product literature aren't available to you, and what you sell is a tangible product, get your hands on a product sample right away. Be like a kid with a new toy: Play with it, experiment, read through suggested demonstrations, and try it out as if *you're* the customer. Make notes on things you find hard to understand. Chances are good that at least one of your prospects will have the same questions or concerns that you come up with. Resolve those concerns now, and you'll be well prepared for your demonstrations.

Try sending the questions you come up with to your customer support department online. See how long it takes them to provide an answer and how detailed the answer is. What you'll receive from them is what a customer would likely receive when using that service after a sale. If the return time is unacceptable for the type of question you asked, see if you can do anything within the company to help speed things up. Or if you know the response time is slow, you may recommend, during your presentation, that your clients contact you directly with questions. This strategy shows that you provide added services *and* that you're knowledgeable about the product.

Make sure that taking care of customer support questions and concerns doesn't take up so much of your time that it interferes with your selling time. After all, you're paid primarily to find and serve new customers for your business, in addition to keeping those you've already gained.

Talking with customers

Get as much feedback as you can from the people who already use and benefit from what you sell. Ask what their experiences have been with your product. Your surveys can be printed pieces mailed to your clients or, for even better response, e-mails or Internet surveys they can quickly complete with a few clicks. If you prefer the personal touch and feel the time is valuable, handle those surveys in a personal phone call. The advantage to talking to people personally is that you can get the client talking and, hopefully, discover something new that will help you serve all your clients better.

Your current customers are an extremely valuable resource — *if* you keep in contact with them.

Picking your colleagues' brains

Veteran and top salespeople have all kinds of information about products that they may never document. Talk with them as much as you can in order to put their knowledge to work for you.

Keep your meetings with other salespeople focused on product knowledge and information; otherwise, your time will not be well spent. When two or more salespeople get together, it's easy to get off the subject at hand and descend into old war stories or other unrelated matters. If you want product knowledge, focus the conversation there. Now is not the time for gossip.

Ask your sales manager for permission to do a ride-along with the top salesperson in your territory. You'll almost always get a thumbs-up, because the request shows your manager that you're sincere in wanting to become the best salesperson you can be. Watch how the salesperson handles everything: herself, the client, brochures, proposals, visual aids, and the product itself. Listen to the word pictures she uses in describing it. Notice the mood she sets. ***Remember:*** The how of handling products and information is as important as the what and why.

Being a student of selling

When you're in a learning mode, you need to set the stage for learning. That may mean gathering pen and paper, brochures, and a demo piece of equipment and locking yourself in the company conference room to study. It may mean setting appointments and interviewing with a training director, company owner, or top salesperson. It may involve watching hours of product training videos or attending classes on the products. It may involve interviewing current customers.

It doesn't matter what the type of education is, you must begin every session with a clear respect for what's to come. Treat the sessions like gold. Show up on time, if not early. Have plenty of paper for note taking. Bring a couple of pens in different colors to highlight the most important information. And be courteous to those who are sharing their knowledge with you. What they are imparting will make you money. Treat them and their messages with the utmost respect. The better you treat the people who are helping you, the more they'll relax. You'll be making them like you and trust you, which will lead them to offer you even more valuable information. Hmm, sounds a lot like selling, doesn't it?

Have the veterans provide you with their research Web site addresses. If they're as good as you think, they'll have a tremendous database of where they get their latest and best information about your product — and that of the competition.

Going directly to the source

Whatever type of product you sell, try to create an opportunity to tour the facility where your product is designed and built. Better yet, try to visit with the originator of the idea. Find out what she was thinking when it all came together.

You cannot know too much about your product or service. Customers love to feel that you have the inside track on the latest and greatest products and services; they want to believe that you are the most competent person in your industry. Face it: No one wants to be represented by a dud!

Keeping an eye on the competition

Most companies designate a person or department to gather information on the competition and to prepare analyses of that information for the sales staff. If your company has this situation under control, sing their praises and encourage them to keep up the good work, because such research can be a voraciously time-consuming feat.

If your company *doesn't* provide this service, you need to take it on yourself. Take advantage, at least once a week, of online searches that will seek out any information for you that includes the keywords you give it, such as your competitor's company name, product name, and so on. This information should include the competition's latest news releases as well as products — good things to know, especially if the competition is in trouble with the government or involved in a lawsuit based on one of its products, for example.

Don't rely on just one source for information. If you're in business on your own, you may want to enlist a family member to find juicy tidbits of information on competitors' products for you. Because you're the one who's out there every day slogging in the trenches, facing off against the competition, you need to keep your eyes and ears open for any information available, too.

If you call on customers who've had past experiences with your competitors, ask them if they would mind sharing their thoughts on the product and service with you. Ask what they liked about the product — particular features and benefits. How were their contacts with customer service handled? What would they like to see improved upon? Asking in a sincere, caring manner will send the message that you want to do better, be better, and help them have a better experience than ever before. When they tell their tales, take good notes and keep them handy for future reference. If a new customer has just switched from the competition to your product, find out exactly what the deciding factor was and work it into any presentations you make in the future where circumstances are similar. Also, be certain that feature has remained in the product if they're thinking about making an upgrade.

Product information doesn't just come from the technical booklet that comes with the product. It's everywhere the product has been. In seeking out as much information as possible, you will earn and keep your expert status, and more people will want to take your advice.

Chapter 6

Taking Advantage of Technology

Gone are the days of 3-x-5 index cards with handwritten notes about clients. Also gone are the giant Rolodex wheels of name and address information. In the 1990s, computers and the Internet took off to such a degree that if you didn't jump on that wave, you may have been left floating along wondering how you missed it. But don't worry: It's never too late to use technology to your advantage. And as a salesperson, you have plenty of opportunities to do exactly that. After all, part of doing your homework is getting up to speed with the technology that can make your life — and your selling — more efficient.

In this chapter, I start by lessening some of your fears and helping you get motivated to get up to speed. Then I share some great resources that can help you sell better — everything from tools to use when making presentations to online map services to help you get where you're going. In this chapter, I don't even come close to describing all the technological resources at your fingertips, but I do highlight the best of the best, letting you know which ones you should check out first. View this as a jumping-off point to the wide range of innovations at your disposal.

Knowing Where You Fit in the "New Economy"

If you've listened to the news anytime in the past few years, you've heard the term *new economy* bandied about. The term *new economy* refers to the dot-com businesses that cropped up with the advent of the Internet, as opposed to the *old economy,* made up of the bricks-and-mortar businesses you grew up with. If you were comfortable selling in the old economy, you may have wondered whether the new economy was turning you into a dinosaur, without your approval.

In the following sections, I help you overcome your fears about technology and help you to get motivated to use it to your advantage. So if you get a chill down your spine when you hear talk about computers and the Internet, read on.

Setting aside your fears

If you've been in the sales profession for decades, the Internet Revolution — and the accompanying technology — may have left you reeling. In the past several years, I've talked with many veteran salespeople — people who consider themselves professionals — who are afraid the Internet will take over their jobs, like the Industrial Revolution took much of the manual labor away from workers. These salespeople fear that if consumers can order online, they won't have any need for a salesperson. They fear that consumers will get the jump on them by knowing more about the competition's products and services and latest announcements than they do. In other words, they fear becoming obsolete.

I firmly believe that the Internet couldn't possibly bring about the demise of the sales profession any more than automation eliminated the need for living, breathing people in the industrialized world. Sales aren't made to machines; sales are made to people. And even though your computer may be able to talk to you and your clients, it hasn't yet mastered people skills — and as a salesperson, you still have the upper hand on the capacity to develop those skills to better serve your customers.

Being able to persuade potential future clients to like you, trust you, and want to listen to you when making buying decisions is still critical. Real people with real challenges will always want to talk with other real people — that's where the fun is. Technology can't empathize with clients. It can't understand their needs and calm their fears the way a living, breathing sales professional can. It can't build a caring, mutually respectful, long-term relationship either.

When it comes to using the Internet — or any other of today's technology solutions — having some fear at first is completely natural. What most humans want more than anything else is to be comfortable. Figuring out how to use something new requires change. And change of any sort leaves most people feeling at least a little bit uncomfortable.

Motivating yourself to change

Many people hesitate to discover something new, even if they're assured it will make their jobs easier or make them more effective — and even if the new knowledge or behavior is guaranteed to extend their lives (like exercise) or help them earn more money (like sales training). They know that in order to get from here to there, they'll have to invest extra time and effort — and who has an abundance of either of those? So where will you find the time in your already busy schedule to master something new, like computers? That question — and the accompanying fear of becoming obsolete — is natural when you have to change your life. What do you give up in order to change? If you're like most people, when you're motivated by your belief of how much better you'll be *after* the change is complete, you'll quickly find the time and be energized to put forth the effort.

Flexibility and adaptability are the keys to success in today's ever-changing business world. As you've seen over the last 15 to 20 years, computer literacy is no longer just a business skill, it's a life skill — just like adding, subtracting, or knowing how to drive a car. Using the Internet, wireless phones, handheld planning devices, and certain common computer software programs all fall under this umbrella as well. The more you know, the more indispensable you will be to your company — or the more valuable you will appear to a new company if you decide to change jobs.

Using Technology to Make Your Life Less Complicated — Instead of More

If you're new to some of the technological tools that are available for you to use, you may think of all those gadgets as time-consuming things you have to spend hours figuring out. And to some degree, you're right. Anytime you use a new product or service, you have to spend a little time upfront learning how to use it — but the reward is definitely worth it if it's the right tool for the job you have in mind.

The techno-salesperson you talk with about any new tool should do a good job of understanding your specific needs before recommending any device. If he doesn't invest that time, he may not have your best interest at heart.

In this section, I highlight some key tools that you can use in your selling career to make your life simpler. If you do your homework and get up to speed on these tools, you can put them to use — and be more profitable in the process. How can these tools make you more profitable? Because, when used properly, they can free you up to focus on your clients' needs more completely (instead of worrying about some of the other details). And that's always a win-win situation.

Using PowerPoint in your presentations

Microsoft PowerPoint is a software program that allows you to create simple or intricate slide-show presentations using your computer. When you're ready to give the presentation, you can use the PowerPoint slides you've created in a couple different ways: You can print the slides and give them as handouts to your audience, or you can display the slides on a wall or screen with a projector. Giving presentations is a key element in selling, and PowerPoint makes it easy for you to tell your prospective clients about yourself, your product, or your service. You can also customize the slide presentation for each prospect — and in much less time than it would take you if you were doing it all by hand, the old-fashioned way. Plus, you can include audio files in your presentation, time music to go along with the messages, or add photos or diagrams to better make your points.

One of my trainers, Ron Marks, takes photos with his digital camera and adds them to his PowerPoint presentations. He can include photos of the company buildings, staff, products, services in use, and, of course, the company logo. Boy, is this powerful when he goes in to provide a truly customized sales training session!

PowerPoint is often bundled together with other Microsoft software programs (like Word and Excel), so you may already have it on your computer. If you don't, you can own it for around $339 directly from Microsoft or from numerous office-supply or software stores.

For more information on how to put PowerPoint to use for you, check out *PowerPoint 2000 For Windows For Dummies* or *PowerPoint 97 For Windows For Dummies,* both by Doug Lowe (published by Hungry Minds, Inc.).

Keeping track of client contact information with contact management software

If your business is a simple one and requires only name, address, and telephone contact information on each client, you can get by with nearly any simple address book, such as the ones found in Microsoft Outlook or Lotus Notes. But if you need to track each contact with your clients and have those contacts coordinate with your daily, weekly, or monthly calendar, using something called *contact management software* makes more sense. Contact management software is a database of information — as much information as you'd like to include — about your future clients and long-term clients. It's where you type things such as:

- Names (make sure to get the spelling correct)
- Company names
- Addresses
- Various phone numbers
- E-mail addresses
- Assistants' or secretaries' names
- Best times of day to reach the clients
- Dates, locations, and times of appointments
- Notes on each conversation with the clients
- Descriptions of correspondences sent
- Products or services ordered
- Delivery dates
- Challenges that arise and how you overcame them
- Future growth plans for the company or division
- Birth dates
- How long they've been with their companies
- Hobbies (to establish common ground)
- Where they took their last vacations
- Just about anything you can possibly learn about the people

The best thing about contact management software is that the information is quickly and easily accessible or alterable as your relationship with each client evolves. Some contact management programs also allow you to link to, let's say, Microsoft Word, and generate a letter or process orders for a client. The name and address information can be automatically placed in the letter so you don't have to worry about misspelling anything after it's entered correctly into the database.

Your company may want you to use a certain software program that's being used by the whole sales team. Many of these programs provide reporting information or sales analysis information for management so they can see how efficient their staff is being and where clients may be dropping off. So, your decision may be made for you by someone higher up. If that's the case, you simply need to take advantage of whatever training is available — even if that's just a training manual to read through.

If your company doesn't offer or suggest a software program to use, you'll need to spend some time researching your options and choose the one that's right for you. Although I don't recommend one program over another (because what will work best for you is your call), I can share some basic information about some of the programs my students use successfully:

- ✔ **ACT! 2000** is an economical investment. It retails for about $190, but you can find it for less at numerous computer stores. If you buy from an online store, you can also download it directly onto your computer instead of having to wait for the CD to be shipped to you. You can also purchase licenses for five or more users so you and four of your associates can use the same program at a discounted rate. ACT! allows you to import contact information from Outlook or almost any other format you may already have been using. If you want to find out more about this software, check out *ACT! 2000 For Windows For Dummies* by Jeffrey J. Mayer (published by Hungry Minds, Inc.).

- ✔ **GoldMine** retails for about $170, but as with any software, you can find better deals if you shop around. It includes a Web data capture tool, a document management center (for those great sales letters you send), and a literature fulfillment center for information you send out regularly. Check out *GoldMine For Dummies* by Joel Scott (published by Hungry Minds, Inc.) for more information on what this software offers.

- ✔ **Salesforce.com online Customer Relationship Management service** allows you to keep your database online rather than on your own computer. That way, you're not bogging your system down with a huge amount of data and the information is available to you online from any computer. No more lugging your laptop home every night. The investment varies depending on the number of people in a company or group who subscribe to the service. Visit the salesforce.com Web site at www.salesforce.com for more information.

- ✔ **SalesLogix.net** helps mid-market companies manage their customer relationships. Like salesforce.com, this service is subscriber-based and offers access to the contact management database as well as many other linked services, including travel information, motivational and training tips, and so on. Visit the SalesLogix Web site at www.saleslogix.com for more information.

- ✔ **Siebel Systems** (www.siebel.com) offers software geared to larger businesses and is a high-end investment. It involves a complete server-based administrative system, including tools for sales needs, service needs, and administrative needs. So you can keep track of your clients, be sent notices from corporate, and file your expense reports all on one system.

Gadgets

If you can think of a task that needs to be handled, there is very likely a bit of technology that has been invented to handle it. The trick to not owning so much technology that you can't carry it all around with you is to concentrate on your own priorities. Which tasks take so much of your time that it would be worth having them mechanized or, at the very least, simplified? In this section, I review some of the more common tools sales professionals are using to get organized, plan their time, and communicate — or at the very least, get from Point A to Point B with clients, both physically and verbally.

Personal digital assistants

A personal digital assistant (PDA) is an electronic device that is smaller than a videocassette tape yet works like a computer. It has a screen display — some in color — and works on a touchpad system. Companies like Palm, Casio, Hewlett-Packard, and Handspring make the most popular ones. You can purchase one at most computer or office-supply stores for as little as $130 up to $600 or more — depending, of course, on how much you want your PDA to handle.

PDAs are wonderful for keeping track of your contact lists, merging your personal and business calendars into one organized program, and getting connected to the Internet for current information. You can even play games on PDAs, but I wouldn't want you to think of them as glorified GameBoys. Most PDAs are compatible with software you are likely to have on your computer (like Lotus Notes or Microsoft Outlook). You can even download your latest calendar changes from the PDA to your computer or download music from the Internet.

The downside of PDAs is that data entry is made primarily with a stylus, which means you hunt and peck on a keyboard display. Some PDAs have keyboards as accessories, where the PDA plugs into a standard keyboard for easy data entry.

You can get all sorts of other fun accessories, such as special cases for your PDA, a portable modem for faxing, a connection to your wireless phone, the ability to check your e-mail, and so on. If you work primarily in an office or store location, a PDA may be more of a fun tool for you. If you're constantly on the road, the PDA can become your best (lightweight) friend.

Wireless phones and smart phones

You have probably seen these phones used on television programs and in the movies. In fact, you probably already have a wireless phone — most of America seems to. *Wireless* means just that: You can be just about anywhere (hopefully, not in a restaurant or watching a movie, unless you want to annoy the people around you) and make and take phone calls.

With the newer *smart phones,* you can also receive e-mail and dial up the Internet for information. All of these services are available for a fee, of course, and those fees vary widely depending upon the types of service you need to make your life easier.

Business card scanners

If you're like most salespeople, you collect a lot of business cards. Then you have to enter the information off those cards into some sort of program in order to keep the information accessible. Lucky for you, some wonderful people decided that entering that information by hand was not a wise use of their time, so they invented business card scanners. These nifty little devices allow you to insert a business card and have the information magically transported in electronic format into your contact management software or other software program.

CardScan is a scanner/software combination. With CardScan you can address e-mail directly from CardScan, launch directly into a contact's Web site, synchronize multiple databases, and transfer information to other programs. The software accurately organizes information into an electronic Rolodex and reads international and two-sided cards. It also synchronizes with PDAs and most digital mobile phones. CardScan Executive (for one person) retails for about $200. (If you're buying for an office instead of just for yourself, you can get special deals for multiple users.) For information on CardScan, go to www.cardscan.com.

Helping your clients locate you

You probably have a lot of information on your business card — your company name, your company address, your direct phone number (or at the very least your extension number), your fax number, your pager number, your mobile phone number, your company's Web site address, and your business e-mail address. So, if I'm your client, what's the best way for me to reach you when I have a challenge? If the challenge is causing me grief or a slowdown in my own business, you can bet I'll use every number and address I have in order to track you down. Instead of allowing your clients to become frantic trying to locate you, consider using a *unified messaging service,* in which you can have all your messages (voice mail, faxes, e-mail, and so on) delivered to one place for collection. You can collect all your messages anywhere around the world using the phone or the Internet. To find out more about this wonderful service, visit Unified Messaging at www.unified-messaging.com, or call 212-252-9258 for more information.

Another good source is uReach.com at www.ureach.com. Sign up online for your personal toll-free number, voice mail, e-mail, fax, calendar, address book, file storage, and more. Or try Onebox.com (www.onebox.com), a free, all-in-one voice, fax, and e-mail service.

Making travel plans and getting maps online

A live person at a travel agency can be a great help when you're planning a business trip. But if you find out at 9:00 p.m., after checking your e-mail, that your boss needs you to be in a city 300 miles away for a client meeting within the next day or two, you're going to want to check the best flight arrangements for your arrival time and to get a reasonable fare — and the sooner, the better.

Most airlines have their own sites where you can check availability and purchase tickets, so if you have frequent-flyer miles with a particular airline, the airline's Web site is a great place to start. (See Table 6-1 for a listing of the contact information for major U.S. airlines.) But if you're flexible and can travel on any airline, you won't want to invest all your time doing individual comparisons at the airlines' Web sites. Instead, visit Travelocity.com (`www.travelocity.com`) or Expedia.com (`www.expedia.com`), both of which offer comparisons of times and fares for nearly all commercial airlines. You can find what's best for you and then book the flight right then and there if you want.

Table 6-1	Airline Web Sites and Contact Information	
Airline	*Web site*	*Contact information*
America West Airlines	`www.americawest.com`	Domestic reservations: 800-235-9292; international reservations: 800-263-2597
American Airlines	`www.aa.com`	All reservations: 800-433-7300
American Trans Air	`www.ata.com`	All reservations: 800-435-9282
Continental	`www.continental.com`	Domestic reservations: 800-525-0280; international reservations: 800-231-0856
Delta Airlines	`www.delta.com`	Domestic reservations: 800-221-1212; international reservations: 800-241-4141

(continued)

Table 6-1 *(continued)*

Airline	*Web site*	*Contact information*
Midwest Express	www.midwestexpress.com	All reservations: 800-452-2022
Northwest Airlines	www.nwa.com	Domestic reservations: 800-225-2525; international reservations: 800-447-4747
Southwest Airlines	www.southwest.com	All reservations: 800-435-9792
TWA	www.twa.com	All reservations: 800-221-2000
United Air Lines	www.ual.com	Domestic reservations: 800-241-6522; international reservations: 800-538-2929

If you'll be traveling by car anytime during your trip, you can find maps online at several different Web sites. Two of the best are MapQuest (www.mapquest.com) and MapBlast (www.mapblast.com). Both sites give you estimated travel times, all the turns you need to take, and the total mileage of your trip. You can print out the information or download it into your computer or PDA. The directions are provided in step-by-step text form, along with maps of the area. You can also find the nearest hotels and restaurants along your route.

As you can see, as the mind thinketh, it shall appear online or, at the very least, be available in version 1.0 software in an e-store nearest you. What I cover in this chapter is just the tip of the iceberg in terms of what current and developing technology can do for you in your sales career. I suggest allowing yourself at least 30 minutes a week to investigate new sites, improved sites, and up-and-coming technology. Keep an eye out for those truly wonderful developments that will help you save time in tracking all the details of your career and allow you more time to do what you're paid to do — acquire new clients.

Part III
The Anatomy of a Sale

The 5th Wave   By Rich Tennant

"GET READY, I THINK THEY'RE STARTING TO DRIFT."

In this part . . .

The chapters in this part cover the seven steps of the selling cycle. Here you'll discover exactly how to find the people who need what you have and how to get appointments with them. You'll find out how to make sure your product is right for your prospects and give a presentation with ease. And you'll discover how to address your prospect's concerns, close the sale, and get referrals so that you can start the cycle all over again.

Chapter 7

Finding the People Who Need What You Have

*T*he first step in the selling cycle is what salespeople call *prospecting*. Prospecting is, essentially, searching for people to sell your products or services to. It's a lot like the type of prospecting that you would use a burro, pick, and shovel for, except that the prospecting you do as a salesperson uses telephones, e-mail, and word of mouth instead.

If you already know the people you'll be selling to, you probably don't need this chapter right now (although the tips and suggestions you'll find here may help you find even *more* prospects, which is always a good thing). On the other hand, if you have a great opportunity, service, product, or idea, but you don't know where to find other people who would be interested in getting involved with it, this is exactly the place to start.

Over the years, my former students have contacted me with news of what they thought were the greatest new products, services, or ideas. They were going to make millions, they said, with their new businesses. Their enthusiasm practically lifted them off the ground. Some of their proposed businesses actually sounded pretty good. But without proper planning — without knowing how to find enough financial resources and the right end users of their products or services — many of those projects turned to dust, and my former students' enthusiasm dissipated like so many wisps of smoke.

Prospecting your way to riches

When you're just getting started, your time should be split between finding out about your product, honing your skills, and finding people who need that product. The key to success in a people business like selling lies in how many people you can see in the time you have. Initially, you'll probably find yourself working very hard just to find a few prospects. But with every experience, you'll discover a little more, refine your strategies and techniques, and eventually find yourself working smarter.

If you're asking yourself, "With all this prospecting, am I a miner or a salesperson?" keep in mind that the two jobs share many similarities. In each, you stake a claim; you bring with you the necessary tools to help dig out your own little niche of success; you have high expectations of success; you persistently and consistently work toward your goals; you have a firm belief in your ability to achieve those goals; and, finally, you refuse to let others' negative reactions to your work inhibit your behavior and beliefs.

If you don't know whom to contact to help you get from Point A to Point B, you doom your product, service, or idea right from the start. You soon lose your enthusiasm or invest too much of your own time and money with little or no payoff at all. You run out of gas before you even get on that road to success. That's why this chapter is vital. You can master everything else in this book, but if you never get the opportunity to get in front of the right people, all the selling techniques you've honed add up to naught. You won't even make enough profit to feed your burro.

Finding the Gold: Knowing Where to Start

When you're finally prepared enough with knowledge about your product, service, or concept, and when you feel comfortable with your selling skills, you need to begin finding the people to sell to. Because you won't have a lot of qualifying, presenting, closing, or follow-up to do when you're new, your primary focus should be on prospecting. In fact, in the beginning, your daily plan should be to invest about 75 percent of your time prospecting. The other 25 percent of your time should go toward developing your product knowledge and presentation skills.

Many successful sales veterans will tell you how important prospecting is even after they have built a large customer base. Successful sales professionals — those with a strong desire not only to reach the top but to stay there — make prospecting a part of their everyday selling strategy. They understand that achieving success doesn't mean they can stop looking for new business opportunities. Successful sales professionals explore every avenue in search of new customers, no matter how long they've been in the business.

The best place to start prospecting is with people who already have paid money for products and services similar to yours. If you're selling exercise equipment, begin with people who jog, belong to health clubs, or join local recreational sports teams. Why? Because you *know* they're already health conscious. The convenience of being able to exercise at home may be just what they're looking for. If you're selling graphic design, start with the people responsible for advertising in local companies. If you've already worked for people in a certain type of business, such as gift shops, you may want to concentrate on other gift shops in the area. The items in your portfolio will then be very appropriate displays of your work.

To some degree at least, where you'll find your prospects depends on what you represent. If you sell products or services for a company, you probably found out during your product-knowledge training where the likeliest places are to find your products or services in use (if you didn't, be sure to ask). Those places are, obviously, the best places to begin prospecting. After you have some sales under your belt, you'll have time to get more creative with staking out other claims.

If you're on your own (as opposed to representing a company), start with your local Chamber of Commerce or your local library; both have listings of all sorts available, including local businesses, national business directories, and international directories. Conduct online searches for businesses of the type that would use your product or service. For example, you may search for all manufacturers of computer software if your product applies to that field. All you need to do to narrow down your list of potential prospects to the right ones to begin contacting is ask the right questions. If you have some money to invest in lists, you may want to contact a *list broker,* which is someone who has all sorts of lists available and can review your particular demographic needs with you to provide you the best list of potential customers to contact.

If you prefer to market via e-mail (a very economical method), ask your list broker if he has *opt-in e-mail lists,* which are lists of people who have agreed to have information about certain things they're interested in sent to them via e-mail. Opt-in e-mail lists receive a response rate ranging from 5 to 15 percent — a huge increase over traditional direct mail response rates. And using opt-in e-mail lists can help you avoid e-mailing unwanted information to people and making a negative impression (making no impression at all is better than leaving a negative one). Check out www.postmasterdirect.com to find out more about how you can benefit from e-mail promotions.

The simplest place to start prospecting is with the people you already know, like the groups I cover in the following sections. Talking with these people first will help you find easy leads and give you an opportunity to practice your prospecting presentation with people who are less likely to give you a dose of rejection than complete strangers are.

Searching for prospects among your friends and family

When you're new in the world of selling, honing your selling skills may help to draw you out of your comfort zone. So prospecting among those people with whom you're most comfortable — your friends and relatives — can take away a little of the stress of this thing called *selling*. I refer to a salesperson's friends and family as her *warm* or *natural market*. Friends and relatives are less likely to reject you (which means you're less likely to fail), and rejection and failure are the two biggest fears among those who are trying anything new. Your friends and family like you, they trust you, and they want to see you succeed. That means they're almost always willing to help. Besides, if you truly believe in the goodness of what you're doing and these people are candidates for your product or service, why would you want to deprive the people you care about the most of the chance to benefit from what you're selling? If you truly care about them, they'll respond in kind — and possibly become some of your best clients.

Be selective when you prospect among your family and friends, though. If you're selling exercise equipment, don't get discouraged if 90-year-old Aunt Minnie doesn't buy two of everything.

Start by contacting your friends and family and telling them that you're in a new business or you're starting a new career and that you want to share the news with them. Unless you've started a new job every six months for the past several years, they'll be happy for you and will naturally want to know more. This interested audience gives you the perfect opportunity to test your presentation skills.

A key phrase to use in getting your friends' permission to share with them your new product, service, or idea is this: *Because I value your judgment, I was hoping you'd give me your opinion.* This statement is bound to make them feel important and be willing to help you — if they weren't already.

After you've contacted all your family members and close friends, move on to acquaintances. Consider talking with your child's baseball coach, other parents, your accountant, and the checkout person you always see at the grocery store. If approached properly, most people are more than willing to give you advice or opinions. Ask the right question, and they can advise you right into a great connection with a big client.

If your friends and relatives are not good candidates for your offering, contact them anyway. The first rule in prospecting is never to assume that someone can't help you build your business. They may not be prospects themselves, but they may know others who are. Don't ever be afraid to ask for a referral. There's gold in them thar hills!

Looking far and wide in the wide, wide world

Unless you represent a unique product or service, the opportunities you have for making contact with prospective clients are practically unlimited. You simply need to test a variety of methods to narrow down those that bring you the best people.

If what you sell is good for businesses, begin with your local Yellow Pages. Businesses invest their money in listings because they're serious about being in business. Their listings also should tell you that they're serious about *staying* in business. If your product or service can bring a business even more business or make that business more efficient, you owe it to them to contact them. And if you want to broaden your field of prospects, check out a toll-free directory. You'll find one online at `www.inter800.com`. Businesses are listed by company, number, and type of industry, regardless of long distance carrier. ATT Anywho directory (`www.anywho.com/tf.html`) allows you to do reverse lookups, when you have the phone number but don't know where the company is located. You can get company e-mail addresses here as well. For the same information about Canadian companies, contact `canadatollfree.sympatico.ca/Search`. If you're not online, your local library will likely have an Internet connection that you can use, or they may even have a toll-free directory in their reference section. Your local library is a wealth of free information. Use it!

Be sure to put the Internet to work for you when it comes to prospecting. Post bulletins on message boards related to your product or service. Provide valuable information *in addition to* selling your product or service. (If you're new to the Internet, refer to *Internet For Dummies*, 7th Edition, by John R. Levine, Carol Baroudi, and Margaret Levine Young [published by Hungry Minds, Inc.] to get a clearer idea of how you can use this phenomenal tool to your greatest advantage.)

Because there is no Big Brother–like editor on the Internet, not everything you see there will be 100 percent correct and accurate. Information posted by large, respectable corporations will probably provide source listings. You should verify information without source listings through a reputable source before relying on it yourself — or passing it on to your clients.

Using the help of professionals

Getting advice from others who have already been where you're going and are willing to share their knowledge is always a wise move — no matter how long you've been in the selling business. The Service Corps of Retired Executives (SCORE) has an excellent reputation for matching people who are new in a field (or those who may be struggling a bit) with retired or semiretired professionals from similar fields. SCORE is a U.S. government program with contact offices in most major metropolitan areas. You can visit the SCORE Web site at www.score.org to find out more about its services and to locate help near you.

The experience the helpful people of SCORE can provide is exceptional, but you must be open to discovery. Although some of their experiences may not apply to your current marketplace, the information available through SCORE can be like a life jacket thrown to you in the middle of the ocean.

If SCORE doesn't have an office in your area, keep an eye out for a mentor who can offer similar assistance. A *mentor* is someone who has more experience than you, an interest in what you're doing, and a willingness to take you under her wing to guide your actions. Mentors want to help others overcome obstacles they faced, to help others learn from their experience. You can find a mentor through Sales and Marketing Executives International, a professional support organization that has offices in most major cities. Check them out at www.smei.org. And you can always contact your local Small Business Administration office for advice by phone or online at www.sba.gov.

Hiring someone else to do the dirty work for you

If you're really pressed for time and able to cough up the money, you can hire an advertising agency and a public relations firm to handle much of your market awareness and prospecting for you. Agency assistance varies; an agency can take on everything for your business, or it can help you with occasional, one-shot promotional ideas.

The fees that agencies charge for their assistance differ across the country, so be sure to do your homework when researching agencies. Ask the agencies you're looking at to send you information on what they've done for other businesses. Always check out the people who give testimonials and references for a business. You never know when an agency's best testimonial will turn out to be from Grandpa Smith, who may have a personal (and maybe even a financial) interest in the agency's success. If an agency hesitates to give you references, don't waste your time considering doing business with them.

Even if you do hire an agency or agent to find prospective customers for you, never, never stop prospecting for yourself. If you ignore this valuable step in the selling cycle, you may walk by your best potential client without even a glance.

If you're new to sales, the company you work for may partner you up with one of its veteran salespeople for a brief training period. This type of company-sponsored mentoring program is working wonders around the world. It gives recognition to the vets for their knowledge and expertise and at the same time helps to train the new people in tried-and-true methods of conducting business. So if you have the opportunity to take advantage of a program like this, be sure to do so. And if your company doesn't have an organized mentoring program, talk with your manager to see if you can be paired with someone anyway. Your interest in learning and becoming the best salesperson you can be will most certainly be looked upon favorably.

Taking advantage of lists generated by your company

When you work for someone else's company, the company usually handles the details of advertising and marketing to generate leads for you and the other salespeople. But in order to become a great salesperson, you should always be prospecting on your own, too. That way, if the company lead program hits a lull, you'll be prepared. A slow period isn't the time to begin developing your prospecting skills. If you're prospecting all along and encounter a minor setback, you'll barely break stride in your business activity level.

You may be in a position to help answer questions that are e-mailed to your company by customers or prospective clients. If that's the case, don't just reply; make the inquirer curious for more information. Do your best to capture more than the person's return e-mail address. Get the person's name, street address, and phone number if at all possible. Add him to your contact list and follow up with him to ensure he's satisfied with your reply. Offer to provide him with additional service as well. This strategy is just one more way to add to your list of prospective clients.

Putting phone, mail, e-mail, and face-to-face interactions to work for you

You can contact your prospects in four major ways: by mail, e-mail, phone, or face to face (I cover each of these methods in the following sections). Keep in mind that when you use any of these four methods, you're asking busy professionals to give up time that they may think can be spent more productively. So before you have a chance to convince your prospects otherwise, they will try to shut you out — and shutting you out is easy for them to do. They can just make a paper airplane out of your letter, delete your e-mail with a simple click of the mouse, leave you on terminal hold, ignore your incoming phone call, or cancel your appointment.

Face-to-face prospecting can be very effective, even though it's much more time-consuming than the other methods of contact. After all, if you prospect in person, one of four things can happen:

- ✔ You can be asked to leave literature and be told that the person you're wanting to talk with will contact you if she's interested.
- ✔ You can be allowed to schedule an appointment for a future date.
- ✔ You can uncover valuable information about the company and who the real decision-maker is.
- ✔ You can actually get the opportunity to present your product or service to the decision-maker herself.

Most professional salespeople integrate all four methods into an effective prospecting strategy. For some, one method works better than others. Different situations call for different strategies, so be well versed in how to handle each. As you gain experience in prospecting, you'll figure out which methods work best for you and at which times.

Telemarketing

Telemarketers' phone calls are easy to hate — especially when you can hear the pages of their script turning as they read it at warp speed, hardly taking a moment to breathe. You may feel like telemarketing calls are intrusions or interruptions in your daily life. The common reaction to a telemarketing call is to say, "No, thanks," and then quickly hang up. So if that's your response to most telemarketers, you probably wonder why businesses keep using telemarketing. The reason is that telemarketers can reach more potential users of a company's product or service in one hour than most salespeople working face to face can meet in a week. Plus, telemarketers don't have to travel from one location to the next; they just dial the next few digits.

But telemarketing comes with (more than?) its share of pitfalls. Salespeople who use telemarketing need to have skin as thick as the backside of a rhinoceros. Plus, they need to use a survey approach to the call instead of just trying to set appointments right away. A certain amount of rapport building needs to take place with every new contact, whether it's on the phone or in person. And that means that you need to ask questions to get the person you call to start talking (this is what I mean by a *survey approach*). When you show concern for the person's time, his needs, and his situation, he'll feel important and want to listen to you.

Hardly anyone wants to listen to a one-minute dissertation. People want to be involved in the phone calls they receive. That's why you need to script your call so that it's courteous and filled with brief questions that your prospect can answer easily. People have to decide whether they like you before they'll consider doing business with you. The survey method is a simple, nonthreatening way of doing exactly that.

When you're using the survey method in your telemarketing calls, you need to create a brief but effective survey. Your survey needs to provide you information about whether to pursue a contact as a customer. It also needs to pique your prospect's curiosity about your product or service. Your goal is to get the person talking — grunting doesn't count. The more the person talks, the more information you'll gather that may point you toward or away from future contact with him. And that's not only in *his* best interest, but yours as well.

Stick with five questions or less. Always tell the person on the other end of the phone that the firm you represent has asked you to conduct a quick survey and tell him that you need his help. If he says it's a bad time for him, acknowledge the bad timing, apologize, and try to get an appointment for a better time to call. If he says, "Go ahead and ask," thank him and get right to your questions. Unless the person appears very interested in what you're saying, each call should take no more than two minutes.

Your questions should generate answers that tell you whether the person you've called may potentially qualify as a good client. For example, If your product is diaper service, you would want to know if there are any children in diapers in the home. If not, does the person have any babies in his extended family whose parents may have such a need?

If your product is family photos, you'd want to know when the last time was that the person had one taken. If it's been awhile, ask how often that photo is looked at and how family members have changed since then. You would then encourage her to consider having a new photo taken to enjoy as much as the last one.

You have two possible goals for a telemarketing call:

- ✔ To arrange a time for a face-to-face meeting
- ✔ To get permission to send information via mail and e-mail and make another brief follow-up call

Mail

If you choose to use mail as your primary method of prospecting, choose your mailing list carefully. Mailing is a great way to prospect, but mail sent to the wrong list of people is a tremendous waste of your time, money, and effort. Nothing is easier to get rid of than a piece of paper that arrives amidst a stack of other papers. And this is especially true if your prospecting piece of paper winds up in the mailbox of someone who wouldn't care about your product or service in a hundred years.

Instead of sending a piece of mail that talks about your product or service, mail a single-page introductory letter to the people you know who are most likely to want to get involved with what you're doing, indicating that you'll be calling on a certain date and time. Include your photograph on the letterhead or on a magnet or other enclosed novelty item. Magnets are great: Every time your prospect goes to the fridge, she sees your smiling face. People buy faces. They aren't as likely, however, to buy from some anonymous voice on the phone. *Remember:* Prospecting is all about establishing rapport.

Whatever you send in the mail, be absolutely certain that it includes your Web site address and your e-mail address. As much as people love talking on phones these days, they're still more likely to check you out first by visiting your Web site to see if there's anything interesting that may make it worth their while to talk with you in person. Or, if the purpose of the mailing is to generate sales, let the recipients know if they can order online. They don't have to wait until they can catch a live sales representative on the phone — especially if they read their mail at 2:00 a.m.

E-mail

You can handle e-mail prospecting in two ways. One is to purchase an opt-in e-mail list from a list broker and send an e-mail message to the group of people who have expressed an interest in your type of product or service. The other is to search out the e-mail address of a consumer or purchasing agent (through an online telephone directory or their corporate Web site) and mail a very specific, customized e-mail.

In either case, you want to use your e-mail like the introductory letter mentioned in the preceding section. Introduce yourself, your company, and the benefits your product would provide to the recipient. For the opt-in list, you may wrap up your letter with a call to action: "Reply to this e-mail within 24 hours and we'll have a specific proposal to you by Friday of this week." Or, in a custom e-mail you may tell the recipient that you'll be calling within 48 hours to ask him two quick questions (this is the survey approach from the "Telemarketing" section earlier in this chapter).

Sending an e-mail that looks like an advertisement is not as effective. Your goal with e-mail is to make a personal connection, pique the recipient's interest, and tell him how to learn more.

Face-to-face interactions

Face-to-face prospecting is almost always the best method, but it's also the most time intensive. Walking from office to office or home to home trying to find someone to talk with is physically exhausting, which is bad enough. But even worse is the sad fact that you may not get many appointments out of all your legwork.

What you will get, though, is a load of information from receptionists. They can be powerhouses who help you either eliminate a company as a prospect or advance your chances of obtaining an appointment for making your presentation with the decision-maker. I've often thought one of the best places to prospect would be a secretarial convention rather than the one where all the executives meet. Secretaries and assistants hold the keys to opening the doors you want to get through.

Treat receptionists or secretaries with the respect they deserve. Their time is valuable, too. If you try to rush past a receptionist or quickly ask to see her boss without first showing concern or interest in her, you may as well not have gone in at all. Introduce yourself, ask the receptionist's name, and then try to have a friendly dialogue with her before asking to see the boss. She will be more inclined to introduce a friend to her boss than she will a pushy salesperson, so try to get her to see you as the former rather than the latter.

When you engage in face-to-face prospecting, remember how lucky you are to be able to get some of the precious time out of the busy schedules of important people. Your prospects are offering something to you, too: an opportunity to show them how they can benefit from your product or service. In today's society, suspicion and distrust are rampant. When you professionally prospect (with the right attitude about your prospects), your contacts will come to trust you and welcome you into their homes and offices.

Finding the Right People: Proven Prospecting Strategies

In this section, I cover ten of the most effective methods I've used to find those people who are the best candidates for what you have to offer. When you apply yourself to finding these people, and if you continue to do so on a regularly scheduled basis, you'll be off and running on a successful selling career.

Mining the people you already know

You don't conduct your normal daily activities in isolation, do you? That means that you already know a horde of people who may be potential prospects for your product, service, or idea.

Think beyond your closest circle of friends and relatives. (Besides, you probably tapped them out during your first two weeks of selling, anyway.) If you're like most people, you shop every week (at grocery stores, hardware stores, discount stores, at shopping malls, and so on). And unless you live in the middle of nowhere, you have neighbors. You may go to church or school functions on a regular basis. You may have a spouse who works or who is involved in other activities through hobbies. And chances are good that several people in this wider circle of acquaintances may be able to benefit from your product or service in some way — or they may know others who do. In prospecting with the people you come into contact with on a daily basis, your job is simply to communicate. Letting others know what you do opens many doors of opportunity for you. All you need to do is start a conversation.

Make a list of all the people you know, and start there. Here's a list to get you started:

- Your parents
- Your grandparents
- Your siblings
- Your aunts, uncles, and cousins
- Your coworkers
- Members of your sports team
- Fellow churchgoers
- Parents of your children's friends
- Your neighbors
- Your hairstylist
- Your friends
- Members of business or civic groups you belong to
- Your mechanic
- Grocery store cashiers
- Your drycleaner
- Your pest-control person
- Your pet's veterinarian
- Your doctor
- Your dentist
- Your lawyer
- Your accountant
- Your kids' teachers
- Your teachers
- Your kids' coaches
- People you used to date
- Tellers at your bank
- Fraternity or sorority friends
- Your kids' babysitters
- Your spouse's friends

Prospecting . . . an imaginative way

One student of mine always wore his company logo on a lapel pin — upside down. He made a specific point of putting it on upside down when he left the house. Hardly a day went by that some well-meaning do-gooder didn't tell him it was upside down, thus opening the door to a pleasant conversation about his business. As soon as he left that person's presence, he would turn the pin upside down again and move on to the next do-gooder.

Tapping your business contacts

Whether or not you're new to selling, you've probably been involved in some sort of business. Even if you're just out of school, you've probably held part-time jobs throughout your school career. Business contacts can be easier to talk with than some social contacts because business contacts prospect all the time, too. You probably can cut to the chase more quickly with business contacts than you can with your personal contacts.

Visit the Web sites of the companies where your business contacts work. Look for the names of other companies they may have affiliations with so you know before contacting them whether they may have another good contact for you. If the affiliates they have posted on their Web site aren't good candidates for your product or service, or if they could be considered part of your competition, don't waste their time or yours in asking for these particular contacts.

Pay attention to the e-mails you get from your business associates. You may have received that e-mail as part of a group of recipients — and one of those people may be a prospective client for you. Getting a new lead may be as simple as having the person who sent you the message give you those other people's phone numbers so you can contact them. Or see if you can get permission to contact each person who received the e-mail along with you.

When you receive a group e-mail from a business contact, you may be able to see the e-mail addresses of all the recipients. If you want to try prospecting with them, call the person who sent the e-mail and see whether the people you want to contact would mind if you contacted them (as opposed to just sending e-mails without checking first). That way, you can contact the person and say, "John Smith asked me to contact you," which is much more professional and courteous to all parties involved.

When you're sending out your own e-mails to more than one person, put your recipients' e-mail addresses in the *blind carbon copy* (BCC) field instead of the *To* or *CC* field. That way, you're not sharing your personal or business lists with others.

When you're prospecting, think not only of the people you know in your business life, but also get involved in clubs or organizations for business professionals and prospect there. Excellent opportunities have been found in sales and marketing clubs and at functions held by Chambers of Commerce.

I can't recommend highly enough Toastmasters (a public-speaking organization) for anyone in sales. When you're involved in Toastmasters, you win through what you give to the group *plus* you gain access to lots of potential clients. Check your local phonebook for Toastmasters, or visit their Web site at www.toastmasters.org to find a chapter in your area.

Many industries also have their own associations through which you can discover valuable new strategies for approaching people in your specific industry. Staking your claim in these groups can be highly beneficial. Ask your business contacts if they have a back issue of an industry publication available. Studying it will give you a good feel for the type of potential business you may find within that organization.

Your local library should have a directory of associations or you can do an online search for specific industry associations, such as the American Heart Association, the American Association of Retired Persons (AARP), or the American Bar Association. You may want to begin a search with the American Society of Association Executives at www.asaenet.org. At the ASAE Web site, you'll find their popular Gateway to Associations — a list of people, businesses, or associations. Another good source of prospects is *American Demographics* magazine (www.demographics.com). At the *American Demographics* Web site, you'll find articles on the latest trends developing in the marketing world as well as statistics on demographics of the American buying public. The site also includes research tools for locating trade shows, exhibitions, and seminars that people who need your product may attend.

When you find a prospective company, do further research with reputable resources. A great one is Dun & Bradstreet. Visit www.dnb.com and request a Business Background Report. Information on over ten million U.S. businesses is available at the Dun & Bradstreet Web site. You'll be charged a fee for the reports, but you'll know the information you're getting is from a reliable source — which makes the fee worthwhile. Other Web sites that offer business listings and specific company information include Hoover's Online (www.hooversonline.com), infoUSA.com (www.infousa.com), and HarrisInfoSource (www.harrisinfo.com).

For free information on businesses, try the Internet Public Library at www. ipl.org. It's an easy-to-use research site, but the information available is not as detailed as what you'll find at Dun & Bradstreet.

Talking to salespeople you currently buy from

Talking to salespeople you buy from is one of the most overlooked strategies of prospecting. Other companies send you highly knowledgeable, professional salespeople who already know loads of other people. They wouldn't be coming to you if you were in a similar business, right? So, because you're in a noncompeting business, why not talk with them about any leads they may have? Or at the very least, ask them to keep you in mind the next time they call on their customers. Any extra sets of eyes that are out there looking for prospects on your behalf are of tremendous value, especially when your only investment will most likely be returning the favor sometime down the road.

I've used the idea of a swap club to generate many leads for my business. I would get between four and six top people in other fields to join me once a month or every other week for breakfast at a local restaurant. Each of us would bring at least five to ten new leads for others in the group. There may be times when one of the people just doesn't have that many, but be sure to emphasize that sharing leads is the goal of the meeting — not devouring the fresh sticky buns. Each person pays for her own breakfast and provides the leads as her "fee" to stay in the group. If you set it up that way in the beginning, no one will have to tell someone else to leave for nonperformance. She'll know she's out if she fails to hold up her end of the arrangement.

Parlaying your adventures as a consumer

Imagine that you're at a restaurant and your server does an especially excellent job. If you're looking for someone to join with you in business, not work for you, and if this person already has great people skills and is competent at performing his duties, he may be a good candidate for being in business for himself. You probably run into these kinds of people every day, everywhere you go — so take advantage of the situation and talk with them about the opportunities (or products or services) you have to offer.

Be careful not to approach people while they're working. Professional etiquette dictates that you don't interfere with other professionals while they're conducting business.

So what do you say to such people when you have the opportunity to talk? Here are some words that have proven to work in this particular situation:

> *I can't help but notice that you have a nice way with people. I'm curious, are you achieving all your goals working here? The reason I ask is that the firm I represent is in an expansion mode and we're looking for quality people to take advantage of the opportunity. Do you have an interest in knowing more?*

If the person asks, "What's this about?" say

> *Ethically, because you're working now, I'm not at liberty to discuss it. However, if you'd like to jot down a number and time I can reach you when you're not working, we can visit and see if it's a win-win possibility.*

You can then either arrange a time to call or, at the very least, leave him with your card and a time to contact you. It's a harmless strategy, but it still gets the person's attention.

Another way to prospect through other businesses is to send the business a letter or thank-you note for providing you excellent service. Many business-people publish or display these letters in their places of business or on their marketing literature. If they have your permission to use your name in promoting their business, they're also pretty likely to list your profession or business name. When other people read your words, they'll see how professional you are and, hopefully, remember your name when they need services such as the ones you offer.

If you market a consumer item, chat with the people you meet when doing your own shopping to see if they're good potential candidates for your product or service as well. Your grocery checker surely needs insurance, doesn't she?

The key to successful prospecting is to acquire the mind-set that *every* person you meet is either a potential client or knows someone else who is qualified.

Benefiting from the itch cycle

Face it: Nearly every tangible product brought to market has a limited life span. At one end of the spectrum are computer software and hardware, which can have a life span as short as six months. At the other end of the spectrum are things like refrigerators and freezers, which have life spans of almost 20 years. No matter how long a product's life span is, every product has one.

The precise life span of your product doesn't matter. What matters is that you know what its life span is. When you know your product's life span, you have a goldmine of opportunity waiting for your pickax to strike. If you're new to the product, ask people already in the business about your product's life span.

When you review your past customer files (see the following section for more information), you'll see that Mr. and Mrs. Lopez's microwave oven will need to be replaced in the near future. It's bound to happen if it's getting up in years — say, 10, 12, or 15 years old. So don't wait for the Lopezes' microwave to break down and then quietly hope they'll come see you again. Get in touch with the Lopezes *before* their microwave breaks down, and let them know you have some great new products with greater energy efficiency, space-saving designs, and other all-around better features. Put a reminder on your calendar or tag their file for follow-up in your contact management software. Your call just may help them move a little *quicker* in replacing that old microwave!

Chances are good that the Lopezes know that their microwave is on its last legs and that they've just been putting off making the decision to shop. Maybe they've been waiting for a good buy or sale to appear in the paper — that doesn't matter. What matters is that they haven't acted *yet*. And these facts matter, too: The Lopezes already know you and/or your product personally — and they know that you're the expert they turn to when the time for decision-making arrives.

Always make sure strategies such as this one are approved by your manager or are acceptable according to company policy before you implement them yourself.

If your company allows it, take advantage of a strategy I call *puppydogging*. How do you sell a little puppy? You let someone take it home for a few days to see how things go. Almost every time, the people — that is, the *prospects* — become so attached to the new puppy that they can't bear to part with it.

If you're a car salesperson, you let a trusted customer try out the latest model of the car you think she'd like, and before a few days are up, the prospect loves the new car and wants to keep it. If nothing else, she's started itching for a new car and will need to get back in touch with you to return the loaner. And you've guaranteed yourself an itchy customer to serve. Such personalized service is guaranteed to keep customers coming back for more. Some salespeople even drop off a high-quality videotape of the latest model of the car their prospects drive so that they can fantasize about owning it, all in the comfort of their own home. Now that's nice!

You can also try e-mailing your client with an attached URL of a Web site where they can see photos and detailed information about the vehicle you think is best for them. Offer to bring one by for them to test-drive. All they need to do is reply with the word "Yes," and you have permission to confirm an appointment with them.

If you don't already know the replacement cycle for your line of products, do some research to find out what it is. When do people begin getting that itch for something new? All you need to do to find out this kind of information is make a few phone calls to people who currently use your products or services. You can treat this like a survey or market study and simply ask for their help. If they know it won't take long, most people love to help you. Begin by verifying that they're still using the product your records show them owning. Then ask what they used prior to the product or service they bought from you. The only time such research will fail is if the product or service that you sold to your customer is your customer's first foray into your market. If it's the second, third, or later product or service of this type that they've owned, ask how many years, overall, they've used such products or services before replacing them.

You can also look at your own records to determine the lifespan of your product or service. For example, if you sell copiers and your customer has used your copiers for 17 years, trading in only 4 times during your association, you know he'll need a new copier after he's owned his present model for about 4 years. When that fourth year rolls around, you may want to ask the client a few questions about his current needs and get permission to send him information about the latest and greatest models. If he won't need another machine for two more years, thank him for his help and make a commitment to stay in touch.

With replacement products, the salesperson who gets to the customer at the right time is often the one who wins. Plan to be that person and you'll be doing a lot of the winning. The early bird makes the sale.

Using your customer list

Any business that's been around for at least three years should have a pretty good customer list. Ask the business owner or manager how many salespeople have come and gone during that time. It may be that those salespeople haven't necessarily gone away but are now in other positions in the company. If you can get in touch with several former salespeople, find out what happened to the people they sold to. If those customers weren't reassigned to another salesperson, you may want to ask to be given the authority to contact those clients yourself. If nothing else comes of your contacts, you will leave a positive impression of the type of follow-up your company provides. And, hopefully, you will have updated your database along the way. Be sure to get e-mail addresses and Web site addresses (for business contacts), too.

With the many changes that occur in business these days, managers don't always take the time to complete the basic task of transferring clients to new salespeople when the former salespeople move on. If the company is growing rapidly, some customers may get left in the dust. Why not be the one to pick them up and take care of them? They've already bought your brand or service before, so they're likely to again.

If your company has lived up to its promises, your customers should want to continue to work with such a fine organization. If they haven't made any purchases lately, it may be simply because no one has asked. Don't leave the door open for a competitor to come in and snatch up valuable customers. Prospect your list of past customers and you may not only solidify their future business but the business that they will refer to you as well.

Riding the wave of technical advancement

Earlier in this chapter, I cover the inevitable itch cycles of various products. Why do you suppose people itch to get something new? In some cases, it's simply because the product wears out. In others, though, it's because of something more personal, like status. They want to have the latest, greatest, shiniest, top-of-the-line products with all the bells and whistles you can provide. When people have the best and latest products, they appear to be doing well.

Think about it. If you see someone with her cell phone attached to her belt and an earpiece subtly hanging over her ear, it catches your attention, doesn't it? And when you see someone who is obviously talking on the phone but isn't holding a phone to her ear, do you automatically assume she's with the Secret Service and start looking around for the President? In years gone by, you would have assumed the person was speaking to an imaginary friend and steered clear of her. But today, you're left with the impression that the person is on the cutting edge of technology, which means she must be successful, a real go-getter.

Few people really want to have the old model of anything unless they're collectors and the old model is a true antique or classic. Because most businesses today sell high-tech equipment, peripherals, and support products and services, knowing and using this method of prospecting is tantamount to success. Whenever you have a new model, an updated version, or even a change in the investment for your product, you have a solid reason to reconnect with the people you've already sold to. Being the kind of people they are, it's only natural that they'll want to be kept apprised of the latest changes. The key to success with this strategy is in how you contact them. Take a look at the following examples to see how you can put this strategy to work for you (and how it can backfire if you're not careful).

Bill invested in a top-of-the-line home entertainment system a couple years ago, but now some improvement has been made in the product that wasn't available when he bought it. Don't just call up old Bill and say, "Hey, I've got something even better for you." That would be both pushy and presumptuous and would very likely have the opposite affect of what you wanted — you may turn Bill off to even hearing what you have to say, because you've just, in effect, criticized his system.

Instead, call Bill and ask him how he's enjoying listening to his favorite music on his home entertainment system. Being sure that he's still happy with what he's got before bringing up anything else is critical. If he has a complaint you didn't know about and you start talking about new products, you could lose Bill as a customer forever.

When you've determined that he's happy, say the following:

> Bill, I know how diligent you were in your research before investing in the T-tronics system. Because I value your opinion, would you mind evaluating something else our company is coming out with?

See the difference? You've complimented Bill, acknowledged his intelligence, *and* asked for his opinion. You've made him feel important. Of course he'll be happy to look at your new toy now. And if it's truly better than the one he has, he'll probably want to upgrade his system.

If you take the time to know what's going on with your current customers, you'll know exactly when and how to contact them with new products or innovations and increase the volume and number of sales you make to each one. Now that's what I call working smarter.

Reading the newspaper

One of the greatest prospecting tools around can be delivered to your doorstep for under a dollar a day in most areas. It has an intimidating, ultra-technical name; it's called a *newspaper*. These days you don't even have to walk out your door to receive it, because many newspapers are also available online. I used to read my printed version with a felt-tip marker so I could circle all the opportunities I found. But today, you can cut and paste the most pertinent information into a single document and print it out.

Unless you do business internationally, you'll probably want to stick to the local news, business, and announcements sections. Stay away from the latest crime statistics and headline-making stories unless that's your field of interest. For most people, the most beneficial portion of the paper is written about John and Jane Q. Public.

John and Jane are the people who get promoted in business. They have babies. They buy or sell homes. They start up new businesses. Do you get my drift here? If John Q. Public has been promoted, what else usually comes along with that promotion? A raise in pay. And what do most people do with their raises? Invest in stocks and mutual funds? Some do. But most buy new cars, bigger houses, nicer clothing, and season tickets to entertainment events — and buy the products and services you sell.

Knowing how to read your newspaper for leads only takes a few days of practice. When you get started, you'll be amazed at the number of leads you used to glance over. Here's just a brief list of some of the things people need and want when they go through life changes (all of which you can find in your local newspaper):

- ✔ People having babies need more insurance, bigger homes, minivans, delivery services, and diapers.

- ✔ Families who are moving into new homes need garage door openers, security systems, ceiling fans, homeowners' insurance, landscaping, and aspirin (lots of aspirin).

- ✔ New or expanding businesses need equipment, personnel, and supplies.

I know of one real estate agent who benefited tremendously from a single news item in his daily paper. The local professional football team had acquired a new player. So the real estate agent sent a note to that new sports player before his arrival, congratulating him on making the move and welcoming him to the area. He included a copy of the news article and offered his services if needed. Being new to the area and to the team, the football player didn't know anyone in town, but he did need a place to live — so he contacted the real estate agent who sent him the letter. The agent not only helped the player find a new home but put him in touch with an insurance agent, local doctors for his family, a dentist, a hairstylist, and so on, illustrating exactly how the newspaper can pay you much, much more than the few cents a day it costs.

Take today's local newspaper and read every headline. Circle those with stories that may hold some business prospects for you. Then do what any top salesperson who's striving for excellence would do and *contact* those people. Cut out the article, make a copy for your records, and then send a brief note, saying, "I saw you in the news. I'm in business in the community and hope to meet you someday in person. I thought you might enjoy having an extra copy of the article to share with friends or relatives." Be sure to include your business card. People love seeing that they were in the news. And they love having extra copies of the articles to send to friends and relatives who aren't in the area. By providing this little service in a nonthreatening way, you can gain a lot of business.

Knowing your service and support people

If you're in touch with the people in other departments of your company, you may be able to discover valuable information that may help you keep the clients you already have (and get more down the road). For example, someone who works in accounting for your company may know that one of your clients has been late several times in making his monthly investment in your product or service. That's a valuable piece of information for anyone in sales.

By reconnecting with that client, you may be able to make other arrangements for him. Perhaps his growth rate isn't as high as he anticipated and your equipment or service just costs too much for him. Instead of letting information like that get away, help the client cut back on his equipment or make other financial arrangements. He'll never forget you and will become a loyal, long-term customer, referring his friends and business associates to you when they need the product or service you provide. If you let such information go without addressing it, you may lose that person as a customer just because he's overloaded with unnecessary equipment and is too embarrassed to approach your company about it.

Get in the habit of periodically checking your company's service and repair records. Even better, see if your company can set up a system so that when a service call comes in, the salesperson is automatically e-mailed a notice of it. Consider asking the folks in your customer service department how many times your clients call with questions about the product or service you've sold them. If your clients are calling frequently, you need to get back in touch with them. Maybe they're in a growth phase and you can help them acquire new services. Or maybe they're having some challenges with particular equipment. If they got stuck with a lemon, you need to be the one to turn it into lemonade — before they demand a replacement, a refund, or your head, and you get squeezed out!

Always strive to provide service above and beyond what the average salesperson would give. You'll build long-term relationships, trust, and referral business in the process.

Practicing the three-foot rule

Many businesspeople subscribe to the three-foot rule when it comes to prospecting: Anyone who comes within three feet of them is worth talking to about their product, service, or business.

When you get comfortable with what you're selling and with talking to people about it, I highly recommend applying this strategy. All you need to do is say, "Hello, it's nice to meet you." Pay attention to the people you talk to. Notice something about them you can compliment. For example, if you're a woman and you're talking to another woman, you can say, "That's a great purse (or dress, or coat). Where did you find it?" After she answers, go on with another question about her response or bring up something else you have in common, such as why you're standing in line at the grocery store at 11:00 p.m. After you establish a little bit of rapport, exchanging names is considered the polite thing to do. And that's when you can bring up the subject of your idea, product, or service. Ask a question such as, "Have you ever found a product to get gum off kids' sneakers?" (if what you sell gets gum off sneakers). Or use a question such as, "Have you been to the new gift shop on Fifth and Grovers?" (if the new shop is your shop). If you market security products, you could say, "I see you carry mace on your key ring. It makes you feel a bit more secure, doesn't it?" When she answers in the affirmative, talk about the great security product that you found (and sell). Personal testimony moves more products than any other method.

I know of one man who has gotten some of his best leads from fellow elevator passengers whom he knew only as long as it took to ride six floors up or down! Many business contacts have been made while standing in checkout lines at the grocery store or order lines at the fast-food restaurant. Be sure to be ready to talk about your product or service wherever you go — and don't pass up any opportunity to talk with a prospective client.

Get creative with how you seek out information. For example, car handlers at valet parking services can be a valuable source of information. They discover a lot about people by their cars and how they treat the valets, and they overhear conversations about business. I'm not advising you to encourage people to eavesdrop on your behalf, but never turn away a valuable source of leads, either. If you've been trying to get an appointment with Mr. Warbucks and the valet knows he's in the restaurant and will be leaving promptly at 9:00 p.m., it may be convenient for you to be next in line at that time, don't you think?

So how do you handle these brief encounters with people and get leads to build your business? I have to admit that this method won't bring you great leads *every* time. Even so, why walk by a potentially beneficial opportunity without knocking? So here's what you do: Grab a few of your business cards. (Salespeople are notorious for ordering thousands of business cards at a time. In fact, you can often tell the people who are newest to sales by the huge bulge of cards in their pockets. So make sure you start with just a few.) Across the front of each card, in very neat handwriting, write, "Thank You." (Hopefully, you haven't printed every one of your vital statistics on the cards; if you did, you may have no room to print your *Thank You.*) When you meet a new person — someone who has entered your three-foot space — be warm and friendly. Introduce yourself and ask her what her business is or why she's at that place. Making such banter sort of obligates her to do the same. When she asks what your business is, you simply hand her one of your cards. Most people take whatever is handed them as long as their hands aren't already full. (Thousands of servers of legal documents requesting your presence in court can't be wrong!) When the prospect gives you the courtesy of looking at the card, she'll probably ask about that *Thank You.* (Curiosity gets the better of most people and they blurt out their questions almost as a matter of reflex.) That's the moment you've been waiting for. At that point, you simply smile and say these words:

I guess I'm thanking you in advance for what, hopefully, will be the opportunity someday to serve your [whatever your business is] needs.

Be sure to use those words exactly. *I guess* makes it sound spontaneous. *Thanking you in advance* shows that you're a nice person. *Hopefully* shows humility. *Someday* places your offer way out into the limbo of the future; it's a very passive, nonthreatening word. *Serve your needs* elevates your prospect to a place of importance in your life — and *everyone* needs to feel important. When she feels like she's important to you, she's more likely to make a move that can help you.

She'll probably do one of four things, any one of which is a move in the right direction for you:

✔ She'll agree to call you to discuss it further.

✔ She'll give you a time to call her to discuss it further.

✔ She'll ask you to send something, either by e-mail or regular mail.

✔ She won't be interested, but she'll refer you to someone who may be interested in what you have to offer.

What have you got now? A lot more than you had a moment ago, standing there in line waiting to order your burger. You've got a prospect . . . with a side order of referrals.

Chapter 8

Getting an Appointment and Putting Your Clients at Ease

In This Chapter

▶ Knowing how to get in touch with your prospects

▶ Using the telephone to your best advantage

▶ Figuring out how to get in touch with the difficult-to-reach decision-maker

▶ Building rapport with your prospective clients

▶ Paying attention to what you have in common

*I*n virtually every situation in which you can use selling skills, if you don't get face to face with the right person, all your hard work developing your selling skills goes for naught. (In telephone sales, being able to speak with someone directly counts the same.) If you aren't live and present to your clients, you'll never be able to discover their needs in order to figure out how you can satisfy them.

So how do you get directly involved with the people you want to persuade? In order to get face to face with people, you first must sell them on scheduling an appointment with you or, at the very least, agreeing to allow you to pop by and visit. And you must schedule an appointment before you can ever persuade your prospect to own your product, start using your service, or consider your idea.

Of course, to begin with, you have to find the right people to contact, and you do this by prospecting, a topic I cover in Chapter 7. But you also have to be firmly convinced that what you have is right for the people you're selling to. If you're not convinced of that, you won't deliver your presentation with enough conviction to persuade them to give you the time of day, let alone consider your product or service.

In this chapter, I let you know exactly how to get an appointment with your prospective clients. Then I take it a step further and give you some great pointers for putting them at ease when you finally do come face to face.

Knowing the Basics of Contacting Prospects

Your first line of approach when you're contacting a prospective client may differ depending on how you received the person's contact information.

- ✓ **If the prospective client contacted you by telephone, returning the call is always the most courteous response.**

- ✓ **If you got the person's name from a referral (another client or business associate recommended you call him), ask the person doing the referring to introduce you to the new prospect.** Or, at the very least, call the prospect and let him know that you'll be contacting him. Then you need to decide whether an introductory letter or phone call would be best — and this will most likely depend on the formality of the situation. If you're selling luxury yachts, dropping a note first may be wise, as opposed to interrupting the prospect's life with a sales phone call.

- ✓ **If the person left his name and e-mail address on your Web site, he would probably prefer to be contacted first by e-mail.** Many Web sites ask in their visitor registration area how the client would prefer to be contacted. If your Web site doesn't already ask this question, start doing so. It's a simple yet powerful courtesy that can open the door to further business if you use it right.

Your goal when you contact a prospective client (whether by phone, mail, or e-mail) is to get in direct, live contact with him, so you must approach the sale of the appointment very carefully. You first have to sell the prospect on the fact that he'd be better off speaking with you than not speaking with you. And that means you must offer benefits to him in your very first contact.

Keep in mind these tips when you're trying to get an appointment or secure an opportunity to pop by and visit:

- ✓ **Always be courteous.** Say "please" and "thank you." Refer to the person as Mr. or Ms. Last Name. Don't be too quick to use their first names.

- ✓ **Do anything to meet the prospect.** Even if you have to drive miles out of your way to be where they are and all you get is an introduction, those miles can turn into smiles when you later close the sale.

- ✓ **Hit the high notes early.** That means you must pique their interest right away. Tell them about a benefit that they would be likely to enjoy — saving money, making money, and improving lifestyles are big ones for most people.

✔ **Confirm all the details about where and when you'll meet.** Verbal confirmation is a must. Written confirmation is even better. You can include in your confirmation note that you'll invest plenty of time in researching just the right information for the meeting to make it worth his while.

These instructions may seem too simplified at first glance, but many a novice salesperson has gotten so excited about getting an appointment that he's let his etiquette slip and said, "Hell yes, I'll be there!" (And although a little swear word among friends may be acceptable, it's something you should avoid at all costs when you're dealing with clients.) Or he's given up too easily when a customer was tough to meet with, losing the chance to meet face to face. Or he's failed to reconfirm details about when and where to meet — and not knowing for sure when the appointment was, lost what was potentially a big opportunity. If you do your best to be courteous, secure an appointment no matter how busy the prospect is, and confirm the details of when you will meet, you're well on your way to a great appointment.

Reaching Your Prospects by Telephone First

The important thing to keep in mind when you've come up with a list of prospective clients is that not all of those clients will need your product or service. You may have to contact 20 people to find 1 who wants just what you have to offer. But every one of those other 19 calls brings you 1 call closer to the right person. So you just need to stay focused on your ultimate goal; don't let a little bit of rejection send you scurrying to the nearest hidey-hole.

So what do you do when you're ready to approach those prospects? What strategies work best? You go through seven steps in that introductory phone call, all of which I cover in the following sections:

1. **Offer a greeting.**

2. **Introduce yourself and your business.**

3. **Express your gratitude for the person's willingness to talk with you.**

4. **Tell the person the purpose of your call.**

5. **Get an appointment to talk with the person face to face.**

6. **Thank the person while you're on the phone.**

7. **Write a thank-you note and send it either by regular mail or e-mail.**

The rest, as they say, is selling.

When you're about to contact your prospective clients, keep three things at the forefront of your mind: your belief in what you're offering, the happiness of your current clients, and your desire to serve others. This advice remains the same whether you're selling yourself as an employee, your skills as a freelance writer, or a million-dollar computer system as a career sales representative for a Fortune 500 company.

Step #1: The greeting

When you call a prospective client for the first time, begin by using the most important thing for anyone to hear: her name. Using a formal approach, such as "Good morning, Ms. James" or "Good morning. I'm calling for Ms. James," is best because it conveys respect. (But be sure to check your watch before you call, and take into account time zone differences. You don't want to look like a complete boob by saying "good morning" when it's 1:00 in the afternoon.)

I recommend the use of *Good morning, Good afternoon,* or *Good evening* because it sounds more professional than just saying, "Hello." This phrasing distinguishes you from all those other people who call your prospective client — and this time the difference definitely favors you.

Too often, people are tempted to use a person's first name over the phone. The use of the familiar Bob or Judy doesn't bother some people (especially those whose names are Bob or Judy), but it does bother others. So don't risk being too familiar with Mr. Robert Smith, whose mother and friends always call him *Robert,* by souring the conversation at its beginning by calling him *Bob.* Wait for Mr. Robert Smith to say, "Call me Bob, why don't you?"

Common courtesy goes a long, long way in making initial contacts. If you aren't confident in your skill level in this area, attend one of the many classes offered on business etiquette. Visit the Web sites I recommend in Chapter 4. Or, if you can't find an etiquette class in your area, pick up a book on the subject at your local library. I don't know of many situations in which you can be *too* polite, except maybe at cockfights and wrestling matches.

Step #2: The introduction

After offering your greeting, introduce yourself and give your company name. If your company name doesn't explain what you do — as it would if your name were, say, Jensen Portrait Studios — then you must also mention briefly what type of business you're in. The key word here is *briefly.* I once asked a salesman what he sold, and I got 45 minutes on the features and benefits of owning my very own magnetic resonance imaging scanner. Gadzooks!

To keep your prospect on the line and awake, you may not want to say that you're in carpet cleaning, for example. Instead, describe your business in terms of benefits to the prospect. For example, you may say,

> We're a local business that helps companies like yours enhance their image with customers and reduce employee sick time.

Clean carpets give a good impression. Dirty carpets harbor germs. Is Ms. James ready to hang up? Probably not yet. Your description is creating all kinds of pictures in her mind because you haven't been so specific as to mention carpet cleaning. Your business could be anything from sneeze guards to high-tech air-cleaning systems. Because she probably doesn't have that clear a picture yet of what you're selling, she's probably curious to know more. After all, no one likes to end a conversation with all the blanks not yet filled in.

Paint a tantalizing picture with the words you use, but keep it simple. If you hear snoring on the other end of the line, you've gone on too long. Keep in mind that this all happens in a matter of seconds. You're trying to get Ms. James to give you anything with which you can extend the conversation.

Step #3: Gratitude

After you've introduced yourself and your business, you need to acknowledge that your prospect's time is valuable and thank her for taking your call. This lets her know you consider her to be an important person.

Say something like this:

> I appreciate your giving me a moment of your valuable time this morning. I promise to be brief.

Or you may want to try this:

> Thank you for talking with me. I'll only be a moment, and then let you get back to the important work you do.

It doesn't matter if she was just walking into the room with nothing in particular planned for the moment. Acting as if you've just called her when she's gotten out of a meeting with the President never hurts the impression you make.

You don't need to gush at your prospects with gratitude, though. Just be professional and businesslike in your manner.

Step #4: The purpose

When you've expressed your gratitude for your prospect's time, you need to get right to the heart of the matter by letting her know why you're calling. You should always express your purpose with a question. Something like this may be appropriate:

> **If I can show you how to reduce employee sick time, while improving the image your company presents to its customers, would you be interested?**

If she says *yes,* ask permission to ask her a few brief questions. When you have her permission, go ahead with your questions.

If she says *no,* be prepared with one more question that may pique her interest, such as:

> **Do you believe an improvement in the image of your business would have the effect of increasing sales?**

If she still says *no,* you may want to be more direct and ask:

> **When was the last time you had the carpets in your facility steam cleaned to eliminate germs and improve your store's appearance to your clients?**

If she says it's only been a week, you may just need to remain polite and ask for permission to contact her when she needs the service again. (**Hint:** Ask how long ago she had her carpets cleaned and you'll find out when she'll need them cleaned again.) Thank her for her time. Put a note in your calendar to contact her a couple of weeks before she needs the carpets cleaned again, and move on to your next potential client call.

Many of my students have benefited from a strategy that I call the *survey approach.* In it, when you get to this phase of the phone call, you say,

> The company I represent has given me an assignment to conduct a quick two-question survey of just ten people. You're the sixth person I've contacted. We would greatly value your opinion. Would you help me by answering these two brief questions?

When you ask for the prospect's help and show that you value her opinion, she's likely to comply. After all, who among us doesn't have an opinion? Plus, by informing her that your company is having you do this, you're likely to gain her empathy and cooperation.

The purpose of conducting this brief survey is to get the person on the other end of the line talking. Hopefully, what she tells you will give you the information you need to build her curiosity enough to commit to that vital face-to-face visit.

Be careful not to just go from one question to the next without really listening to your prospect's answers. She'll know by how you phrase the next question whether her last answer was heard. If she thinks you're just waiting to pounce on her with a canned list of questions rather than sincerely trying to get valuable information, she'll quickly hang up and send you off into the dial-tone void.

So how can you show that you're really listening to what your prospect is saying? Paraphrase her responses before moving on to the next question. When she hears that you cared enough to listen, she'll be more inclined to continue — and you escape your instant journey into the vortex.

Step #5: The appointment

If, after sharing with your prospect the purpose of your call and asking the questions you've prepared, Ms. James seems inclined to set a time for a visit, be prepared to tell her just how long you'll need. I recommend that you keep your initial contact as short as possible. Most people will balk at giving you an hour or even 30 minutes of their time. Twenty minutes or less seems to be an acceptable time commitment for most people. When Ms. James agrees to give you the 20 minutes you need, give her an option of when to meet, with an alternate advance question such as this:

> Would tomorrow at 10:20 a.m. be good for you, or is Wednesday at 2:40 p.m. better?

This question lets your prospect choose yet keeps you in control. What's she doing if she chooses either option you've given her? Committing to the appointment, which is exactly what you want.

Notice that my example mentions off times, as opposed to 10:00 a.m. or 2:00 p.m., for example. Using off times differentiates you from all the other salespeople who call. It also shows that you must know the importance of punctuality if you can keep a schedule using those times. If your visit will last only 20 minutes, it also lets your prospect schedule other appointments around you in the more standard time slots. *Remember:* It all comes down to courtesy.

Step #6: The over-the-phone thank you

When you've secured an appointment, you move on to thanking your prospect again, reiterating the time that has been agreed to and verifying the location of her office (or the place where you'll be meeting). Nothing is worse than showing up late and presenting the excuse of getting lost. If the location is difficult to get to, *now* is the time to ask for explicit directions. If this is The Big Sale you've dreamed about for years and you finally have the appointment, drive to the office the day before and get familiar with the area. Know at least one alternate route in case traffic presents a problem or a road crew decides that's the day to repair potholes.

If an appointment is important enough, schedule at least the earlier part of that day in the prospect's part of town so that you're already in the area when the time for the appointment arrives. You never, ever want to take a chance that you'll be late for a first appointment because you don't know where you're going or because of circumstances beyond your control.

Making sure you don't set yourself up for disappointment

When you set appointments for people to come to your place of business or to a meeting, give yourself a reality check and expect only 20 percent of those who committed to you to actually show up. Between the time you contact the person to set up the appointment and the time the appointment arrives, any number of conflicts may occur. They may decide to sleep in that day. An important call may come in. They may just be running late. Or they may just plain forget.

The only way to guarantee that a person will come to an appointment with you (short of offering her a bribe) is to go and bring her to the appointment yourself. And when your appointment is at her place of business or her home, your odds improve tremendously.

Making sure you don't come up cold when cold calling your prospects

Most appointments today are made over the phone, but that powerhouse of a device can be your best friend or your worst enemy. Phones are friendly, little, lightweight things when prospective clients call in for information and want to set appointments, because they present no threat of rejection. But that same lightweight little device can transform into a nasty, 60-pound ball and chain when you make outgoing calls to people you've never met in an attempt to get appointments. Making calls under such conditions is often called *cold calling,* partly because it can send shivers down your spine and partly because you're calling someone cold, with no prior contact. But cold calling doesn't have to be that scary. Just think of it as a slot machine — eventually, it's going to pay off. And if you use it right, it can bring you a jackpot!

Your success at cold calling depends on your perspective. The best way to sell or persuade anyone is in a face-to-face situation, and the most effective way to get face to face is by using the telephone. If you focus on that simple point, you will overcome those clammy hands, the beads of perspiration dancing on your upper lip, the churning in the pit of your stomach, and all those cotton balls rolling around in your mouth when the time to make the call arrives. With practice, you can easily overcome those emotional reactions to your fear of saying the wrong thing or of being rejected.

If you doubt that you'll ever get comfortable making cold calls, think back to when you first started talking with members of the opposite sex — probably somewhere in your preteen or teen years. Your physical reactions then probably resemble those you experience now if you're not used to cold calling, don't they? Your reactions were pretty much the same then because you wanted to impress someone and you were afraid you'd look like a fool. Your fear arises partly because you know how you've treated people who have called you — and now, you fear, it may be payback time.

Step #7: The written thank you

If your appointment is more than two days from when you call, immediately send your prospect a thank-you note (either by regular mail or e-mail), confirming the details of when you spoke and what was agreed to. A professional-looking piece of correspondence can solidify any doubts she may have about this commitment.

Keep in mind that if your prospect has given you a home e-mail address as opposed to a work one, she may not check that e-mail account on a daily basis, which means it may not be the best method of reaching her. In most business situations, however, people communicate primarily by e-mail, so the recipient will likely see your message right away.

Including your picture on your letterhead or on your business card and then enclosing that with your thank-you note never hurts. Get a professional portrait taken if you choose to use a photo — sending something that looks like your driver's license headshot is bad news. Knowing what you look like increases the prospect's comfort level when she meets you.

An excellent program at WellConnected (`www.wellconn.com`) allows you to generate thank-you notes via the Internet that are then mailed to your potential client and include both your photo and a high-quality gift that can be imprinted with the client's name. It makes a wonderful, professional impression.

Getting to the Elusive Decision-Maker

When you're seeking an appointment with a prospective client, what you really want is to get in with the person who has the ability to make decisions about the products and services the company uses, otherwise known as the *decision-maker.* Unfortunately, in addition to facing the challenge of that initial phone call with a prospect, you may find yourself not even able to get through to the person you want to reach. In fact, that person may have so many people contacting her that she's established a hierarchy of people around her who screen calls quite heavily on her behalf. This situation may cause you to wonder exactly where your prospective client is and what she's doing. Images of her jetting to exotic locations for meetings or floating in a sensory-deprivation tank may come to mind. But it doesn't matter what she's doing, as long as you can eventually get to her.

When you have trouble getting through to the decision-maker, you get the opportunity to be a little creative. Yes, this situation requires more work. But keep in mind that those people who are hardest to get to will be tough on your competition as well. So if you stick it out, get in to see them, and win their business, you'll be on the inside of that same protective wall. And those same support people will keep not you, but your *competition,* at bay.

Gentlemen, start your engines: Going head-to-head with the receptionist

If you're having trouble getting through to a decision-maker, begin with the receptionist who answers the phone when you call. If at all possible, get the name of the decision-maker on your first contact. Tell the receptionist that you need his help and ask, "Who would be in charge of the decision-making process if your company were to consider getting involved in a [whatever your product or service is]." The receptionist is the person who has to know what each employee's area of responsibility is in order to direct calls properly, so he should be a great help. Then, whenever you make follow-up calls, use the decision-maker's name.

Be sure to ask for the correct pronunciation and spelling of any names the receptionist gives you. Never guess about names or take the chance of writing them down incorrectly; business practices like that are likely to haunt you later. It never hurts to get the receptionist's name as well.

If the receptionist is especially helpful — as receptionists tend to be — take a moment to send a thank-you note to him along with your business card. Businesspeople often tout the value of a good receptionist when they need to hire one, but only smart businesspeople reward other people's receptionists well. A little bit of recognition now can prove valuable later on. When you have built a solid relationship with the receptionist, he will always look forward to seeing you and future visits will be much warmer. He will also help guard your account against infiltration attempts by your competitors.

Working with the decision-maker's assistant

If the decision-maker has an assistant, the receptionist probably will put you through to that person first. Expect it, and don't be put out by it. Treat this person with the same respect and courtesy you would use with the decision-maker herself. The assistant can make or break your chances of ever getting an appointment, so the best thing to do is to ask for the assistant's help as well. You can accomplish a great deal of research with the assistant's help — and you may even be able to prequalify the decision-maker through her assistant (see Chapter 9 for more information on qualifying).

First tell the assistant that you have a way of increasing efficiency while decreasing the costs of a service the company is already using. This provides that assistant with just enough information to either want to know more or to want to help. (And if you live up to a promise like that, the assistant could be seen as a hero by taking your proposal to the boss right away, so he'll probably be eager to listen.) Finally, tell him you need his help, and simply ask how to get an appointment with Ms. Decision-Maker.

Most businesses have an established procedure for setting up appointments with the head honchos. By asking what that procedure is, you show that you're not trying to beat the system; you just want to find out what it is so that you can work with it. When you show respect for the system that's in place, you move up a notch on the respect scale.

Unless the procedure for meeting the honchos is too complicated or your offering has a stringent time deadline, try it their way first. If the system doesn't work, consider how much effort the company's business is worth. If it's a once-in-a-lifetime proposition, then you need to get creative (see the following section for more information).

Getting creative in your efforts to meet with the decision-maker

Whatever unusual method you choose for getting in touch with the decision-maker, always consider how the other person will receive it. Your goal is to find an inoffensive method for getting people's attention — but your method has to be creative, too. You don't want to risk alienating anyone, but if she's important enough to contact, you need to find out what her hot buttons are and build your contact method around that. Again, this is where receptionists, secretaries, and assistants can come to your rescue.

I know of a salesperson who sent a loaf of bread and a bottle of wine in a basket to a hard-to-reach decision-maker. She included a note that said, "I hate to w(h)ine, but I know I can save you a lot of dough if you'll just meet me for ten minutes." It broke through the barrier in a creative way and she did get a confirmed appointment.

Before sending alcohol to a prospective client, find out whether she drinks or abstains from alcohol. If she doesn't drink, this bit of creativity could make the wrong impression.

Another creative way to make a good impression on the decision-maker is to ask her receptionist or assistant who she respects and listens to in her field. Our planet of billions of people really is a small world when it comes to making contacts. If you find out that your prospect is a member of the Rotary Club, think about who else you may know who's a member and try to network your way into an appointment that way.

If you're working your business correctly, you're bound to find some way that your circle of contacts connects with the prospect. The real skill in meeting people is turning those points of contact into strong links.

If the decision-maker's schedule really is strict and all else fails, try to arrange for a telephone meeting instead of a face-to-face one. You'll have to adjust your presentation to give it impact over the telephone. But it may be a method worth trying.

Making a Good First Impression

Your prospective clients make many decisions about you in the first ten seconds after they meet you for the very first time. That's right. Within *ten seconds,* you're either chopped liver or Prince or Princess Charming.

Take a stopwatch or check the second hand on your watch right now and find out what ten seconds feels like. When you're watching your clock, it seems like a long time — but when you're walking into a room and meeting someone for the first time, it passes by in an instant. Your job is to come up with a way to help the people who meet you for the first time see that they made a good choice in agreeing to see you. Your clients must *immediately* see some benefit from investing their time with you. Knowing how to maximize those first ten seconds allows you to make the impression you really want to make, so that you can comfortably move forward in your selling.

If you're new to the sales profession, be careful not to cram everything you know (or think you know) into the first ten seconds. Instead, that time needs to be natural and comfortable. That way, you'll help your prospective client to relax, which always makes a good impression.

Dressing for success

Before you arrive for your appointment or visit with a potential client, consider the way you dress. Your goal is to ensure that your prospects like you and see that you're like them, so how should you dress to accomplish this? Dress like your clients dress. Or, even better, dress like the people they turn to for advice.

Keep in mind that some folks turn to their ministers or priests for personal advice . . . so you may want to rethink your goal of dressing like that — a cleric's white collar under a suit may not be the best way to dress for success. And some folks turn to good old Mom, so I'd caution you against a housedress and a pair of sensible shoes. *Remember:* You want to dress like the people your clients turn to for *business* advice.

Use good judgment and common sense when it comes to the way you dress, and you can't go wrong. If you sell farm equipment and show up at a client meeting dressed like a banker, the farmers you're selling to aren't likely to feel very comfortable around you. After all, in the past, bankers have foreclosed on farmers, so you want to dress less like the banker and more like the farmer himself. This doesn't mean you have to show up at your client's farm in a pair of dusty overalls, but more-relaxed clothing is probably in order — maybe a pair of khaki pants and a nice shirt. On the other hand, if you sell to a corporate purchasing agent and you show up in slacks and a casual shirt, you won't make the impression you want to make either. Know your clients, and you'll know what to wear.

If you're new in sales or new to a particular group of clients, pay attention to what the other successful salespeople at your company wear, and then dress like they do. If your company has a dress code, there's probably a good reason for that — they've probably done some research and determined that clothes in line with the dress code are what customers expect to see. Be sure to abide by it.

If you show up at a meeting with your prospective client wearing something that's a good bit different from what the prospect is wearing, then you must work during the first few minutes of your meeting to find a way to get yourself on even footing with him. After that, it's too late.

Paying attention to your body language

In addition to the message you communicate to your clients with what you wear, the body language you use also expresses something. Your carriage, your facial expression, the placement of your hands, the amount of bass in your voice, the frequency with which you have to pry your tongue from the roof of your mouth as you talk . . . all of these govern first impressions just as much as what you wear.

Being aware of your body language may require some time in front of a mirror or video camera, or you may need to spend time with someone who truly cares about your success and is willing to give you an honest opinion. But dress for work and walk your normal walk. If your normal body language doesn't present an image of success and confidence, watch someone who does and emulate her. Basically, you'll want to walk with your shoulders comfortably back (not like Miss America in the swimsuit competition). Your arms should be at your side (no hands in pockets!). Make good eye contact with the people you meet. Don't stare them down or eye them as if you're assessing their clothing. Smile warmly — with both your mouth and your eyes. Keep your tone of voice confident. When you rehearse, if your voice sounds shaky, keep rehearsing until you've got it down. If you're truly nervous when meeting new people, take a few slow, deep breaths to calm yourself before entering the room.

Walking into a yes

In a study of 10,000 people conducted by U.C.L.A., each person was asked what their initial impressions were of someone they later said yes to. Seven percent said the person had good knowledge of the topic, product, or service. Thirty-eight percent said the person had good voice quality — he sounded confident and intelligent. And 55 percent said the person walked with an air of confidence and self-assurance rolling off of him even as he approached. If you doubt the power of projecting positive body language, think again.

If you're sincere about your pleasure in meeting people, this behavior will be automatic.

Establishing Rapport with Your Clients

Your clients feel comfortable around you when you know how to establish *rapport* with them, which is what selling situations are all about — establishing common ground. People like to be around other people who are like them. Bringing out the similarities you share with your prospects proves that at least one salesperson is not an alien being from another solar system. You're not even from the dark side of the moon — you're just like them: You have a family, you have a job, you have similar values, and when you're seeking any product other than the one you represent, you work with salespeople, too, just like your prospects. You just happen to be more of an expert on the particular product line or service you represent than your prospects are — and you're happy to use your knowledge to their advantage.

In fact, I have a phrase just to get that point across. If you sense that the other party is concerned that you're on the same page as they are, say something like this:

> Mr. James, when I'm not helping people get involved with my product, I'm a consumer, just like you, looking for quality products at the best price. What I hope for when I'm shopping is to find someone who can help me understand all the facts about the item I'm interested in so I can make a wise decision. Today, I'd like to earn your confidence in me as an expert on state-of-the-art stereo systems. So feel free to ask any questions you may have.

Don't wince at the thought of using these words — they've been proven to work successfully in lowering barriers people put up when dealing with salespeople. Although no one likes hearing "canned" material, it's only canned if you let it sound that way. In sales, how you say it is as important as what you say. Always remember to speak with a sincere concern for your customers. If you're not truly concerned for them, you shouldn't be in this field.

In order to build rapport with your clients, you have to be truly interested in them. You need to be sincere in wanting to get to know them well enough so that you can help them have more, do more, and be more. Even if you're selling to a loved one, he needs to feel that high level of personal concern as well. If your clients believe you're being real — talking from your heart — they'll put their confidence in you much more quickly.

Winning over Hell's Angels

After about my third year in sales, I had been working hard and had done pretty well. I was driving a brand-new Cadillac, which was the real estate car of the 1960s. It was long, sleek, and beautiful. I'd even earned enough to invest in a few nice suits.

I received a call from a woman who asked me to come by and look at the home she and her husband were thinking of selling. Driving over in my new Caddy and nice suit, I was feeling pretty good about myself. When I pulled up to the house, there in the driveway leaned six Harley-Davidson motorcycles parked in a line, the way serious bikers park their bikes.

Judging from the looks of these hogs, my Cadillac and suit weren't going to help me establish much rapport. A huge, bearded man wearing a Hell's Angels jacket answered my knock. Glancing into the home, I could see five other guys just like him sitting in the living room. If there were ever a time when a salesperson did not have instant rapport, that was it.

Nervous, I walked on into the home and decided to stick with what I normally did for starters. I said, "Before I can give you any figures on what your home is worth, I need you to show it to me." We started in the living room and went into the kitchen. Because the garage was just off the kitchen, it was the next stop. As we went into the garage, there on the floor was a motorcycle all in pieces, one they were obviously customizing. I asked them how they distributed the weight when they extended the front wheel, explaining that I had a motorcycle, too, and that I had been riding for years. Of course, it wasn't a Harley, but I was a motorcycle enthusiast.

We talked bikes for about ten minutes and all of a sudden the entire situation changed. I was no longer a guy in a fancy suit, but a fellow motorcyclist. I ended up listing the home and getting them happily moved. And I learned an interesting lesson about the importance of making my customers comfortable.

Getting Your Clients to Like and Trust You

When you meet people, your main goal is to help them relax with you. No one gets involved in a decision-making process when they're uptight. You want your prospective clients to like you and trust you because, if they don't, they won't do business with you. Always remember that your goal is this: to be a person whom other people like, trust, and want to listen to.

So how can you help your prospective clients like and trust you? Start in those first ten seconds after you meet, and move through five important steps to making a stellar first impression (covered in the following sections in more detail):

1. **Smile deep and wide.**

2. **Make eye contact.**

3. **Offer a greeting.**

4. **Shake hands.**

5. **Offer your name and get the prospect's name.**

If you handle these steps properly, you'll earn you the opportunity to continue building rapport and lead into the next phase of selling, which is qualifying (I cover that in Chapter 9). Qualifying is where you determine whether you can help your prospective client, but if you can't get to that stage by making a good first impression, all your previous efforts will be about as useful as a box of wet Cracker Jacks.

Most of the time, people will be the kind of people you expect them to be. That's because your demeanor — what you say and how you say it — sends them a distinct message of what you think of them. People are, for the most part, reactive and will respond according to what's given them. So if you expect them to be cordial, open, and friendly, they will be. When your body language and opening statements are pleasant, they'll very likely respond in kind.

Step #1: Smile deep and wide

When you first come into contact with a prospective client, smile until you're almost grinning. A smile radiates warmth. If you're not smiling, or if it looks like it hurts when you do, your prospect will want to avoid you and he'll put up a wall of doubt and fear in just a few seconds.

Long-term relationships begin in the first ten seconds. So smile! But keep it pleasant — you don't want to look like a grinning hyena.

Some people forget how to smile because they don't do it much. I've had to ask some of my salespeople to go home, stand in front of a mirror, and practice smiling for a solid 30 minutes. (If you try this at home, make sure the door is closed when you practice, or someone may just throw a net over you and haul you away!)

If you're contacting people over the telephone, smiling still counts. Believe it or not, people can hear a smile (or a lack of one) in your voice. When I was a manager, I put little mirrors by the telephones of each salesperson, because I wanted them to see themselves when they were talking with clients. If my people saw that they weren't smiling, chances were good that the person on the other end of the phone could sense it — and it would certainly have a negative effect on the relationship. I had the salespeople turn the mirrors over or slip them into drawers when clients were actually in the office, but believe me, having those mirrors made a big difference in the success of our telephone contacts.

Step #2: Make eye contact

When you meet a prospect, look in his eyes. This is a part of body language that builds trust. People tend not to trust those who can't look them in the eye. Think about it: People usually glance away when they're lying to you. So when you don't look your clients in the eye, they may doubt what you're saying. Developing the ability to look someone in the eye and lie to them takes a good bit of intentional practice, which is what con artists do.

Although looking your clients in the eyes is very important, be sure not to go to the extreme and lock onto their eyes. Getting into a staring contest is dangerous in any selling situation. Give your prospect a couple seconds of solid eye contact while smiling, and he'll most likely be the first to glance away.

Step #3: Say hi (or something like it)

The style of the greeting you offer depends on several factors, such as whether you're calling a longtime friend, a new acquaintance, a total stranger, or the Pope. Your greeting will also be affected by the particular circumstance of how you're meeting your prospect. If you have any doubt at all about what kind of greeting is best, err on the side of formality.

Depending on the situation, any one of the following greetings may be appropriate:

- Hi.
- Hello.
- How do you do?
- How are you?
- Good morning, good afternoon, or good evening.
- Thank you for coming in.
- Thank you for seeing me.

If you already know your prospect's name, use it with your greeting (for example, "Good morning, Bob"). If you don't know your prospect's name, don't rush to get it. Pressing strangers for their names so they're no longer strangers is fine in many parts of the country and in many situations. But in others, it's seen as being pushy. If you're in a situation where you're obviously a salesperson, be atypical and establish a bit of rapport *before* asking for your prospect's name.

Step #4: Shake hands

Salespeople are well known for having a tremendous desire to press the flesh, so most people expect to shake your hand when they meet you. But, to avoid appearing awkward with those who don't feel comfortable shaking hands, I recommend that you keep your right arm slightly bent and held by your side. If you see the other person reach toward you, you're ready. If he doesn't reach toward you, then you haven't committed the grand faux pas of reaching out too eagerly.

Some people don't want to shake hands because they just don't like touching other people. Then there are those people who go to great lengths to avoid physical contact for health reasons — they may be unusually susceptible to germs and don't want to touch anything they don't have to touch. Other people suffer with arthritis and find hand shaking extremely painful. Instead of opening a first meeting with their list of physical ailments, they'll simply avoid shaking your hand.

The handshake is appropriate in most instances, but only if you do it properly. If you're skeptical about the value of spending time practicing a good handshake, take some time to notice how others shake your hand. If you've ever shaken a hand that feels like a dead fish, you'll understand what I mean. Or, if you've experienced a bone-crushing handshake, you'll also see the importance of having the right kind of handshake.

To convey the highest level of trust, confidence, and competence, you need to grasp the whole hand of the other individual and give it a brief but solid squeeze — not too tight, but definitely not loosey-goosey either. Keep it brief. There's nothing more uncomfortable than to have someone keep holding your hand when you're ready to have it back.

If you're meeting a married couple, shaking the hands of both the husband and the wife is appropriate. If they have children with them, shaking the kids' hands is a nice gesture as well. After all, if the product you're selling involves the children, you want to earn their trust, too. If you can tell a child would be uncomfortable with having his hand shaken, simply give him a moment of eye contact as well. Don't do any cheek tweaking or hair tussling of the kids. Remember how you hated it when Aunt Minnie did it to you?

Step #5: Your name for their name

The handshake is the most natural time to exchange names. Depending on the situation, you may want to use the formal greeting of, "Good morning. My name is Robert Smith with Jones & Company." If the setting is more casual, you may want to give your name as Rob or Bob — whatever you want your prospects to call you. Make sure they get your name right, though. Nothing is more difficult than correcting a potential prospect who calls you Bob when your name is Rob. Besides, when you've won them over and they've begun sending you referral business, you don't want the referrals asking for the wrong person and letting someone else earn your sales.

If a woman says her name is Judith Carter, use Ms. Carter when you first address her. Don't jump to the familiar Judy. Why? Because that's what a typical salesperson would do, and calling your prospect Judy will cause her to raise her guard against you. Visions of suede shoes, pinkie rings, and gold chains start to dance in her head. Getting familiar too fast is also impolite. Let your prospect decide when you may become more familiar, and let *her* give you the appropriate first name to use. Don't shorten someone's name (from Judith to Judy, for example) unless she tells you to. Some people prefer their given names to the more common nicknames.

When you're involved more deeply in the qualification or presentation stages of selling and you feel some warmth building, using first names with most people will be more comfortable. If they haven't given you permission to do so, politely ask for it. With Judith, just ask, "May I call you Judith?" If that's what everyone calls her and she has built some confidence in you, she'll probably say yes. Or she may say, "Call me Judy." Although this may seem like an old-fashioned approach, it's what sells. People yearn for a time when they were treated with more respect and courtesy.

What's in a name?

If you're being introduced to a group of people, be careful to use the same level of formality with each member. Don't call one person Mr. Johnson and call Mr. Johnson's associate by his first name, Bob, just because you can't remember Bob's last name. That's more offensive than having to ask again what Bob's name is.

Early in my career, I spent an entire afternoon with a couple, failing to get their names clearly during the initial greeting. The day concluded with them making an offer on a home. When it came time to fill out the paperwork, I asked the husband very warmly and sincerely, "And how do you spell your last name?" He responded, "J-O-N-E-S." Boy, was my face red!

Knowing How to Respond to Prospects in a Retail Setting

Selling in a retail environment is really no different than selling in any other environment — you need to get each customer to like you and trust you enough to ask for help instead of immediately pouncing on your customers with a reflexive "May I help you?" Wouldn't you love to have a dollar for every time you've heard a retail salesperson ask, "May I help you?" when you walked into a store?

As a customer, you may have heard variations of the "May I help you?" greeting, including something like this: "Hi, I'm Bob. What can I do for you today?" What kind of response does Bob hear 99.9 percent of the time he says those words? "Oh, nothing. I'm just looking." If something doesn't work 99.9 percent of the time, doesn't it make sense to try to come up with a better initial greeting?

If you work in retail sales, I have two important suggestions that will increase your sales and the sales of anyone else in your company you share these suggestions with:

- ✔ When people enter your establishment, never walk directly toward them.
- ✔ When you do approach customers, don't rush.

Think about a time when you've been approached by a quick-moving, overzealous salesperson, and you had to step back away from him. You don't want that to happen to you. Let your customers know you're there in case they have questions. Then get out of the way and let them look around.

Figuring out what to say instead of "May I help you?"

So what can you say instead of "May I help you?" Try saying,

Hello, thanks for coming in. I work here. If you have any questions, please let me know.

What does this greeting do? It projects a warm, welcome feeling rather than an overwhelmed feeling. You've just invited your customer to relax, and, when people relax, they're more open to making decisions.

Another greeting you may want to try is this:

> Hello, welcome to Standard Lighting of Arizona. I'm happy you had a chance to drop by today. Feel free to look around. My name is Karen, and I'll be right over here if you have any questions.

Pause momentarily in case the customer does have questions. Then step away.

When you step away from the customer, instead of toward her, you distinguish yourself from all the typical salespeople she's ever encountered — and for most customers that's a very good thing. When you leave customers alone, they walk toward what they want. By observing them from a discreet distance, you know exactly what they came in for. When they finally stop in front of something for a moment, that's when you want to move closer to be ready to answer questions. Don't hang over them like a vulture, though. Just be where they can find you when they look around for help.

Recognizing the signals your customers project

If a customer doesn't look around but remains by one item for a while, then you may walk up and ask a question. Use an involvement question right off the bat, because she'll have to answer it with more than a *yes* or a *no*. Plus, you'll discover something that will help you keep the conversation going.

If it's a piece of furniture she's looking at, ask,

> Will this chair replace an old one, or is it going to be an addition to your furnishings?

When she answers, you'll know why she's interested and you can then begin guiding her to a good decision.

In any place of business where you have a display area or showroom, let your customers look around before you approach them. Being laid back is much less threatening and far more professional than mowing down your fellow associates and careening toward your potential customer like a runaway freight train the moment she walks in the door.

I know of some places of business, such as automobile dealerships or some furniture stores, that are so large that people usually *do* need a guide (or at least a map) in order to find their way around. If you work in such a setting, you have to take your customers to the type of product they want. But, again, step away from them when you get them where they want to be, and let them relax. When they're ready to talk with you, they can still find you quickly, but you haven't invaded their space and taken control of their shopping experience.

Building Common Ground

When the introductions have been made and you're out of those first ten seconds of a meeting with a prospect, you need to smoothly transition into establishing common ground. How do you do that? By being observant.

If you just walked into Mr. Johnson's office, and you noticed that he has family photos all over the place, ask about his family. You don't need to know details now. Just say, "Great looking family," and let him decide how much to tell you. If you see trophies, comment on them. If you can see that he's a fisherman and you're a fisherman, too, bring up the subject of fishing.

The power of observation is incredibly important to develop as you work on your overall selling skills.

By allowing your prospect to first see the human side of you rather than the sales professional side, you will help him break through the natural wall of fear that encloses him when typical salespeople walk through his door.

Someone may have referred Mr. Johnson to you. If that's the case, mention the mutual acquaintance — that's usually a great starting point. "Good old Jim" may have an excellent talent, great family, or wonderful sense of humor. Those are all nice, noncontroversial topics to cover.

If Ms. Smith has an accent, you may ask where she's from. Perhaps you've traveled there or know people in that part of the country. Be careful here, though: Ms. Smith may be self-conscious about the accent or tired of people always asking about it, so don't dwell on it too long, especially if she seems uncomfortable.

In the following sections, I cover ways to reach common ground with prospects or existing customers with whom you may not yet feel entirely comfortable.

Keep the conversation light, but move ahead

Don't let the conversation part of rapport building become too hard for you. If all else fails, bring up something in the local news. Just make sure it's a non-controversial subject. Try your best not to bring up the weather — if you start off talking about how hot or cold it is today, your prospect will know you're struggling for something to talk about or that you're nervous.

Another good tactic is to give your prospect a sincere compliment. *Sincere* is the key word here. Sincerity takes you everywhere; blatant, insincere flattery gets you nowhere. A stale line like "Gee, Mr. Gargoyle, I'll bet everybody tells you that you look just like Warren Beatty" does not qualify as sincere.

To keep the conversation moving forward, try an approach called *piggybacking.* In this technique, you simply ask a question, and when your prospect gives you an answer, acknowledge it with a nod or an *I see,* and then ask another question based on the prospect's response. For example, if you meet someone at a party, the piggybacking may go like this:

> You: *Good afternoon, Mr. Johnson. I appreciate your time. Nice looking family you have there.*
>
> Prospect: *Thank you.*
>
> You: *What grades are your children in?*
>
> Prospect: *The oldest is a freshman in college. The middle one is a junior in high school. And the youngest is a freshman in high school.*
>
> You: *You must be very proud of them. What's your oldest studying in college?*
>
> Prospect: *Business. She wants to work for me when she graduates. I told her I would only hire her if she had straight A's. A degree is a degree, but grades will tell me how much someone really learned.*

Or

> You: *Good afternoon, Ms. Thompson. I appreciate your time. I was wondering how long the company has been in this location? I know I've seen your sign on the building for many years.*
>
> Prospect: *We've been here 25 years.*
>
> You: *That's great. And how long have you been with the company?*
>
> Prospect: *I started ten years ago in the area of inventory control. For the past five years, I've handled all the purchasing.*

When you piggyback, don't make a hog out of yourself by asking too many questions unless you think that the other person is agreeable to answering more.

Acknowledge their pride

If you happen to be working in a business where you give a lot of in-home presentations, and the people you're presenting to have a nice home, say this:

> *I want to tell you that I spend a lot of time in the evening in other people's homes, and you should be proud of what you've done here. Your home is lovely.*

Look for signs of hobbies or crafts that you can comment on. If a woman is an artist and has her paintings on display, you could say, "You did that? What a great talent to have." That way you're not lying if you think the painting is really poor. Painting *is* a great talent — whether or not your prospect has any is in the eye of the beholder. If your prospect has any hobby he's obviously proud of, give him a sincere compliment about it. People always enjoy hearing compliments.

Avoid controversy

Be cautious that the prospect doesn't tempt you into a conversation about a controversial subject. Some people do that just to test you. Specifically, avoid discussing politics and religion at all costs.

Here's how to get around any topic that may lead you down the wrong path:

I'm so busy serving clients, I haven't had time to stay current on that topic. What do you think?

By tossing the ball back at the prospect, you've dodged what may have been a fatal bullet, plus you got in a plug for your professional abilities. If the prospect comes back at you with a very strong opinion, you'll know to avoid that subject in future meetings. Or you may feel the need to brush up on it if he's deeply involved, so you'll have a better understanding of this person before you build a long-term working relationship with him.

In any business contact, be certain to never, *ever* use any profanity or slang. It doesn't matter if such language is widely used on today's most popular television programs; it has no place in the business world. You never know the values of the person you're talking with and you don't want to risk offending him. The same goes for off-color, political, ethnic, or sexist jokes. Be sensitive to the values, beliefs, and morals of the person sitting or standing across from you.

Keep pace with your prospect

Taking time to become aware of your normal speed of talking is extremely valuable. And notice the rate of talking of everyone else you encounter. When you become tuned in to it, it happens naturally.

When you're aware of your speaking rate, you need to know what to do about it. If the person you're trying to persuade talks faster than you do, you need to increase your rate of talking in order to keep her attention. If she speaks much more slowly than you do, you should slow down or pause more often in your side of the conversation. Any distortion in your rate of speaking can be deadly. You may lose her if you talk at the rate of a professional auctioneer, or her mind may wander if you're too slow. Try to time your rate of talking to your prospect's rate of talking.

Chapter 9

Qualifying Your Way to Success

- -

- -

*A*t the qualification stage in the selling cycle, you've found your prospect, made an initial contact, and gotten an appointment. The prospect has shown a certain level of interest in your product, service, or offering. Now you need to determine not only whether your prospect needs what you're offering but also whether your prospect has the power to make the decision to buy. Both of those factors must be present in order for you to consider this person a qualified buyer. If they're not, you will need to politely withdraw and move on to another potential client. If you pursue presenting and trying to close an unqualified buyer, all you're doing is wasting his time, getting in a little practice with your presentation, and allowing your confidence to take a hit. That type of situation is part of what has given sales a bad name in the past. Don't go there!

This step in the selling cycle is particularly important in situations in which you don't have a close enough relationship with your prospect to know whether he needs your product or service. And the person needs to make a financial commitment or a personal commitment in order to go ahead.

So what circumstances would keep someone from being able to make a commitment? If it's a financial commitment, he'd have to have the money or some credit to draw upon. If it's a personal commitment, he may need to check with someone else, like a spouse, before going ahead. It could be a situation, as with insurance, in which the person must qualify in terms of their health. You need to know your prospect's circumstances *before* you go into a full-fledged presentation and try to convince him to go ahead.

One of the biggest mistakes people make when they try to convince or persuade others is going into a full-blown presentation before they know whether the listener is a qualified decision-maker or needs what they have to sell. There's nothing worse for either of the people involved than to be caught up in something that is a total waste of their valuable time. So, for goodness' sake, when you see the word *receptionist* on a desk, don't give the person behind the sign your whole presentation.

In my experience, using this step in the selling sequence is the single greatest factor separating those who win most often in their selling presentations from those who don't. Statistics from our surveys of over 250,000 sales professionals show that the biggest gap between six-figure income earners and those averaging around $25,000 per year is their skill in qualifying. That statistic alone would make me want to master this area of selling. And all it takes is asking the right questions.

Taking a Few Sales Pointers from a Scruffy TV Detective

So how do you get started in qualifying your prospects? You need to ask the right questions. In some cases, you wait and watch for the perfect opportunity to ask. Other times, you have to create the opportunity to ask. Think of yourself as a detective, a gatherer of information to solve the mystery of your prospect's buying needs. If all you had to do was come up with a couple of questions that would always be answered completely and honestly, your life would be simple. But it isn't always that easy. Being able to discover your prospect's needs and concerns, as well as successfully incorporate such information into the opening of your presentation, takes a lot of time and practice before you ever walk through the doors of each appointment.

I can think of one person — a real character, actually — who exemplifies what effective qualification is all about. In the 1970s, this character was quite popular on network television, and he even resurfaced in the 1990s. See if you can tell who it is by this description: He drives a battered old car. He walks with a slight limp and has a bad eye. He has poor posture and a five o'clock shadow most of the day. His trench coat is always wrinkled and his tie askew. He carries a cigar and a small spiral notebook.

If you watch any television at all, by now you've probably guessed that I'm not talking about Lassie. It's Columbo, of course. I love using the example of Lieutenant Columbo when I cover qualifying tactics and strategies, because Columbo does a wonderful job of adjusting his questioning techniques to fit every situation. He also acts as if the person he's questioning is better, more important, or smarter than he is. Columbo's demeanor throws his "prospects" off guard, and they often drop their defenses. Their lapses allow him to ask the same question in several different ways. If they come up with a different answer to the rephrased question, he knows that they're not telling the truth or that they know more than they're letting on. Such information is valuable for him in continuing to seek out answers. In the following sections, I highlight some of the key strategies Columbo uses to solve every case. And they're strategies you can put to work for you when you're trying to get information from your prospects.

Keep out of the limelight

Columbo never presumes to be the top dog or the smartest person in the world. He doesn't enter with a flourish, like Sherlock Holmes might. Instead, he lets the selling situation or the product be the star, explaining it in great detail to the suspects. Throughout this book, I tell you that you need to be an expert. That's still true, but you need to get your points across in an educational style rather than a know-it-all style. When you enter the classroom of a great teacher, is the teacher the star? No. She's not. The education — the learning is the star. The teacher is just the facilitator.

Your prospect believes you know more about the subject than he does or he wouldn't invest his time with you. The prospect needs to share certain information about himself in order for you to know what to share with him. Your goal in qualifying, then, is to involve the prospect in an educational experience where he learns through the use of questions. Each of your questions builds on his answers to the previous ones.

Always take notes

Taking notes is vital, but Columbo doesn't rush to get every word of vital information. Instead, he seems to jot things down casually. His notepad isn't large and threatening. It's small enough to fit in his pocket and rather nondescript. And he refers back to this information again and again during his investigation. The information he turns up helps direct his future efforts with each suspect (which, in selling, is called the *prospect* or, more optimistically, the *future client*).

Take a look at the device you use to take notes. Is it imposing? Does it have 100 blanks that your prospect will feel you must fill in with information about him? If so, it's likely to be somewhat threatening.

When you state a fact back to the prospect, glance or point to where you have it in your notes. This shows that you have the correct information and that you're on top of the details.

Make the people you're questioning feel important

Ever the humble searcher of truth, Columbo always reminds his suspects how accommodating they are to let him impose on their busy schedules. He thanks them profusely for their time and the vital information they provide. No matter how small the tidbit of information, he makes them feel as if it's the single most important key to solving the case.

Don't just jot down the notes. Make comments on the facts and figures the people provide you with. Compliment them on being on top of things enough to know these details without looking them up. *Note:* If they did look up some of the figures, compliment them on their dedication to accuracy by not calling out numbers from memory.

Ask standard and innocent questions

Columbo rarely comes out and asks a suspect "Did you do it?" Instead, he asks what sounds like typical police-type questions about times, people, and places in order to gather background information and disarm the suspect.

In sales, sooner or later, you need to talk about money. Money is an uncomfortable subject for many people. So, you don't just ask: "How much have you got?" Instead, you're more discreet: "Mike, if we were fortunate to find just the right widget for you today, how much did you plan to invest to own one?"

Listen to both verbal and nonverbal responses

Columbo notices *how* people tell him what they have to say, not just noting the words they use but paying attention to their body language as well. He knows and evaluates not only their postures, but also what they're wearing, the surroundings they spend their time in, and even the cars they drive.

If someone lives in a $500,000 home and drives the latest Mercedes, it's likely she'll be interested in owning the top-of-the-line model of your product as well. In other cases, if someone is looking at the top-of-the-line model and then steps away when you approach her, it's possible she's hesitant about whether she can afford it.

Build on the answers you get

Rarely do Columbo's suspects realize they *are* suspects until they've let their guard down a bit and said something that doesn't jibe with a previous answer. They often find themselves uncomfortable in having to explain the difference in the two answers. They try to give credence to their errors and still keep their innocent attitudes.

Someone may tell you he invested $40,000 in his last series of widgets. You would then assume he'd be comfortable investing in that price range again. If, when you get to your presentation, your bottom line is that same amount and he says he can't afford it, something was missing in the information you were provided. Don't call the client out on the detail — as important as it is — just ask more questions. "Mike, I thought you told me you invested this much the last time. Was I wrong in my understanding that it was an acceptable amount?" This gives Mike an opportunity to explain further without you coming out and saying, "Hey you gave me bad information!"

If a potential client initially says she has to have a car that seats six, then due to the higher investment, backs off to wanting a model that only seats five, she's potentially embarrassing herself with that discrepancy and may be uncomfortable if you bring it up.

Relieve any tension your questions create

One of Columbo's most famous tactics is to change the subject. For example, he asks about a plant that's like one his wife has or acts as though he's finished and begins to leave. This tactic momentarily gets the suspect thinking about something else or answering by reflex. Then he asks another question while the suspect is in the reflex mode and tries to get him to hang himself.

Another of Columbo's most famous tactics is to return, as if he's forgotten something, to ask just one more question . . . just as the suspect is breathing a sigh of relief and letting her guard down. This usually catches the suspect off guard, and she trips herself up. I love that part!

If your potential client has not gone ahead with the purchase, I strongly recommend that you pack up your things and get ready to leave. This usually causes the prospect's guard to go down simply because she starts thinking about whatever it is she's going to do after you leave. Then, use the lost-sale close in Chapter 23. This close is an excellent demonstration of how Columbo would handle the sale.

Use nonthreatening language and a sympathetic tone

Columbo doesn't create scary images of "going downtown" for a chat. In fact, you'll rarely see Columbo in the police headquarters at all — because he knows it's intimidating to his suspects. He also uses lay terms or defines police lingo in words the suspect understands.

Meeting potential clients on their home turf will make them more comfortable. Many business negotiators will tell you that you need to meet on your turf to hold the power — the home court advantage, so to speak. In sales, you're not in a win or lose situation. The goal is to reach a win-win agreement. Making people feel comfortable with you is the first step you take in coming together to determine what the best solution will be.

Let them know you'll be in touch

Any good salesperson who doesn't make a sale on the first contact will do whatever she can to leave the door open for further discussion with a prospect:

> Mr. Scales, I know you haven't agreed to do business with my company, but may I have your permission to stay in touch with you regarding our latest developments in case something in the future would be of benefit to you or your company?

Of course, with Columbo, letting the suspect know that he'll be in touch is plenty to think about in its own right.

Knowing the Nuts and Bolts of Qualifying Prospects

Good qualifying is one of the basics of selling that you cannot overlook or slough off. Don't set yourself up for failure. Work on your style and questions, and then watch your income and your base of happy customers begin to grow.

The average salesperson today either lets the consumer totally make the decision as to what he wants, or she tries to steer the person to what that salesperson likes best. Both of these approaches are wrong. You will recognize steering by the use of these phrases, especially prior to qualifying:

✔ I know just what you're looking for.

✔ This is my favorite.

✔ I have the best thing for you.

✔ We have the best products.

✔ This one looks so good in red.

To help you stay focused on what matters most when it comes to qualifying your prospective clients, I've come up with an easy-to-remember acronym: NEADS. I cover the five parts of the NEADS equation in the following sections, but the acronym itself is what's most important. Granted, my spelling is a little creative, but that new spelling will help you think of meeting the needs of your customers. Each of the letters stands for a question you should ask your prospective clients in an effort to discover their needs.

The success ratio for your entire company would rise if you could get all the salespeople to say to themselves when they meet a customer, "I am concerned about my customer's NEADS. I will discover my customer's true needs and lead my customers to the right product or service for them." Satisfying NEADS helps you accomplish more in your business.

WII-FM: What's in it for me?

An old sales training lesson goes like this: What's everyone's favorite radio station? The answer is always WII-FM. The call letters in this case stand for "What's In It For Me?"

People have a WII-FM mentality, whether they admit it to themselves or not. Human beings are selfish creatures whose natural propensity is to make themselves as comfortable as possible. Be painfully honest: When was the last time you did something for someone else with absolutely *no* expectations of getting anything in return? Now before you tell me what a self-sacrificing person you really are, think about that answer for a second. I'm asking you to remember a time when you did something for someone else without expecting *anything* in return for what you did — no thank-you, no undying loyalties, no promises that the object of your benefactions would someday return the favor, nothing . . . zip, zero, zilch, nada, nienti, goose egg.

If you're like most people (myself included), you'll have difficulty thinking of such a time. Most people are motivated to do for others only if they themselves expect to receive compensation that they value in return. The compensation may not always be monetary, but people *always* want something, anything, even a crust of bread in exchange for their efforts. Even if the sought rewards are intangible and emotional — hugs, kisses, pats on the head, a warm smile— a reward is a reward is a reward.

And that's the same philosophy your customer holds every time you contact her. She sees you as someone who can eliminate a discomfort from her life. To her, you're someone who can give more than he receives, which is why she expects you to provide customer *service*. You contact your customer for one reason: to serve her needs, whether you do it by providing information, a service, or a product.

N is for "now"

The N in NEADS stands for "now" — as in, "What does the customer have now?" Why should you ask this? Because average consumers don't make drastic changes in their buying habits. If you know what your prospect has now, you have a good idea of the type of person he is — and you have a good idea of what he will want to have in the future.

If past experiences often dictate future decisions — as they undoubtedly do — then you need to explore your customer's past experiences. You need to know what he has now so that, in your mind's eye, you can see the type of buying decisions he will make in the future.

Show me your current vehicle, home, style of dress, or style of jewelry, and I can probably tell you what your next version of each of those products will look like. I'm not prejudging here. I'm simply observing that most people are creatures of habit. People usually don't make drastic changes in their lives unless they've recently won the lottery or received a large inheritance or windfall.

E is for "enjoy"

The second letter in NEADS is E. As I'm using it here, E stands for "enjoy." You need to know what your customer enjoys about what he has now. What was his major motivation for getting involved with his existing product or service?

To discover what your customer enjoys, you need to structure your questions so you can discover the customer's past. There's a good chance that what he *enjoyed* about the product or service in the past, or what he *enjoys* about what he already has, is exactly what he will want again. That's usually true — unless you can demonstrate a benefit in *your* product or service that is even better than the one he enjoyed when he purchased his present product or service.

A is for "alter"

The A in NEADS stands for "alter," as in, "What would the customer like to alter or improve about what he has now?"

Because it is constant, change is a potent force in business. In some ways, everyone is looking for change — more benefit, more satisfaction, more comfort. Your customer's normal urge to improve his present condition is why you want to develop questions to find out what he would like to change. What would he like to be different? When you know your customer's answer to that question, you can structure your presentations to show him how your company can provide the changes he wants in his present product or service.

D is for "decision"

The *D* in NEADS stands for "decision." Specifically, you need to know who will be making the final decision on the sale.

Many times salespeople meet a customer who is looking for a car, a home entertainment system, maybe some furniture, and they meet only that one person. Is it wise for the salesperson to assume that the person she's met will be the decision-maker? No. Never assume anything about your customers. The customer may be scouting or researching, planning to bring a spouse or parent in later, when it's time to make the final decision.

So you need to ask qualifying questions to discover whether the person you're talking with is the decision-maker. Here are some examples:

> Will you be the only person driving the car?
>
> Who, other than yourself, will be involved in making the final decision?
>
> Is there anyone else you usually consult with when making decisions of this type?

You've probably heard the standard response to a decision-qualifying question: "I'll have to talk it over with my husband/wife/parents/best friend from college." Many times the salesperson who hasn't properly qualified the prospect will go too far in the presentation before finding out that the real decision-maker is not present. You do nothing more than practice your presentation when you present to non-decision-makers.

You need to be just as enthusiastic to everyone you meet. Even though the person is not the decision-maker, he can be an influencer or a champion of your cause.

Network marketing is a type of business where you build your own business by distributing a product, then getting other people to join you in using the products and sharing the opportunity with others. Some prominent network marketing companies you may be familiar with are Amway, Discovery Toys, and Mary Kay Cosmetics. If you're in network marketing, also known as *multi-level marketing,* never *ever* give your business-opportunity presentation to potential new distributors without both the husband and wife present. This is the kind of business that requires the spouses' mutual support if it's going to work, because it's most often based out of the home and many of the meetings are in the evenings and on weekends. If you present when you don't have that mutual support, you're wasting your time. Wouldn't you rather give your best to someone who can truly benefit from your product or service?

S is for "solutions"

As a salesperson, you're in the business of creating solutions. And, coincidentally, that's exactly what the *S* in NEADS stands for. You are in the solution business. You find out what your prospects need, and then you come up with a solution. In most cases, the solution is that your customer owns the benefits of your products or services.

At my seminars, one casual but effective introduction to the qualifying process that I ask people to adapt to their product or service is this:

> As a representative of [name of your company], it's my job to analyze your needs and do my best to come up with a solution to satisfy those needs so you can enjoy the benefits you're looking for.

You serve customers by finding out what they need and then creating the right solution. When you do this, you create a win-win relationship where people want to do business with your company and they get the products or services they need. They give you business and, in turn, you both grow and prosper.

Avoiding déjà vu when you ask questions

To save yourself from needlessly repeating questions, make written notes of your prospective client's responses during the qualification sequence. Referring to your notes in order to remind yourself what questions you already asked and what the client said his needs were is perfectly okay. Inadvertently asking the same question twice (or more) doesn't inspire confidence in the customer about you or your product. Not only do written notes help you during the presentation, but they also help you to remember what you've already covered when you follow up with the prospect after he's become a regular, happy client. In fact, that's part of how you keep him happy.

Don't forget to ask permission to take notes before you start taking them. Some people get nervous when you start writing down what they tell you. For all you know, they may visualize themselves being grilled in a court of law on what they say to you. If you think you're with someone like that, give her a pad or piece of paper and a pen (preferably with your company name on it), so that she can take notes, too. Being prepared for this situation helps you avoid, or at least to handle, uncomfortable situations.

Getting permission to take notes is easy. All you need to ask is this: "I don't have the best memory in the world, and I do want to do a good job for you. So would you be offended if, while we chat, I make a few notes?" Putting it that way gives you an opportunity to admit that you're human and that you're also smart enough to have learned how to overcome that human failing of a poor memory. And even if you happen to have a photographic memory, these little sentences will help put your clients at ease and build their confidence in you.

Questioning Your Way to Success

Part of qualifying your prospects includes knowing the right questions to ask. But questioning is a technique you use throughout the selling cycle, so don't be afraid to use these strategies when you're presenting, addressing customer concerns, or closing as well.

So why should you ask questions of your prospects? You can use questions to acknowledge or confirm a statement your prospect made that is important to your final request — the decision you want your listener to make. For example, if your prospect tells you that gasoline mileage is very important to her in buying a new car, when you're getting ready to ask her for a final decision, you would include a question like this in your summary of the reasons she should go ahead with the close:

> **Didn't you say that fuel economy was your primary concern?**

Such a question starts the *yes* momentum you need in order to encourage her to go ahead and agree with you. The *yes* momentum is what every persuader strives for. After you get your prospect agreeing to things, if you simply keep asking the right questions — kind of like following a flow chart — she'll follow where you want to lead her. Plus, she'll have enough information at the end to make a wise decision, which you hope is that she can't live without your product or service.

Questions also create emotional involvement. If you're marketing home security devices, you can ask:

> **Wouldn't you feel more confident about entering your home knowing you would be warned beforehand if there were any danger?**

What does that question do? It raises a prickle of alarm on the back of your prospect's neck about the unknown possibilities of walking into an unprotected home. That's emotional involvement — and it's a requirement in any selling situation. ***Remember:*** Think of at least two ways to build emotion, through the use of questions, into every presentation you make.

ANECDOTE

Asking the right questions kept me in high school

I was in high school when I first realized the value of asking the proper questions. In those days, I was recognized as something of a leader, not academically by any means, but in sports and some of the various clubs — the more social aspects of school. I didn't always lead my classmates down the straight and narrow path, though. In fact, our class had a reputation for being pranksters. I was a great instigator and pretty good at hiding these types of "leadership" activities from the teachers.

For three years, I led my classmates to do things they probably shouldn't have done. At that point, our principal, Father Wagner, learned of my part in the pranks and called me into his office. This was the first quarter of my senior year. Father Wagner listed about six "unusual occurrences" that had been attributed to me, so I knew he had a reliable source of information. Father Wagner said that ours was the worst class to go through our school in many years and that he'd decided to make an example of me: I was to be expelled from school! My heart and mind raced. What would my parents say? What would I do? I *had* to graduate with my class.

Father Wagner went on to say that our class was the first class not to have a gift to leave to the school at the end of the year. I was trying to think fast before he dismissed me and I was out of school forever. Suddenly I asked, "Would things be different if our class *did* have something to leave the school and *I* was the one to lead them to giving it?" He said he'd never considered that option. He left the door open for further discussion, though, so I told him I thought there was enough time for us to raise money for a class gift.

Then I asked another question: "What did the school need most?" Father Wagner challenged me with the biggest single item that the school had a need for: an electric scoreboard for the football field. As captain of the football team, I thought that was a great idea. Then he told me how much it would cost: $2,500.

This was 1962, mind you, and $2,500 was a lot more money then than it is today I couldn't let the amount stagger me, though, because I was trying to resuscitate my dying senior year. So I asked another question: "If I raise the money for the scoreboard, will you let me graduate with my class?" Father Wagner again expressed doubt that it could be done, but I stuck to my guns. "If I make a commitment to doing this, will you let me stay in school with my class and graduate with them?" After what seemed an eternity, Father Wagner asked if I'd give my word to make it happen. I jumped at the opportunity and we shook hands on it.

Our class began with a car wash. It raised $200. We went to a junkyard and got the body of a car that wasn't in too bad shape, hauled it to the school grounds, and sold chances to hit it with a sledgehammer for 25 cents each. That raised $50. We were getting nowhere fast.

Then I heard a local car dealership advertising that they were giving away a new Thunderbird to whomever could find the right key. I knew I had my answer: All we needed was a car! I went to the dealership and talked with the owner. He was pleasant and offered to make a cash donation to our effort. I told him I didn't want his cash; I wanted to work with him to get him a lot of publicity while working toward our goal. He was interested all the way up to the point where I told him all we wanted was a new Thunderbird. He leaned back and laughed for a long time. Then he told me that I had a lot of guts asking for a car and that there was no way he could do that.

So I started asking *him* questions. "You do want to help your community, don't you?" Of course he did; he was a well-respected businessman. "Would you like to see the largest group of teens ever assembled, teens who will be car buyers in the near future, applauding your dealership?" Now I had his attention. How would I accomplish this great goal? I explained how we would give presentations at all the other high schools in the San Fernando Valley to invite their students to the biggest dance ever held in the area. Tickets to the dance would be $1, and each ticket held the opportunity to win a Thunderbird. He was interested, but he still wouldn't give us a car. I looked around the room and saw a gold-plated ashtray on his desk in the shape of a Thunderbird. I asked if he could donate the ashtray. He was puzzled by my sudden change in tactics, but he agreed.

The end result was that 2,450 teenagers showed up at our dance. It was the largest dance in the history of the San Fernando Valley at the time. We raised the money we needed, and Father Wagner smiled the whole time he counted it.

Our class gave the school the electric scoreboard, and I gave one of the most winning presentations of my life the night of the dance when I had to present the winner with a gold-plated Thunderbird ashtray. Fortunately for me, it was a fellow student who held the winning number. He was so excited by the recognition from over 2,400 other kids, as well as by our feat of getting the scoreboard, that he didn't even get upset about the prize. In fact, he laughed. Then everyone laughed and had a great time at the dance. It was truly a win-win situation.

At the end of the evening, I got another call to come to the principal's office. This time a smiling Father Wagner gave me a talk I will never forget. He told me that if I could take all the talent I had shown in making that evening a success and apply it to business, I would be a very successful man, regardless of how terrible a student I had been. That's when I realized how vital it is to ask the right questions. And to this day, I thank Father Wagner every time the answer to one of my questions adds to my success.

Tying down the details

I teach many questioning techniques to my students at my live seminars, on my videos, and on my audiotape programs. One of the most popular techniques is called the *tie-down*. A tie-down does not involve tying clients into their chairs until they say yes. Instead, tie-downs involve making a statement, and then asking for agreement by adding a question to the end of it. Here are some of the most effective tie-downs:

- **Isn't it?** For example, "It's a great day for golf, *isn't it?*" When your partner agrees, you set a tee time.

- **Doesn't it?** For example, "Jet-skiing at the lake this weekend sounds like fun, *doesn't it?*" When your friend agrees, call the rental place or get the jet ski tuned up — pronto.

- **Hasn't he?** For example, "The previous homeowner has done a great job with the landscaping, *hasn't he?*" When the prospective new homeowner agrees that he likes the landscape, he's just moved one step closer to liking the whole package — house included.

✔ **Haven't they?** For example, "The manufacturers have included every detail about the questions you asked in this proposal, *haven't they?*" Having all the details covered and having the buyer agree she's covered helps reduce the possibility of stalling when it's time to close.

✔ **Don't you?** For example, "Cleaning up the area where our children play is important, *don't you* think?" When the person agrees, sign him up for one hour of cleanup duty at your neighborhood park.

✔ **Didn't you?** For example, "You had a great time the last time we went hiking, *didn't you?*" Then schedule a time to go again while your friend is in a positive frame of mind about the last trip.

✔ **Shouldn't we?** For example, "We should come here for dinner more often, *shouldn't we,* honey?" If it was an enjoyable meal, the next time you're in the mood for one, this restaurant will pop into your spouse's mind.

✔ **Couldn't we?** For example, "We could let the children organize the games for the neighborhood picnic, *couldn't we?*" Delegation at its finest!

The goal of using tie-downs is to get your prospect thinking in the affirmative about the subject you've just tied down. While he's agreeing with you, you can confidently bring up whatever it is you're trying to get a commitment on.

Professional salespeople often use tie-down statements such as this:

> A reputation for prompt, professional service is important, isn't it?

Who can say no to that? The salesperson who asks such a question has begun a cycle of agreement with the prospect who, hopefully, will continue to agree all the way through the selling sequence.

Giving an alternative

You've certainly seen or heard the *alternate of choice* questioning technique used before, but you probably didn't recognize it as a sales strategy. This strategy involves giving your prospect two *acceptable* suggestions to choose from, and it's most often used for calendar events such as appointments, delivery dates, and so on. Here are some simple examples:

✔ **"I can arrange my schedule so we can visit on Thursday at 3:00 p.m. or would Friday at 11:00 a.m. be better?"** Either answer confirms that you have an appointment.

> ✔ **"This product comes in 55-gallon containers or 35-gallon containers. Which would you prefer?"** No matter which container your prospect chooses, he's still chosen to take one of them.

> ✔ **"We'll have our delivery truck at your home on Monday at 9:00 a.m. sharp. Or would 2:00 p.m. be more convenient?"** Whichever option your prospect chooses, you've nailed down the delivery.

You can also use the alternate of choice technique when you want to focus or limit the conversation to certain points. For example, if you're on a committee to revamp the playground in the neighborhood park, you may want to find a way to gather information without getting into a debate about other aspects of the project. Perhaps some of the neighbors want the playground placed on the northeast corner of the park, and others want it on the southwest corner. Your total involvement may be just to work with the construction crew — not to make or alter placement decisions. In that case, you can ask, "Which do you think would be a better surface under the equipment, wood chips or sand?" It helps you get right to the point of the matter and gives only the two solutions you need addressed.

Alternate of choice questions are particularly effective in surveys. The market researchers are seeking particular information, not general answers, so they build the questions in such a way that the prospect is limited in his responses.

Getting them involved

Another questioning technique is the involvement question, in which you use questions to help your listeners envision themselves *after* they've made a decision to agree with you. If you're marketing office equipment, you can involve your prospect with a question like this:

> Who will be the key contact for us to train on the use of the machine?

Now you've got her thinking about implementing training *after* she owns the product, not about whether or not she'll own it.

Similarly, if you want to involve someone in business with you, use a question like this:

> What will you and Janet do with the extra income that our business plan says we'll generate in the next year?

Ask what they know

Before you ask any question, remember this: In order to sell or persuade, you need to make the other person feel important. Your prospect needs to feel smart, too. So never, never, ever ask a question that your listener cannot answer. For example, if you ask someone what the available memory is on his computer and he doesn't know, you've just made him feel uncomfortable. Yuck! Avoid that result at all costs. If he hasn't brought up the subject of available memory, you should ask whether he has the information available on his current computer. Chances are good that he does. If you tell him specifically the information you need, he can get it. But if you assume that he knows it, and he doesn't know it, you've just embarrassed him. And he may find someone else to buy from who is a little more sensitive and able to make him feel important. And where does that leave you? Without the sale.

Is your listener thinking about whether to get into business with you? Nope. He's just envisioning spending the money he'll earn *after* he goes into business with you. If what he plans to spend the money on is something he wants badly enough, there's a good chance that he'll find himself *having* to go into business with you to satisfy a need he's been feeling without knowing how to fulfill it. Aren't you the good little fairy bringing him just the right solution?

Chapter 10

Winning Presentations

- -

In This Chapter

▶ Getting your clients emotionally involved with your product or service

▶ Making sure the product is in the spotlight

▶ Using visual aids to your advantage

▶ Avoiding Murphy's Law in the world of presenting

- -

*T*his stage of the selling process is the show, your chance to get your prospective client's senses involved. Major companies prepare for the presentation stage by investing hundreds of thousands of dollars and a great deal of time in creating graphics, models, and samples.

A presentation can be as simple as giving out a brochure with a quick explanation or as complex as what you may see at a trade show — complete with bells, whistles, food, clowns, and fireworks. How you present your show depends on what product or service you represent and the potential investment of the prospect.

In this chapter, I steer you through the often-frightening territory of the sales presentation — everything from finding the power players in the room to giving a presentation over the Internet. I also give you some great tips for avoiding common presentation pitfalls. So before you give a presentation, read on.

Getting More Than a Foot in the Door

When you've earned the right to give a prospective client a presentation of your idea, concept, product, or service, you're nowhere near done. The decision-maker has chosen you — probably from several other contestants — and given you the opportunity to prove that your offering is as dazzling as you've been saying. But having an appointment to give a presentation doesn't automatically grant you favored status or guarantee you a warm welcome. It doesn't mean that you will become the prospect's favorite supplier. What many prospects are saying when they let you in the door is, "Okay, wonderboy, impress me!" or "Okay, wondergirl, back up your claims." No pressure here, is there?

In any selling situation, understanding the perspective of your contact person is vital. (I cover this point at length in Chapter 7.)

Every day, salespeople just like you probably bombard your prospect with overtures for their business. Your contact person may be a real decision-maker or someone designated to narrow the field to two or three potential suppliers for the real decision-maker to talk with. Many times, a purchasing agent will bring in several competing companies to give presentations to a committee. If you've done your homework well, you'll know exactly who will be present and why each one of them is there. Think of this as the opening to *Mission: Impossible*. The first aspect of the mission is to identify the players and what's in it for each of them. This way, should you decide to accept your mission, you'll know who will need more persuading and how to go about doing just that.

Find the power players

When you begin an in-person presentation, thank and acknowledge the person who invited you, make eye contact with each person in the room, and see if you can tell which member of your audience is the power player. There's one in every group, and she may or may not be the person you've already been talking with. Just by watching how the other members of the group treat each other should clue you in. Workplace behavior isn't much different from what you see in a documentary about the social habits of wolves. Just as in wolf packs, in most workplaces the subordinates usually defer to the power players when important issues arise. Another hint for identifying the top dogs in a workplace: They often take the best seat in the house during presentations. The best seat is usually at the head of the table or at the 12 o'clock position at a round table, with you at the 6 o'clock position. Or the power player may sit closest to the door in anticipation of an interruption for a vital call or message. You won't be able to make a perfect call every time, but as you hone your skills at the people game, you'll start picking out the power players in minutes.

Some power players don't play the game the way you'd expect and may sit unobtrusively in the back of the room. By watching everyone else's body language, though, you should still be able to recognize that person.

Be quick or be sorry

In today's world of the ten-second TV commercial, few people bother any-more to develop their ability to concentrate. In fact, the average person has a short, downright gnat-like attention span, which means that you must com-press the heart of your presentation down to a matter of only a few minutes. After those few minutes, spend the rest of your time involving your prospects directly in the presentation through questions, visual aids, or a hands-on demonstration.

To help your prospect focus on your presentation and to help yourself stay on track, state your objectives prior to beginning your presentation. Limit your objectives to three. For example, you might say the following:

> Bob and Linda, today I would like to cover three things. First, I would like to better understand your business. Second, I would like to demonstrate a product I think you will find beneficial to your com-pany. And finally, if you see the value in what I am presenting to you today, I would like to discuss the action steps required to help you benefit from it as soon as possible.

I've long taught my students that they should practice, drill, and rehearse their presentations to get through the nitty-gritty in just under 17 minutes. Go past 17 minutes, and your prospect's mind wanders and her eyelids droop. Besides helping to keep your prospect awake, brevity and conciseness demonstrate concern for her valuable time. She may not realize that she appreciates your concern for her time, but on some level she will appreciate it — and the concern will make a difference.

This 17-minute time constraint may challenge you if your product is, say, a complicated mechanical system. If that's the case, you may want to plan for a short break or a summary or question-and-answer period after the first 17 minutes are up. Letting your prospect stretch her legs will increase the level of concentration she gives you. When the blood stops circulating in your extremities, paying attention is difficult. The mind can only absorb as long as the body can endure.

The magic 17 minutes do not begin the moment you enter the room or while you're building rapport. The 17-minute period begins when you get down to the business at hand and cover the finer points of your product's features and how those features can benefit your client.

Break well, and prosper

If you choose to schedule a break, or even if an unplanned break occurs, here's a vital piece of advice you must take to heart: Always do a brief recap before starting back into your presentation. A *brief recap* is just a restatement of the major points that you've covered so far, a quick way to bring everyone back to where you were before the break. Any break in the action allows your listener's mind to wander. She starts looking at her watch, she thinks about lunch or her next appointment, or she wonders what the rest of the office is doing. She may even leave the room to make a call. If she does leave, her mind focuses on the person on the other end of the call, not on your presentation. And you'd better believe that the emotional level your prospect was at when the break began will not be the same when she comes back. Before you can move on with your presentation, you must take a moment or two to bring her back to where she was.

Studies have proven that, after any interruption, it will take you ten minutes to get back to the same level of concentration and emotional involvement you were at before the interruption. Just thinking about all the interruptions you have in a normal day makes you wonder how you ever get anything done, doesn't it?

Knowing the ABCs of Presenting

The general guidelines for giving effective presentations are simple. They're the same ones you learned in English class for writing a good story: Tell them what you're going to tell them, tell them, and finish by telling them what you've told them.

This method serves the same purpose in oral presentations as it does in written ones. It helps the person on the receiving end understand and remember the story you've told him. And when you're selling, you want your presentation to be a memorable occasion for the decision-maker. Master the four basics of presentations — talking on your customer's level, pacing your speech, using the right words to create ownership, and interpreting body language — and you're on your way to earning favored status in the mind of every prospect who hears your presentation.

Being multilingual (even if you're not)

Know enough about your prospect — going into the presentation — that you can talk with him on his level. What does it mean to talk on someone else's level? Consider this example.

Suppose you're in your 30s, and you're trying to sell a refrigerator to an older couple who want to replace a 20-year-old appliance. What do you say to them? Well, with these prospects you'd probably talk about dependability and the new features that your product displays. You'd also point out the benefits that would accrue to the couple if they owned those features. The benefits would be lower utility bills with increased efficiency of new appliances, longer food storage time (which means less waste and greater convenience of getting at things), whether it has an outside drink door, and so on.

Now cut to a different scene: You're trying to sell the same refrigerator to a newly married couple for their first home. Do you talk to them the same way you did to the older couple who were replacing an old appliance? No, with the younger couple you would accent the features and benefits that apply to their situation and satisfy their present needs. The features are the same, but the benefits are seen in a different light when viewed from their perspective. They may want something less expensive because that's all they can afford. But if you can show them the overall savings of getting a bigger or better fridge now, as opposed to the replacement costs down the road, you'll be farther ahead because they'll be more comfortable making the investment when the decision is rationalized for them.

I call this versatility of message being *multilingual*. You speak senior citizen. You speak yuppie. You speak single parent. You speak high end. You speak economy. Being able to converse with someone at his level — whatever that level is — pays big. If you want to test this theory, try talking at your normal business level to a 5-year-old and see how long you keep her attention. Then talk with her on her level and watch the animation in her face as she realizes that you've just entered her world.

Recognizing the posted speed limit

When you give a presentation to a prospect, you need to be sensitive enough to recognize the proper demeanor to have with each client. This part of your presentation is kind of like what stage actors and actresses do: They play off of the attitude and enthusiasm of the audience. If you're too energetic for your audience and speak at too fast a rate, they'll be turned off. Then again, if you're too mild mannered for them and speak too slowly, you may lose them as well.

The ideal approach is to pay attention to the rate and pitch of your prospect's speech and then closely match it. When this happens, on some subconscious level, your prospect gets the message that you're like he is. Plus, he'll understand you better. Be careful if the other person has an accent different from yours. If you adopt his accent, he'll think you're mocking him or that you're insincere. Also, if his pacing is slow, you can speak at a level slightly above his.

Forcing yourself to get down to his level can have an adverse effect on your entire presentation. With a little practice, you'll develop a good sense for what's right.

Using words that assume your prospect will buy from you

Speak as though your prospect already owns what it is you're selling. Don't say, "If you join our neighborhood safety awareness group . . ." Instead, say, "When we meet, you'll enjoy the value of participating in our neighborhood safety awareness group." Giving your prospect the ownership of your idea, product, or service helps to move him closer to making a decision. This is called *assumptive selling*.

Assumptive selling is not the same as *suggestive selling* — when you order nothing more than a chocolate shake but your friendly McDonald's server oh-so-sweetly asks if she can get you an apple turnover today anyway. With suggestive selling you're being offered something you haven't yet asked for or about. Assumptive selling is operating as if you have made the decision to own a product or service you have expressed an interest in.

Deciphering the human body's grammar, syntax, and vocabulary

You don't necessarily need to learn to speak Spanish, French, or Russian to conduct business (though in our global marketplace, it wouldn't hurt you to do so). What I'm talking about here is body language. The study of body language has been around for a long time. In fact, most people are aware of body language, but they don't consciously read it and benefit from it. Pick up a book in the library or bookstore on body language and peruse it. When you find out a little bit about body language and start studying the body language of others (as part of your full-time hobby of selling), you'll quickly see how to benefit from it. Plus, studying body language gives you a perfectly valid alibi the next time you look a second or two too long at someone you find attractive.

Here are just a few examples of the kinds of messages your body language communicates to those around you:

- **Leaning forward:** If you lean forward when you're talking to someone, you're showing that you're interested and paying attention. When you recognize that positive sign in other people, you should keep moving forward, too. In fact, you may be able to pick up the pace of your presentation a bit if your audience is leaning forward.

✔ **Leaning back or glancing away:** When you lean back or glance away from someone who's talking, that means you're losing interest in what he's saying. What do you do if you recognize this body language in your audience? Pause if you're in the middle of a long monologue, summarize the last couple of points, and ask him a question to bring him back. Or, if it's a group presentation and you see several of them displaying this body language, suggest a short break or a question-and-answer period.

✔ **Crossed arms:** If you cross your arms when you're listening to someone, this indicates that you doubt what the other person is saying. When you receive this sign from your audience, move to a point-proving demonstration, chart, graph, or diagram.

Just as important as knowing how to read the language is knowing how to speak it. When you understand positive body language cues, you should practice them as a part of your presentation. They can be as critical as the words you say. If you want to successfully persuade your prospects, you need to be able to give positive, warm, honesty-projecting gestures, such as the following:

✔ **Sit beside the person you're trying to persuade instead of opposite him.** You're not on an opposing side. You're on your prospect's side.

✔ **Use a pen or pointer to draw attention, at the appropriate times, to your visual aids.** Some people hesitate when they use a pen or pointer, and that hesitation says that they are uncomfortable. (You always want to avoid any suggestion of discomfort during demonstrations.) If you wonder about the effectiveness of this technique, watch magicians. They would never be able to keep their "magic" if they didn't master the ability to draw your attention to (or away from) what they want.

✔ **Use open-hand gestures and eye contact.** Open-hand gestures and lots of eye contact say that you have nothing to hide. Don't use the palm out (or pushing) gesture unless it's when you're trying to eliminate a prospect's negative concern. Even then, push to the side, not toward the prospect.

These are the basics of body language, but the whole field of study on body language can help you so much more. When you begin paying attention, you'll find that many other body language cues will become obvious to you. I highly recommend that you research what's available at your local library if body language piques your interest.

Being comfortable with long-distance presentations

When you can't possibly meet in person with your prospective client and you have to conduct business over the telephone, you need to be aware of certain strategies to apply. First, because you can't see your clients, you may have trouble knowing whether they're being distracted or interrupted. Even though you can't read body language over the phone, you can definitely listen to their voice inflections (just as they'll be listening to yours). You can tell fairly easily whether someone is paying attention by counting the length of pauses between their comments, and the number of *uh-huh*s or *hmm*s you hear. If you're in doubt as to whether your prospects are on the same page with you, ask a question of them. Don't, of course, ask if they're paying attention. Instead, ask how something you just covered relates to their business or what they think of it. Restate that point or benefit clearly so they're not embarrassed if they really weren't paying attention.

Another strategy to use when you're giving presentations from a distance is what I call the *pregnant pause*. If you briefly pause during your presentation, the pause will make your prospects wonder what happened and draw their attention to what you'll say next, thus drawing them back to the point at hand.

The product needs to be the star of the presentation — especially if you're not meeting in person. If at all possible, be sure to send a sample product or, at the very least, an attractive visual of it to the client so she'll be seeing what you want her to see during your presentation.

You may also be asked by a prospective client to join him for a presentation via videoconference or through an online service. If you're not savvy to these types of communication tools, you'll need to find someone who is and take a quick lesson. They're not too difficult to work with, but the logistics of setting the stage just right can be tricky. For example, when videoconferencing, you'll probably use an "eyeball" sort of camera attached to your computer. You may even be doing this from home. When you participate in videoconferencing, you need to be aware of what else is in the picture with you. Check your camera and be sure that it doesn't allow your next potential major client to see a torn poster hanging on the wall behind you, or a neglected plant. Believe me, these kinds of objects can harm your credibility. Be certain you have an attractive background even if you have to borrow something to put up behind you. If you do decide to place a plant behind you, beware of putting it (or any other object) in a position in which it may look like it's coming out of your head (in other words, anything positioned behind you, at the level of your head).

Take note of how your local newscasters appear and act on camera. They are in the talking-head type of shot, which is what you'll be in — your head and shoulders will be in the frame, but not much else. Newscasters make great eye contact with the camera — they smile into it, smiling with their eyes.

If your presentation online requires you to show slides or other visuals, maintain as much control of how the flow goes as you can. For example, you can control a PowerPoint presentation from your computer while it's being viewed online from someone else's computer. In PowerPoint 2000, you can save your work as *ready-to-view HTML* documents. Clients and coworkers can then launch the presentation in a browser, even in full-screen mode. They can view slides in any order or repeat important slides at their convenience. *Presentation on demand* is another feature within PowerPoint 2000 that allows people to rerun your presentation at any time that's convenient for them. Visit `www.microsoft.com/office/powerpoint` for a tour of the latest features you may benefit from.

Other services, such as HorizonLive (`www.horizonlive.com`) allow you to provide live audio and/or video of yourself online while pushing PowerPoint slides, Web sites, or other video to the other person's computer.

Letting the Product Be the Star

The first key in presenting or demonstrating anything — a new hobby, a multimillion-dollar piece of high-tech equipment for a Fortune 500 company, or anything in between — is really pretty simple: Let the product shine, let it be the star. You're just the host who introduces the key players (your product and your prospect) to each other and then fades into the background to let them get acquainted.

Even though one of the players may be an inanimate object, even an intangible one, you need to think of that object in terms of the future primary relationship between the product and its new owner. And you need to let the possibilities for that relationship develop (with your encouragement, of course).

Getting out of the picture

As a salesperson, you are not unlike the matchmakers of old. You may help me find a mate, but after we've met, you step out of the picture. Of course, you may occasionally monitor the progress of our relationship, but you won't be coming to live with us.

Even though the product must be the star, never forget that your prospective client needs to always remain the focus of your presentation. Never give so much attention to the product and what it can do that you ignore what it will do *for* the person sitting there with you — your prospective client.

Staying in control

Don't let your prospects see what you want them to see until you're ready for them to see it. The product has to be the star, but you need to be the guide — or the bodyguard — letting them close only when it's appropriate.

If your demonstration involves the use of a piece of equipment, don't let your prospective client come in and begin punching buttons or demanding answers to a lot of questions — taking control of the presentation away from you. Just tell the prospect that he has great questions and that you'll cover most of them in your presentation. Then ask that he hold his questions until after the demonstration. When he recognizes that you've planned something special for him, he'll probably settle down and let you do your thing.

Keeping control can become a challenge when you have several things to display. If your demonstration falls into this category, I recommend that you bring something (like a cloth) to cover your display items, uncovering only those items you're prepared to discuss. If you're using a video or computer screen, be sure to have an attractive screensaver that you can go to when you need your prospect's attention focused back on your planned presentation. Otherwise, your prospect will probably try to read ahead on the screen instead of listening to what you're saying.

The primary need of all humans is the need to be comfortable. If your prospect isn't comfortable with what you're offering, he'll never part with his money for it, give his commitment to it, or follow through with it. So, your number one goal in any presentation is to get the prospect to an acceptable comfort level with your offering.

Mastering the Art of Visuals

The majority of people learn and understand best when they involve as many of their senses as possible; however, each person usually has one dominant sense. Some people learn best by closing their eyes and listening. Others have a strong need to touch and feel things. Most people, however, gain the best understanding by seeing things.

I'm sure you've heard the phrase "seeing is believing." That phrase comes from the desire of most people to be shown the proof that what they're being told is real, or at least that it can come true. Take a moment to see the difference between *telling* someone about a new product and letting her *see* it, either in picture form or through a product demonstration. Obviously, letting the prospect see it will involve more of her senses. And that's where visual aids come into play.

Visual aids should show three things to new clients:

> ✔ **Who you (and your company) are.** Visual aids should identify your company and the industry to which it belongs. If you are worldwide suppliers of your particular type of product, put that information in your visual aids. The story of your company builds credibility.

✔ **What you've done.** If the Space Shuttle uses software developed by your company, brag about it in this portion of your visual aids. Be careful not to belabor the point, though. Being proud of your company is one thing; being a bore is another thing altogether (and something you obviously want to avoid).

✔ **What you do for your clients.** This is the part your prospective client is most interested in. This is where you tune in her favorite radio station, WII-FM, on which she will ask the pressing question, "What's In It For Me?"

The best visual aids include all three of these key points. If they don't, be sure to try to verbally incorporate these points into your presentation.

Using the visuals your company supplies

If you represent a company's products or services, you've probably been exposed to their visual aids. These are usually slick, high-quality sheets with graphs, charts, diagrams, and photos. Such visual aids often contain quotes from various well-thought-of authorities about your product or service. For organizing and storing printed visual aids, many companies provide you a great-looking binder that also stands up like a miniature easel.

You may work for a company that's much more high-tech than this. For example, you may get computer-generated graphics that appear on a projection screen and include music and professional announcers, such as those created using PowerPoint. For computer presentations, you'll most likely have a laptop computer and multimedia projector. When you prepare for one of these high-tech presentations, be sure that your prospective client has a white board or screen for you to project your images onto. Presenting your product professionally is tough when all you have to work with for a background is wood paneling or flowered wallpaper.

You may also find yourself working with videotapes for your presentations. Videos often include recorded testimonials from actual customers your prospect can relate to. When your prospect sees someone just like herself who is benefiting from your product or service, the relationship between the prospect and your product grows a little stronger.

Whatever your specific visual aids depict, the important thing to remember is this: Your company invested in the creation of your visual aids for a reason. And that reason was not to make your life more complicated by having to carry all this stuff around and keep it updated. Instead, they did it because many, many years' experience has proven that visual aids are very effective when they are used properly.

So what's the best way to use visual aids? Most likely, it's the way your company recommends. Few companies succeed in business by putting out garbage as visual aids and then leaving their salespeople to figure out how to use them. Typically, companies rely on a task force of some sort that includes top salespeople, manufacturing people, and marketing people. All of their suggestions usually have to be approved by a director or manager of the marketing department — someone who will ultimately be held accountable if the brochures, videos, or sample products do the job of moving product into the hands of consumers (or if they don't).

If for some reason you don't like or have trouble using the company's visual aids, talk with the people who trained you on how to use them. If their suggestions don't satisfy you, talk with a top salesperson, someone who uses them effectively. You may even want to go on a customer call with that salesperson to watch how she handles things. After you master her suggestions for using the visual aids as well as possible, if you still think you have room for improvement, ask to meet with the people who put them together. They'll probably be glad to offer you constructive suggestions and, hopefully, listen to yours.

Developing your own visual aids

If you aren't involved in formal selling or you have no visual aids to work with, put some thought into what you can develop on your own. Involvement of the senses in attempting to persuade others is critical. In fact, I recommend that you involve as many of a prospect's senses as possible.

For example, say you want to sell your family on vacationing in the woods when you know they'd rather go to the beach. You may want to rent a video on all the outdoor adventures available to them in the woods. Many vacation spots now offer free videos as promotional items in information packages. Or you can get a video on nature in general, with flowing waterfalls, gentle breezes blowing in the trees, canoeing, horseback riding, whatever appeals to your audience (in this case, your family). Such a video would involve two senses: sight and hearing. And what's that I smell out front — smoke? If possible, you may even want to have a little campfire going in the yard while the family watches your video. Or prepare some hot dogs and s'mores ahead of time so that they get their sense of taste tied in to the joy of that vacation in the woods. Invest in hiking boots, lightweight canvas backpacks, or canteens filled with spring water in order to get the sense of touch involved.

All these things (the video, the campfire, the food, the equipment) are sensory aids that are vital to your presentation if you're serious about persuading your family to go on this type of vacation. When they accept ownership of all these feelings, it'll be an easy sale (unless you have a family member with a very strong phobia of bugs or wide-open spaces).

The same strategy applies to formal business sales presentations: The more senses you can involve, the better. If your aids limit you to sight and hearing, find ways to get additional sensual involvement (no, I don't mean *that* kind of sensual involvement). You can involve your prospects' sense of touch just by handing them things. Smell and taste are a little tougher, especially if you're selling an intangible object like a service. With intangibles, you may want to paint visual pictures that bring those senses into play.

For example, say you're selling a cleaning service to a working mother. You may not necessarily want to have her smell the cleaning agents you use — but you can talk about how fresh the home will be after your professional crew has completed its duties. And to get a homeowner prospect's senses completely involved, always refer to his residence as his *home* — not his *house*. (A house is made up of lifeless bricks and boards; a home is made up of the people who live there and the events of those people's lives.) Bringing a small box of candy or mints as a new-client gift involves the sense of taste in your presentation, even though it doesn't directly apply to your service.

Demonstrating Products to Your Prospective Clients

When you demonstrate a tangible product, you have to be like a game show host. You want a lot of excited contestants, and the way people get excited is through involvement. Who cares if Regis Philbin knows all the answers to the questions on *Who Wants to Be a Millionaire?* He's a nice guy and all, but the fun is in using those lifelines and playing the game.

Selling is not a spectator sport; it's an involvement sport.

If you sell copiers and you don't have the people you are demonstrating to push the buttons, change the paper, and open and close the machine, you're not selling. You're showing. Let your prospective clients perform the functions, and they will feel involved.

It won't matter to the office manager that you've won all the time trials at your office for making the most complicated copying challenges come out perfect. Instead, what matters is how simple it is for everyone on your prospect's staff to meet those challenges — and you should build into your demonstration the proof that they can do so. During your demonstration, your prospect and her staff members should be able to make normal copies simply and to find out something about a new feature that's going to make their job easier. Your key contact person should see exactly what all the warning lights are on the machine and what to do about each one.

The best computer salespeople stand or sit at their client's shoulder, giving him instructions on how he can do whatever it is he just asked about. They make sure the client's hands are on that keyboard and mouse. That way, he has a positive experience with the product and builds his confidence in the capabilities of the machine. What's really happening is that the client is learning something new and building his confidence in his own ability to use the machine. He may even be overcoming a fear of computers altogether. And if he overcomes that fear and gets comfortable using the product, you can bet he'll be much more likely to want to own it.

One of the greatest fears all clients have in selling situations is that they will trust what the salesperson tells them, buy the product or service that's for sale, and then, after they own the product or service, find out that it doesn't meet their expectations or meet their needs. The best demonstrations give people the opportunity to prove to themselves that what the salesperson is telling them is true.

Avoiding the Crash-and-Burn Scenario of Presentations

If I were to tell you all the horror stories I've heard about failed sales presentations, I'd need the better part of an afternoon. The unfortunate thing is that those same salespeople could have avoided the problems they came across if they had taken a few simple precautions. But fortunately for you, hearing so many of these horror stories has helped me develop effective suggestions for avoiding your own demonstration faux pas. In the following sections, I cover just a few things you may not think of, but all of them should become a vital part of your preparatory checklist when you're getting ready to make a presentation.

Find the electrical outlets and know how to reach them

If your demonstration requires the use of electrical power, find out in advance exactly where the available electrical outlets are and how you can plug into them. If you're running the show on your computer battery, check and double-check that it's fully charged prior to your presentation — and bring a spare, fully-charged battery with you, just in case.

A woman I know of invested hours in preparing her computer-generated demonstration with high-quality graphics, customized charts, graphs, and diagrams. Her only problem: The power cord she brought to her presentation was too short. She had to place all her equipment right next to a wall, which was about 20 feet from her audience. As a result, she lost vital eye contact and other rapport-building closeness with her audience, and probably the sale, too — all because she brought the wrong extension cord.

ANECDOTE

Being prepared for the worst . . . and hoping for the best

Jim is a manufacturer's representative for a line of products sold to automotive service shops. He travels a great deal around the country, servicing his clients. Once or twice a year, Jim coordinates large-scale presentations of the latest innovations in equipment from his company. He invites two or three representatives from each of his best, noncompeting clients' companies. Jim puts weeks of work into each presenation, including building models, coordinating slides, conducting interviews with end-users — in other words, doing whatever it takes for his presentation to succeed.

Jim is so detailed in these presentations that he's often invited to company headquarters to show other representatives his presenation methods. Jim's customers always enjoy his presentations, and he often leaves with much larger orders for his products than he would if he were to meet with them one-on-one. In addition to placing orders for the latest and greatest products for their stores, his various clients can compare notes with each other on the latest industry trends. The Big Presentation is a win-win event for everyone involved.

At one of Jim's last presentations, however, he stayed at a new hotel. He heard it had a great reputation and thought his repeat attendees would enjoy the change of scenery. All was going well until the alarm clock in Jim's room failed to work, and he overslept on the morning of his presentation. Waking up with only ten minutes to go before showtime, he quickly showered, dressed, and dashed to the meeting room. He was going to be able to start on time, thank goodness. However, about ten minutes into his well-planned presentation, the lightbulb in his slide projector burned out. Being the detail person he is, Jim had put a new lightbulb in the evening before, but he didn't count on a new bulb being bad. It took him half of a very embarrassing hour to find the correct staff people to locate a replacement bulb so he could move on with his presentation.

Luckily for Jim, his clients already knew his track record, and they all ended up having a good laugh about it later in the day. However, if Jim had been giving this presentation to new clients, his credibility could have fallen so much that he would've had to spend many hours following up in order to gain their business — if he ever got it at all.

The best thing of all in this incident is that Jim took the time to analyze what went wrong and how he could prevent it from happening again. He's a professional who sees every experience, whether good or bad, as a learning experience. Today Jim's checklist for presentations includes at least two extra lightbulbs, knowing the name of the audiovisual person who can help in case of an emergency, and carrying a backup alarm clock — a key-wind alarm clock, at that, to beat power failures.

Be sure your visual aids are in order

Food stains and bent corners on your presentation materials give the impression that you don't care about details. And if your materials are confiscated by a roving band of evil, invisible little gremlins who mischievously rearrange your slides into a state of utter chaos, your audience will be less than thrilled. So before your presentation, be sure to review each and every piece of equipment or presentation material that your audience will see. You'll sleep better knowing things are in order.

Never use your materials after someone else has been through them. Misplacement is rarely intentional, but it does happen.

Test everything ahead of time

You may have a very dependable demonstration model of your computer software. In fact, it could be one you've used for several weeks or months without any challenges. But on the day of your big presentation, Murphy's Law may strike. You remember Mr. Murphy. He's the poor bloke who deduced the most prevalent law in the known universe: If anything can go wrong, it will. Having a bad cable for your equipment or your computer can wreak havoc on the best-laid plans. So always arrive early enough to test your equipment on-site. And test it early enough that, if you find something isn't working, you can replace it.

Customize as much as you can

Don't you love it when someone gives you a generic presentation that you just know they've given, word-for-word, to at least 40 other people before? I didn't think so. No one does. By making the extra effort to customize your materials, you will appear competent and knowledgeable about your customer's specific needs. And that's just the kind of person they're looking for.

Don't customize by skipping over materials in your generic, full-blown presentation. People will feel slighted by the absence of this information. Instead, remove pages or slides you won't need. Page past graphics on your computer screen that are unnecessary. If you can't skip them, go ahead and show them. Just make sure you offer a brief explanation that you know those particular graphics don't apply to your present audience's needs and that you won't waste their valuable time going over them in detail.

Bring a protective pad

If you're scheduled to make a presentation in someone else's office, don't take a chance that any of your equipment will mar their furniture. I know of a salesman who, when it was time to fill in his order form, placed it on the client's table and, because it was a three-part form, printed heavily on the paper. The only problem was that the table was made of a fine, soft wood. Because the salesman didn't have a pad of paper under the form, his heavy printing etched itself into the tabletop. Needless to say, his lasting impression wasn't favorable. To prevent damages from a similar source, always check the bottoms of your equipment before placing anything on a potential customer's furniture. Rough edges can easily leave scratch marks.

Chapter 11

Addressing Customer Concerns

- -

- -

*U*nless you sell balloons at a parade, few customers will contact you, make an impulse purchase, and go away happy. What really happens is that customers have concerns. What concerns will they have? Questions such as these:

- ✔ Will the product or service do what you say it will?
- ✔ Will you really be able to make their required delivery date?
- ✔ Have they negotiated the best investment?
- ✔ Are they making a good decision?
- ✔ Is it something they need right now?

All these little fears creep up on customers when they feel the urge to invest in your product or service or to commit to your idea. The concerns that arise when a customer makes any commitment that involves his time or money are completely natural.

Unfortunately, most people new to persuading think that a "No" or a sign of hesitation means "Good-bye, Charlie." The seasoned persuader, however, knows that customers can have good reasons to hesitate. The best reason of all is that they feel themselves leaning toward "Yes." So your client's hesitation can simply be a sign that he wants to slow down the selling process so he can absorb all the information you're giving him. Or hesitation can mean that the customer needs *more* information. In such a case, the customer objects in order to show you that you need to back up and resell him on a certain point. When a potential client hesitates or gives you a stall, just think, "He needs more information."

If you get nervous or afraid when you hear an objection and start beating a hasty retreat for the door, you're leaving empty-handed. And if you try to overcome your client's objection and he doesn't like the way you handle it, you're going to be heading for the door anyway, and he'll have it open before you get there! So why not experiment with ways to address your client's concerns or handle his objections? The worst that can happen is that you won't get what you want and you'll move on to the next likely candidate. The best that can happen is that your customer sees how competently you handled his concern and that his concern wasn't strong enough to keep him from going ahead with your offering.

Until you come to expect customer concerns, you won't know how to handle them. And until you know how to handle customer concerns, you won't come close to reaching your highest earning potential in sales. So go into every presentation anticipating objections, and you'll come out ahead.

Reading Your Prospect's Signals

Prospective clients tell you three important things when they voice objections or raise concerns during your presentation:

- ✔ They are interested, but they don't want to be thought of as an easy sale.
- ✔ They may be interested, but they aren't clear about what's in it for them.
- ✔ They may not be interested, but they could be if you educate them properly.

All three situations tell you one thing: The prospect needs more information.

If you've properly qualified the prospect (see Chapter 9 for more information), you know what he has now, what he enjoys most about it, what he would alter, and that he is the decision-maker. Armed with that knowledge, if you're confident the prospect would benefit from your offering, then chances are he's interested, but he just doesn't want you to think of him as an easy sale. In that case, you want to slow down the pace, encourage questions, and generally get him relaxed and chatting before you ask him to make a decision.

If your prospect is already asking lots of questions and looks somewhat perplexed or doubtful, he's interested, but he just doesn't have a clear picture of what's in it for him. This situation is especially common when the prospect doesn't have previous experience with a similar product and you're educating him from ground zero. To respond to this kind of prospect, you have to cover the features and benefits in a bit more detail — asking questions along the way that will help you create the right word pictures in your presentation.

When the fish aren't biting, change your bait

Most persuaders find it hard to influence people who voice no objections and raise no questions. In other words, the most difficult people to persuade are like dead fish: Their eyes wiggle every now and then, but they don't respond.

In negotiation situations, you carry the presentation forward by directing and redirecting your course of questions and information based on what your prospect tells you. If she tells you nothing, the communication often stalls. When that happens, you have to guess which direction to follow next — and guessing is very bad, because when you guess, you're no longer in control. Guessing is like casting your line with no bait on it.

The people who don't get verbally involved in your presentation likely have no intention of going ahead with your proposition. Those who *do* bring up challenges for you to address are, at the very least, interested. If they're really tough to convince, they'll probably become your best customers when you finally do convince them. So the next time you hear an objection, be glad. Getting objections and getting past them is a necessary step in the selling cycle.

Finally, if you face the third kind of questioning client (the one who's disinterested because of a lack of information), you must first earn his trust so he'll give you the time you need to educate him on your product. You also have to build the prospect's curiosity about the product, service, or idea so he wants to know more.

By backing up and clarifying exactly what it is the prospect is objecting to, you find out just which direction to take for your next step.

Using Some Simple Strategies to Address Your Prospect's Concerns

Objections from prospects are just part of the business of selling. What's important is that you know how to handle them. Fortunately, you can use some key strategies to address your prospects' objections so that they come away with more information *and* more respect for you and your product. In this section, I show you how.

Condition versus objection

If your customer's objection is "I'm totally broke," and you're selling a luxury item, chances are pretty good that you've just heard a condition, not an objection. And there's a big difference between the two.

A *condition* is not an excuse or a stall. It's a valid reason that the prospect cannot agree to what you're proposing. If you're trying to exchange your offering for your potential customer's money, and the customer has no money and has no credit, just thank him for his time and move on. With so many potential customers out there who have no conditions, you have no good reason to beat your head against the wall with those who *do* have valid conditions.

Always leave people who voice valid conditions on a positive note, though. You never know how

that person's situation may change down the road. He may win the lottery in the next 24 hours. Old Aunt Thelma may leave him an inheritance. He may borrow the money from his rich grandpa. Or, better yet, he may convince Gramps that your offering would make a great birthday or Christmas gift for him.

Remember: If he wants what you have to offer badly enough, he'll call you. And you can rest assured that his calls won't go to someone else with whom he doesn't have a positive relationship. After all, why would he call a stranger when he can rely on a salesperson whom he knows to be knowledgeable, competent, and considerate?

Bypassing your prospects' objections completely

If you know your prospect wants and needs the product or service you're offering, but she feels a natural inclination to object — in these situations, you can often bypass the objection altogether. Simply say, "That's a good point, Ms. Smith. I believe it will be addressed to your satisfaction by the end of my presentation. May I make a note of it and come back to it later?" If she gives you permission, she'll be watching the rest of your presentation for a satisfactory answer. Or, she may see enough benefit during the balance of the presentation that the value outweighs her concern and it becomes a moot point.

If you're new to persuading, don't ignore any objection without testing the waters to see how big a concern it truly is. Sometimes just acknowledging the concern is enough. Your prospect will be satisfied that you're really listening, and then she'll move ahead.

When your prospect raises a concern, it doesn't necessarily mean, "No way." It may simply be a way for the prospect to say, "Not *this* way." If that's the case, you just need to take another path to the same destination.

Helping your prospects to see that they're trading up

If your prospective client has money, credit, or both, but he just doesn't want to part with it now, you haven't convinced him that he'd be better off with the product than he would be with his money.

If an investment you're offering requires the person's time, "No time" is not a valid condition. It's an objection. Everyone has the same 86,400 seconds in every day. How people use them is their choice. If you want someone to invest his time with you, you have to show him enough benefits for him to *want* to spend his time on your offering instead of on what he's already planned.

Beating your prospects to their own objections

If you know that your prospect is likely to voice a particular concern, beat her to it. By being in control and bringing the issue up when *you* want it brought up, rather than when your prospect thinks the time is right, you can brag about it and turn it into an advantage. For example, if you know your product costs more than others on the market, you can be fairly certain that your prospect will be concerned about that cost. But you can beat the prospect to that objection by explaining upfront that your product requires a higher investment because it contains only the highest-quality ingredients. And those high-quality ingredients make people feel better, last longer, or perform in a superior manner. Those benefits are worth bragging about *before* your prospect gets busy laying bricks for that wall of defense against the investment.

Trusting your instincts

Selling instincts (expressed by that little voice inside your head telling you what's right and what's not in a selling situation) develop through practice and experience. Everyone has these instincts, but some people's selling instincts are more developed than others.

To start developing and using your selling instincts, carefully listen to your customers' concerns and genuinely put their needs before your own. Then, and only then, can you trust your own instincts. If you can't honestly say that your customers' needs come before your own, then you place your own desires before what you instinctively know is right for the customer — and your self-centeredness will show. Your customers will see the dollar signs in your eyes and won't trust you. And why should they trust someone who only thinks of himself?

Here is a specific script for how you can handle an objection to your product's investment:

> CLIENT: Tom, I'm sure I can find this product, or one just like it, for a lot less money.
>
> TOM: Well, Jim, I understand your concern. You know, I've learned something over the years. People look for three things when they spend money: the finest quality, the best service, and of course, the lowest investment. I've also found that no company can offer all three. They can't offer the finest quality and the best service for the lowest investment. And, I'm curious, for your long-term happiness, which of the three would you be most willing to give up? Fine quality? Excellent service? Or the lowest fee?

This client is going to have a tough time coming back at you and saying, "Well, poor quality and crappy service are okay as long as they're cheap."

Here's another way to handle a concern about money. Your choice between two methods is going to be a judgment call. When the customer raises the concern, if you think that he has developed a certain belief in you — in your competency — then you may prefer to use this approach:

> CLIENT: Tom, I'm sure I can find this product, or one just like it, for a lot less money.
>
> TOM: Jim, I could have chosen to work for any company in the area in my particular industry. After careful research, I chose my company because I wanted to be able to sit with my clients and look them in the eye and say, "You are doing business with the very highest quality company in the industry." I know you appreciate quality and, because of that, those few extra pennies you'll invest per day to enjoy the finest quality will benefit you in the long-term scheme of things, wouldn't you agree?

With this approach, you enhance the credibility you've already established. In effect, you're telling your client that you're not an amateur. You have a concern for your own reputation and you plan to be around in the business awhile.

One of my former students uses this tactic to her tremendous advantage. She markets fax machines to small businesses, and she's so good at it that sometimes her company has trouble keeping enough inventory in stock to keep up with all the orders she writes. Her favorite strategy accounts for much of her uncommon sales volume. Rather than waiting until a prospective customer asks about a delivery date, she brings up delivery date early in her presentation by saying something like this:

> Jim, I'm confident that at the end of my presentation you'll want to own my fax machine, as so many of my happiest clients have done. I must say that we're excited about that. You see, if you had decided to get a fax machine from one of our competitors, they probably would have it available immediately. Maybe that's because there's less demand for their machines — I don't know. If you decide on our machine, I'm going to have to ask you to be patient because we're currently in an oversell situation — everyone seems to want this particular machine. Its popularity speaks for itself, doesn't it?

Having product that's back-ordered can be a serious challenge if you let it. But bringing it up and bragging about how popular the product is puts back-ordering in a different light — a light that many customers will accept.

Take advantage of this tactic with objections that you know are most often heard about your product or service. If people object to the cost, have a testimonial at hand from a happy client who had the same objection and now feels her return on investment was well worth it. Many companies post such testimonials on their Web sites. You can easily impress your prospect by calling up the Web site on your laptop right then and there to address the prospect's concern. Let him read it rather than telling him about it. In fact, asking your prospective client to take a look at your company's Web site prior to your presentation is always a good idea. Send the prospect an e-mail with your Web address and a few suggestions of areas within your site he may find helpful.

This method of beating prospects to their concerns — by bringing it up, bragging about it, and then elaborating on it — has proven successful for many of my students who used to see common challenges as stumbling blocks. Now they see them as springboards to success, and you can, too.

Understanding the Do's and Don'ts of Addressing Concerns

Before you get too deep into dealing with your prospect's concerns, you need to be aware of some basic do's and don'ts of this important step in selling. In this section, I fill you in on a couple of each that will guide you through any selling situation.

Do acknowledge the legitimacy of the concern

Dismissing your prospect's concerns as unimportant can cause those objections to get completely blown out of proportion. In many cases a simple "I see" or "I understand" is acknowledgment enough. In other cases, you may do well to say, "Let me make a note of that so we can discuss it in depth after we cover everything," and then jot it down. Jotting down the concern validates the concern and shows professionalism on your part.

Do get the prospect to answer his own objection

The most important "do" of addressing concerns is: Get the other person to answer his own objection.

That advice may sound tricky to follow, but here's why it's so important. You're trying to persuade your prospect, so he'll have reservations about anything you do or say. Why? Because anything you say must be good for you, too. Until the prospect realizes that you're acting in his best interest, he will doubt you.

Here's something to help you remember that last point: When *you* say it, they tend to doubt it. When *they* say it, they tend to think it's true. And *that's* why you want to get your prospect to answer his own objections — because he's much more likely to believe *himself* than he is to believe *you*. All you need to do is provide the information that answers his concern and let him draw his own conclusions. You let him persuade himself.

This technique often works well when you persuade a married couple (children, take note). When one partner objects to something, don't respond immediately. Average persuaders are quick to defend their offering. But there's a better way: Learn to sit tight. Many times, one spouse jumps in with the next comment and you have a 50/50 chance that the originally silent spouse will answer the objection for you. If the second spouse agrees with his partner's objection, then you know you'll have to work a little harder to overcome it. The point is that these two people already have a positive relationship (you hope) and trust each other's judgment. Being quiet while they think it through can cause the objection to evaporate into thin air right before your eyes.

When something important to you is hanging in the balance, being patient is difficult. During such moments, seconds feel like hours and you can quickly become very uncomfortable. To keep yourself from jumping in too soon, try this trick. Silently count to 30. Or you may want to count the seconds by saying to yourself, "one-thousand-one, one-thousand-two, one-thousand-three," and so on. (Just remember to count to *yourself,* not aloud.) Some salespeople recite a short poem to themselves to kill that time. Whatever method you choose, just be careful not to let them see your lips move.

What you never want to do when you're waiting for a response is look at your watch or at a clock in the room. Even a slight glance at a timepiece can distract the prospects, because they're already looking at you, waiting for your next move. So practice this step until you're comfortable with it.

Don't argue with your prospect

Although not arguing with your prospect may seem obvious, when you're negotiating with someone, emotions can take over and things can get out of hand. Arguing or fighting an objection or concern raises a barrier between you and the person you're trying to persuade. You're trying to persuade her to something, not go ten rounds with her. If you keep the perspective that objections are simply requests for further information, you shouldn't have much of a challenge with this advice.

Don't minimize a concern

To the person you're persuading, every point he raises is valid. Remember to put yourself in his shoes. How would you react to someone who acts as though your concerns are stupid or unimportant?

Handling Objections in Six Easy Steps

In the following sections, I give you six steps for handling objections or addressing concerns that almost always work in your favor. They also work pretty well in diffusing unusually tense situations, so heed them well.

Sometimes you'll hear more than one objection or concern from a prospect. If you start running through all six steps with each objection you hear, you can spend a lifetime trying to persuade. Experience helps you tell which concerns you need to address and which you may be able to bypass (see the section "Bypassing your prospects' objections completely" earlier in this chapter).

If a concern or objection is raised during a group presentation and you have to do a bit of research and get back to them, be certain you have the contact information (specifically, an e-mail address) for each person in the group. Never rely on one person to relay vital information in the manner that you know to be best for moving the selling process forward. Send the exact same e-mail message to each person, and let them all see that they're part of the group e-mail. If each person receives it individually, they could all wonder what else you may have shared with the others.

Outsmart your prospect's last objection

Construction work was my first job. It was tough, physically demanding, and ultimately, for me, unfulfilling work. In my part of the country, real estate was booming, so I studied and eventually got my license. My next step was to get a job with a local company. I had two strikes against me at this point: My only means of transportation was a motorcycle, which made it tough to drive people out to view properties, and even worse, I didn't own a suit.

After being turned away by several real estate companies, I finally talked with a man who told me he probably could help me work around the motorcycle challenge, but having a suit was critical. It dawned on me then that this was his final objection. I asked, "If I have a suit, then will you hire me?" To my surprise, he said yes and told me to show up in a suit at the next company sales meeting. He didn't specify what *kind* of suit I needed, though, so I took the liberty of cleaning up and wearing my band uniform. You see, when I was 16, I played in a band. We were greatly influenced by the Beatles, and our band uniforms were silver lamé. Technically, my band uniform was a suit.

I walked into that sales meeting just as he was informing everyone that they had a new agent on board. You should have seen his face when he realized that my "suit" was my old band uniform. It got a lot of laughs and the guy agreed to let me stay on if I could produce. I was the only motorcycle-riding real estate agent in a band uniform in the country at that time, and my nonconformity turned out to be an advantage. People talked about "that crazy kid, Hopkins." It was free advertising.

Identifying and outsmarting my prospect's last objection to what I was selling was a turning point in my life. It can be in yours, too.

Include the link to your company's Web site for each member of the group to peruse. Often in a committee decision-making situation, only one or two members get the whole package of information. They then break it down for the balance of the decision-makers. This may be the way the *company* wants the process handled, but what *you* want is to get as much information as possible equally distributed.

Step #1: Hear them out

When someone trusts you enough to tell you what's bothering him, do him the courtesy of listening. Don't be quick to address every phrase he utters. Give him time; encourage him to tell you the whole story behind his concern. If you don't get the whole story, you won't know what to do or say to change his feelings. Don't interrupt either; you may jump in and answer the wrong concern.

Step #2: Feed it back

By rephrasing what his concerns are, you're in effect asking for even more information. You want to be certain that he's aired it all so that no other concerns crop up after you've handled this one. You're saying to him, "Go ahead. Lay it all on me. Get it off your chest." In doing this, you're asking him to trust you.

Step #3: Question it

This step is where subtlety and tact come into play. If a guy objects to the fact that you are asking Block Watchers to wear a reflective vest while out walking the neighborhood, don't say, "What's wrong with it?" Instead, gently ask, "Wearing the vest makes you uncomfortable?" If it does, he'll tell you why. Maybe he's shy. If so, you have to build his confidence in the respect the uniform generates and in the authority it lends to him as a participant.

Step #4: Answer it

When you're confident that you have the whole story behind his concern, you can answer that concern with confidence. If the prospect's concern is cost, you can engage in the following dialog:

> SALESPERSON: I can certainly appreciate your feelings. But I think we ought to keep that $1,000 in the proper perspective. Over the years, most of my happiest clients received true enjoyment/value from this product for at least five years. This fact really makes that $1,000 only $200 per year, doesn't it?
>
> PROSPECT: Yes, it does.
>
> SALESPERSON: If you're like most people, you'll receive the benefits of this product for 52 weeks per year, which means that $1,000 breaks down to about $3.85 per week. Then, of course — and this may sound ridiculous — it finally boils down to about 55 cents per day. Do you think you should avoid enjoying all the benefits we've discussed for 55 cents per day?
>
> PROSPECT: Well, when you put it that way, it does sound a little silly.

And you've just gotten the prospect to answer his own concern.

Step #5: Confirm your answer

When you've answered the objection, confirming that your prospect heard and accepted your answer is important. If you don't complete this step, the prospect very likely will raise that objection again.

You can confirm your answers simply by completing your answer with a statement such as, "That answers your concern, doesn't it, Bob?" If Bob agrees with you that your comment answered his concern, then you're one step closer to persuading him. If he isn't satisfied with your answer, now is the time to know — not later, when you try to get his final decision to go ahead.

Step #6: By the way . . .

By the way are three of the most useful words in any attempt to persuade or convince another person. You use the phrase to change gears — to move on to the next topic. Don't just keep talking. Take a conscious, purposeful step back into your presentation. If it's appropriate, turn the page in your presentation binder or booklet. Point to something other than whatever generated the objection. Take some sort of action that signals to the other person that you're forging ahead.

The lady doth protest too much

If prospects bombard you with objections, you may want to ask a few questions to get them to express their *real* objection. If people protest too much, they're either not interested and don't have the guts to tell you so, or they're hiding the real reason they aren't going ahead. For some people, liking your offering but being unable to afford it is hard to admit. So instead of admitting that they're strapped, they come up with a hundred other reasons why your product, service, or idea isn't right for them. Eventually, you may need to say something like this:

Mrs. Johnson, obviously you have quite a few concerns about our product. May I ask, what will you base your final decision on, the overall benefits to your family or the financial aspects of this transaction?

This way you're asking, as is your right, for the real objection to your product or service while still being nice, warm, and friendly. *Remember:* You can't move beyond this step in the selling cycle until you identify and handle that real final objection.

These six steps, if you practice and apply them properly, will take you a long way toward achieving your goal of selling others, even when they raise objections or concerns.

Chapter 12

Closing the Sale

Closing is the fun part of sales, the moment when you tie it all together, the moment when what your client needs and what you're selling become one. If you adopted this book's philosophy of selling, you know that, in effect, you work on closing the sale from the moment you first contact any prospect. That's just a given of the world of selling. But unless you hone your *instincts* for closing into finished *skills,* you're just winging it. And in this chapter, I help you hone to your heart's content, giving you specific strategies for closing the sale.

The bottom line with this most bottom of all lines in selling is this: If you want the sale, sooner or later you need to ask for it.

After you get past your own version of first-timer's jitters and you've done it a few times, I'm confident you'll agree that closing a sale is downright fun.

In closing, the end is really at the beginning

Closing the sale starts at the beginning of the transaction, when you first make contact with your prospect. If you're weak on making original contact, on qualifying, on handling objections, on presentations, or on any other area of the sales process, or if you're generally weak in asking pertinent questions, I don't care how great a salesperson you think you are, you're costing your prospect, yourself, and your company a lot of money, time, and aggravation. No one closes every sale, but just think how much better you can become when you put your best effort into it.

A perfect ending needs a perfect beginning.

Recognizing That Sometimes All You Need to Do Is Ask

Salespeople are often uncomfortable if they have to go beyond putting their offering out there. If a prospect doesn't quickly see the value and jump right in to own it or to participate in some way, a salesperson may start to lose confidence. And this wavering of confidence weakens the salesperson's desire to close the sale. In other words, the salesperson doesn't ask for the order, call for a decision, or otherwise try to get a commitment from the prospect.

My company, Tom Hopkins International, conducted a little survey and asked people who were not persuaded to buy why they didn't go ahead with whatever it was they were offered. Interestingly enough, the most common answer was that (drum roll, please) *they were never asked.* The prospects were contacted, a product or service was demonstrated to them, and their questions (or objections or concerns) were answered. In some cases, they were convinced of the value of the offering and probably would have gone ahead, but nothing happened — the salespeople didn't ask the prospects to make a commitment or to part with their money, so they didn't.

Don't ever let the fact that you didn't ask someone to make a buying decision be the reason a prospect doesn't go along with you.

Knowing when to ask, however, is just as important as doing it in the first place. Sometimes salespeople wait so long to ask for the sale that the right time to ask passes them by. To get past this timing challenge, figure out how to take a prospect's buying temperature. You do this by asking an ownership question like the following:

Not to be assumptive, but if everything we've discussed here makes sense, how soon would you want to begin benefiting from your new computer system?

Because you're asking an assumptive question, soften it by beginning with "Not to be assumptive, but . . . ." (If you were asking a personal question, you would start with, "Not to be personal, but . . . ." Sure you're being personal, but by stating it that way, you show respect for the prospect's privacy and give her an option not to answer if she's uncomfortable. You never want to purposely make a customer uncomfortable, but you will face selling situations in which you need to ask questions of a personal nature.) If the prospect answers such a question enthusiastically, in the affirmative, she's probably ready to go ahead. But if such a question brings up another concern or hesitation, then she's probably not ripe yet to make a commitment. This strategy is commonly referred to as the *trial close.*

When you ask your prospect for the close, what you're doing is using a question to confirm what the prospect wants. This type of question is called a *confirmation question.* In the following sections, I give you several ways to confirm your prospect's level of interest.

Give your prospect alternatives

This strategy (called the *alternate advance*) involves giving your prospect two choices — but either one advances the sale. This way, no matter which option your prospect chooses, the sale moves forward, because the prospect isn't given the option of saying no. Giving your prospect positive choices helps him focus better on what would be best for him — and that's what you really want, isn't it?

SALESPERSON: Mr. Hall, which delivery date would be best for you: the 8th or the 13th?

MR. HALL: I'd need to have it in my warehouse by the 10th.

What has happened in this exchange? As long as the salesperson can meet that delivery date, she owns it. If Mr. Hall is uncertain, he'll raise an objection here or try to change the subject.

Here's another example of the alternate advance:

SALESPERSON: Jim, would you be the one trained on the use of the new system, or would you want someone else to be involved?

When Jim tells the salesperson whom to train, she knows that he's going ahead with the sale.

Jump to an erroneous conclusion

The *erroneous conclusion* is an intentional error you make to test how serious the prospect is about going ahead with the sale. If the prospect doesn't correct you, you may have missed some information along the way that would have told you he wasn't serious. If he does correct you, his buying temperature is heating up. In this kind of test, all you want to do is take your prospect's buying temperature to see if it's warm enough to go ahead.

For example, if a salesperson is selling home improvements to John and Cathy in their home, and during her demonstration Cathy tells John, "Honey, my mother is coming in July. If we decide what we want today, we ought to have it finished by then." Many salespeople would ignore that remark or regard it as an interruption. But the champion salesperson hears that comment and remembers it. Later, when it comes time to close, the salesperson may smile at the wife and have the following exchange, using an erroneous conclusion:

SALESPERSON: I can see that you're kind of excited about this addition. Now, your mother is coming in August, isn't she?

CATHY: No, in July.

SALESPERSON: So the first week in June would be the best time to get started?

CATHY: Yes.

SALESPERSON: Let me make a note of that.

The salesperson *knew* that Cathy's mother was coming in July, but she asked whether her mother was coming in August, because she knew Cathy would correct her. Then, when Cathy offers the correct answer, the salesperson can segue right into the best time to begin with the home improvements, getting one step closer to that final close.

You can use the erroneous conclusion test close on almost anything. For example, Cathy may have said to John during the presentation, "I think I'd like a bay window on the south wall." Later, the salesperson can use that line for an erroneous conclusion test:

> SALESPERSON: Let's see. You said you wanted the bay window on the *east* wall . . . .
>
> CATHY: No! I want it on the south wall.
>
> SALESPERSON: Yes, that's right. Let me make a note of that.

You can also put erroneous information in your paperwork. Then, if your prospect corrects you, he may be agreeing to move forward by letting you write down the correction.

The purpose of this method is not to tell a lie or trick the customer — I would never recommend that. It's simply a test for you to determine whether the prospect is sincere in moving ahead. After all, the prospect wouldn't correct you if he weren't interested. But if you're at all uncomfortable with this method, don't use it.

Playing the porcupine game

If I were holding a prickly porcupine right now and tossed it at you, what would you do? Instinctively, you would probably either jump out of its way or catch it and quickly toss it back, kind of like a game of hot potato. You can use a method of questioning called the *porcupine method* in much the same way. When your prospect asks you a question, you just ask another question about that question.

Here's an example of the porcupine method in action at a car dealership. A young woman is walking through a car lot looking at convertibles. Suddenly she stops, points at a car, and says, "This is the convertible I'm interested in. Do you have it in red?" The average salesperson would answer her by saying, "If we don't have it in red, I can call around and get one for you in a hurry." When a salesperson gives an answer like that, is he looking to help himself or the customer? He's looking to help himself, by making a sale as soon as possible. Plus, the response the salesperson has given is a pushy statement.

The real power in selling is in pulling with questions.

Unlike the average salesperson, the champion salesperson would answer the customer's question this way:

SALESPERSON: Would you like it in Red-Hot Red or Cranberry Red?

How is the customer going to respond to the salesperson's question? She's already said that she's interested in the convertible and she wants it in red, so she'll most likely choose one color or the other and he can note that on his paperwork. The salesperson is now one step closer to getting the customer's autograph on that dotted line and having her drive away happily in her new Red-Hot Red convertible.

Knowing when to go for the close

The crucial question in any selling situation is, "When should you close the sale?" A certain electricity is in the air when the prospect is ready to go ahead with the close. Here are some positive buying signs to watch for:

- **The prospect has been moving along at a smooth pace, and suddenly he slows the pace way down.** He's making his final analysis or rationalizing the decision.

- **He speeds up the pace.** He's excited to move ahead.

- **The prospect suddenly starts asking lots of questions.** Like anyone else, he asks questions only about things that interest him.

- **He asks questions about general terms of purchase before he settles on one particular model.** Some people immediately start asking questions about initial investment, delivery, and so on. They feel safe doing this because they know you can't sell them everything. But if they ask these questions after you know exactly what they want, it's a good sign.

If you've noticed any of these positive signs, test the waters. If you think that your prospect is ready to close the sale, ask a test question to make sure you're reading him correctly. When you ask this question (from which you expect an answer confirming that the prospect wants to go ahead with the purchase), one of two things will happen:

- The prospect will give you a yes or an answer that indirectly confirms his desire to go ahead with the sale.

- The prospect will give you an objection or ask for more information to enable him to make a decision.

Don't start talking before he answers. You want to be sure to get either a confirmation to go ahead or an objection. If you get the former, you can go ahead with the close. If you get the latter, you need to answer the prospect's questions and address his concerns (see Chapter 11 for more information).

Using Closing Questions and Statements

Closing is where you make it all happen, where all your hard work pays off and you — and your client — reap the rewards. Unless what you're selling is the latest, greatest, everyone-has-to-have-it whatchamacallit, you're likely to hear the word *no* quite frequently. In fact, the average consumer will say *no, nada,* or *pass* to a new product or service approximately five times before he'll give it serious consideration (by that I mean saying *yes*). If you, as a salesperson, only know one or two ways to ask for his business, you'll run out of closing material before he runs out of "no-sale" material.

Always use a legal pad and your paperwork for making notes — and always let the prospect stop you from writing your notes. Letting your prospect stop you doesn't hurt — it helps. Your desire to take good notes shows the prospect that you're a professional salesperson who knows how to get things done.

The basic oral close

When you're talking with your prospects in person, you have the perfect opportunity to close the sale through your conversation. Here's an example of a simple closing statement:

> John, Mary, I'm excited to help you take a major step toward financial independence. We can do that right here with your approval.

If you know everything is right and that all the cards are on the table, go ahead and ask for the order. Don't keep selling — that's one of the biggest mistakes novice salespeople make. They don't always recognize when they can close; they simply continue to talk, re-demonstrate the product, or even change the subject while searching for a reason to continue in the company of their prospects.

The basic written close

If you use order forms in your selling, this closing method works especially well: Walk into the meeting with your prospects with a leather binder. Have an order form under a cardboard protector. That way, you can flip to it instantly when the time is right. Here's how the situation might play out:

> PROSPECT: Does it come in blonde wood?
>
> SALESPERSON: Is blonde the best color accent for your furniture?
>
> PROSPECT: Yes. I think that would look fantastic.
>
> SALESPERSON: Let me make a note of that.

Then you write down the prospect's preference on the order form. Be careful, though. Some people panic when they see you filling out a form:

> PROSPECT: What are you doing? I haven't agreed to anything yet.
>
> SALESPERSON: Mrs. Palmer, I like to organize my thoughts to keep everything in order. I do that on the paperwork so I don't forget anything.

Keep filling out that order form. By the time you finish your conversation, the form will be almost completely filled out. In most cases, the forward momentum you've developed while completing the form will be enough to get it approved. If the prospect gets used to seeing you write on the order form, you're almost home.

The reflex question

Go into every closing sequence by asking a *reflex question* — a question your prospect can answer without thinking. By this point in the selling cycle, you should have earned the right to use your prospect's first name, but if you're not sure if you've earned that right, you probably haven't. **Remember:** Never jump into the familiarity of using that first name unless you're certain it's okay with them.

If you have a prospect's first name, you can ask a reflex question like this to get a response:

SALESPERSON: Mary, do you have a middle initial?

PROSPECT: It's K.

If you're dealing with a corporate executive, a good reflex question is to ask for the company's complete name and address. If the executive hands you her card and lets you copy all the information, you get to move ahead. Congratulations!

The sharp angle close

In some situations, your prospect will, in essence, throw down the gauntlet and challenge you to give him exactly what he wants. The key here is to accept the challenge — but with the understanding that if you can come through, you win by getting the sale and he wins by owning the product or service just the way he wants it. This method is referred to as *sharp angling* your prospect into ownership.

For example, your prospect may ask you an assumptive question of his own, a question that assumes that he will buy your product or service. What should you do in response? Answer with a question that shows that, in his own mind, he has bought your product or service:

> MR. STEWART: If I decide I want this boat, can you handle delivery by Memorial Day?
>
> SALESPERSON: If I can guarantee delivery by Memorial Day, I bet you can guarantee me that you'll be prepared to have a great time enjoying the holiday on your new boat, can't you?

The salesperson is still guiding her prospect, Mr. Stewart, toward what he wants to do: Buy a boat.

> MR. STEWART: If I decided to go with this boat, I'd want delivery by May 15. Can you handle that?

The average salesperson would be tempted to jump in and say yes, whether or not she could "handle that." Pay close attention to how a champion salesperson takes advantage of this same opportunity:

> SALESPERSON: If I could guarantee delivery by May 15, are you prepared to approve the paperwork today?

Or, if the salesperson really doesn't know if she can make delivery on that date, she may want to respond this way:

> SALESPERSON: If I could guarantee delivery by May 15, and I am not certain yet that I can, are you prepared to approve the paperwork today?

Then you remain silent until Mr. Stewart answers. Remaining silent is the key here. The first person to speak owns the product. It will either be you keeping the product in inventory or Mr. Stewart keeping the product at his home or business. So unless you need to keep inventory up rather than sales, keep your lips sealed.

To use the sharp angle method, your prospect must first express a demand or desire that you can meet. (Although my example here uses delivery, you can sharp angle many other demands or needs besides delivery.) For you to use your prospect's own demand as your way to get to yes, always remember that sharp angling involves two pivotal points:

 ✔ You must know what benefits you can deliver.

 ✔ You must know when the delivery can be made.

Be aware that sharp angling can be hazardous to your selling health: A dangerous part of the sharp angle is that you may be tempted to apply it before you've gathered enough qualification information or before you've built enough rapport. I recommend that you do *not* use the sharp angle too early in the selling process. If you sharp angle too soon, you may offend some people, because the method is not smooth and can be interpreted as overly aggressive. But if the prospect's thinking and the rapport you have with him are in good shape, the sharp angle is a wonderful way to get agreement early in the sales process.

The following exchange shows you how to time your use of the sharp angle:

PROSPECT: Can you get it for me in red?

SALESPERSON: Are you ready to go ahead today if I can?

PROSPECT: Yes.

Or

PROSPECT: I may be, but first I need a lot more information.

Before you ask, "Will you go ahead if I can?" you must be absolutely sure that you can deliver your product. Saying you can deliver the product won't do much good if you can't. Overselling and over-promising are the two worst enemies of a professional salesperson. Always be honest and your reputation will bring you more business. One of the reasons trained salespeople outsell average salespeople is that the professionals know more about their products and what their companies can deliver. How do you get this information?

The answer depends on your product, the company, and your attitude. Salespeople often make enemies in production departments and on shipping docks by promising clients things the company can't deliver. When the client gets angry over a missed delivery date, the production department or the shipping dock usually takes the blame. Know what your company can deliver. And always thank the people in your company who help you get your job done, especially if fulfillment requires extra effort on their part in order for you to keep your sale.

The higher authority close

Every happy client is a potential higher authority for another prospect. This closing method keeps that in mind and is very effective if you know it thoroughly and set it up correctly. No matter what your product or service, all you need to do is adapt the wording to your own style of selling.

The *higher authority* must be exactly that — someone who is respected by and known to the prospect. The prospect doesn't have to know the higher authority personally, but he must know of the higher authority's existence and position. If you sell industrial equipment, you want a prominent decision-maker at a well-known company; if you sell advertising, you want a high-profile businessperson.

Here are the steps for using this close successfully:

1. **Select your higher authority figure.**

   You should constantly be on the lookout for higher authority figures. For example, imagine that you're the sales-record smasher for BuiltGreat Computer Systems. A prominent businessperson in the area invested in a computer system for her company, MarketShare, Inc., and she's very pleased with the system's performance and increased productivity. This businessperson, Katharine Steele, is an ideal higher authority figure for anyone interested in your computers.

2. **Recruit your higher authority figure.**

   On one of your visits to MarketShare, Inc., after they have had plenty of time to know the system inside and out, ask Katharine Steele if she'd be willing to share her knowledge of your product with other businesspeople. Katharine agrees because you've done a solid sales and service job for her on a good product, and you've assured her that you'll only call when you need help with an occasional prospect who may be in a similar situation. In other words, you promise not to bother her if you're working on selling a two-computer system to a small business. Remember to give Ms. Steele a small gift of appreciation.

3. Schedule your higher authority figure for the sales situation.

You're out to update the computer system at Southwest Advertising with your newest system. George Phillips is the decision-maker there. While planning your appointment with George, you decide that you may need the higher authority figure confirmation, so you call Katharine Steele to determine if she'll be available to take a phone call while you're with George Phillips. With Katharine's cooperation, you complete your plans for a powerful presentation to George at Southwest.

4. Use the higher authority figure confirmation effectively.

You know that George will have concerns about your system similar to those that Katharine had. (Will the software that makes your systems superior be the right one to increase productivity for Southwest? Is your service department as good as you say it is?) And in planning your presentation, you know that George will have specific technical questions. The primary purpose of your interview with George Phillips is to isolate the specific technical and other reservations that he has about your equipment and company. After you clarify these questions for him, and after you agree that these are all reasons why he questions the idea of installing your system now, you're ready to bring in a higher authority — Katharine Steele.

Be sure to make the list of George's reservations specific, and to get George's agreement that these are all the reservations he has. Write them out on a piece of paper. After you clarify and write down the causes of George's reservations, you're ready to appeal to a higher authority:

> YOU: Do you know Katharine Steele of MarketShare, Inc.?
>
> GEORGE: No, but I know of the company.
>
> YOU: Katharine is the owner, and she's a client of mine. George, so that I can relieve your mind of some of the questions you may have about the system or our services, would you be offended if we called Katharine and asked her your questions? You see, she had the same concerns you did before she invested in our system.

When Katharine is on the phone, tell her, "I'm here at Southwest Advertising with George Phillips, and he has some questions about BuiltGreat." Then hand the phone to George and let him take it from there. He has the list of questions in front of him, so he'll miss none of his objections when he talks to Katharine.

5. Close after the call.

After Katharine Steele has discussed the technicalities and reassured George that the BuiltGreat computers are performing well in her office, George's objections have vanished. When the phone call ends, you're in a position to smile and ask, "By the way, which delivery date is most convenient for you: the 1st or the 10th?"

If something keeps Katharine from taking George's call, even though you set it up with her in advance, you may not be able to close the sale that day. Try to set up a specific time to contact her again, when you can be present with George, or try to arrange a conference call among the three of you.

Take a copy of George's objections and hot buttons with you to the re-contact meeting so that, at the start of the re-contact, you can get back to where you left off. Remember to do a brief recap with George before you get Katharine on the line.

Some salespeople turn away from the higher authority confirmation because they think that all competitors hate each other and won't cooperate. But in general, most people at competing companies are friendly with each other. If you do happen to run into a case of bad blood between competitors, simply back off.

Don't settle for just one higher authority — you can wear out any one person when you rely on her too much. When you do your job with the utmost professionalism, most clients will be happy to help you out. It's an ego boost for them to be considered a higher authority.

Overcoming Your Prospect's Stalls and Fears

When you're closing sales, you may come across situations in which closing isn't quite as simple as the example I provide earlier in this chapter — situations in which your prospects stall or hide behind a wall of fear. So in the following sections, I show you exactly how you can help the prospect work through that stall so that he has no more objections or concerns . . . and you can close the sale.

Close with empathy

Empathy is understanding another person's feelings, thoughts, and motives — and it's extremely important in the world of selling. When you have empathy for your prospect, you put yourself in his shoes. You know and feel what your prospect is feeling — which means you know exactly how to proceed based on the information the prospect has given you.

Until you develop empathy for your customers, you probably won't make it in selling. Your prospects need to sense that you understand and care about helping them solve their problems, not think that you're just out looking for a sale. As a professional salesperson, you must truly believe that you can satisfy the prospect's needs. You must see the benefits, features, and limitations of your product or service from your prospect's view; you must weigh things on the prospect's scale of values, not your own; and you must realize what is important to the prospect. Your prospect must always be the star of the show.

Taking a lesson from Benjamin Franklin

This decision-making strategy — in which you make a list of the positives and negatives surrounding a choice — was developed by the great Benjamin Franklin, and millions of people have used it successfully for years. Everyone can understand its effectiveness because it's so simple, basic, and easy to understand that it rarely fails to get the point across.

Here's an example of a situation in which a salesperson may want to use this approach with Kevin and Karen Smith in a real estate office:

> SALESPERSON: Do you think that the home on Third Street may be the best decision for your family?
>
> KEVIN: [hesitant, noncommittal] Well, you know that a home is a pretty big investment. I don't know that I'm ready to make a decision on this right now.

The salesperson has asked a lot of questions up to this point, and now she's ready to put the answers to work for her in order to close the sale. She can see that Kevin and Karen really don't want to make the final decision. They're impressed with the home, they need to get the family moved quickly, and the numbers work out. But they're trying to avoid committing to the home. In other words, they are behaving like typical buyers. This is a perfect opportunity for the Benjamin Franklin decision-making process.

SALESPERSON: [calm, determined to help Kevin and Karen to make the decision they want to make, to help them make the best decision for them] Could it possibly be, Karen and Kevin, that the problem is that you haven't had a chance to weigh the facts involved?

KEVIN: [nodding, open to reason] Yeah, I don't think we've really gotten to the heart of this thing yet.

SALESPERSON: Well, a decision is only as good as the facts on which it's based, don't you agree?

KAREN: [seeing the wisdom of the salesperson's reasoning] I think that's probably true.

SALESPERSON: [reflective and sincere] You know, it's interesting. A while back I was reminded of a man we Americans have long considered one of our wisest men — Benjamin Franklin. What Ben used to do when he was uncertain about making a decision was take a sheet of paper and draw a line right down the middle. On one side of the page he would write all the reasons in favor of the decision, and on the other he would write all the reasons against the decision. Then he would simply add up the reasons on each side and see which decision was the best. It's a funny thing. One day I decided to try Ben's system, not only in my professional life, but in my personal life as well. Pretty soon, my whole family was using it to make all kinds of decisions. Would it be okay with you if we tried it now just to get a feel for the facts of your decision?

The important thing here is to keep going with the flow of the conversation. After you master this strategy, you'll know how to weave this story into any conversation.

SALESPERSON: Ben Franklin said that if a decision was the right thing to do, he wanted to be sure to go ahead with it. If it was wrong, he wanted to be sure to avoid it. So why don't we analyze the decision and "get down to the heart of it," as you put it?

KEVIN AND KAREN: [as one voice] Okay, yeah, let's do that.

SALESPERSON: Great. So the reasons *for* the decision go on one side, and all those *against* the decision go on the other side. Then you can add up the columns and the right decision should be clear. We have time, don't we? It'll take us just a couple of minutes.

KEVIN: Yeah, okay.

The salesperson has a long list of things Kevin and Karen like about the home because she's made notes on every positive comment they've made since they drove into the neighborhood. If Kevin and Karen run out of positives off the tops of their heads, the salesperson will remind them of those on her list.

When you make note of each item, do it with a check mark. But don't write down their actual reasons. You're just tracking how many there are now. If you start writing each one out, this strategy takes longer and the prospects start weighing each reason against the others.

SALESPERSON: [waits a beat for Kevin's agreement, then draws a line down the center of the page she holds in front of her] Okay, let's start it off here. Let's think of the reasons favoring the decision. You agree that the home has all the features you were looking for, isn't that right?

KAREN: Yes, it does.

SALESPERSON: And we've already established that, with the right financing, you can actually have a smaller monthly investment than what you have on the home you're in now.

KEVIN AND KAREN: [as one voice] Right.

SALESPERSON: You said you wanted to be close to the elementary school, and this home is just three blocks away. That's certainly a plus, don't you think?

KEVIN AND KAREN: [as one voice] Absolutely.

SALESPERSON: Let's go on. You thought the professional landscaping in the backyard was impressive.

KAREN: [looking at the salesperson, but seeing the future] Yeah, the kids would have a lot of fun in that yard.

SALESPERSON: Wouldn't they? Let's write that down. And what about the outside of the home? When we first pulled up, Karen, remember how you got so excited?

KAREN: It really is a beautiful home.

SALESPERSON: [counting the positives] Let's see; that's five. Can you think of any others?

> KEVIN: Well, we really liked the extras in the newly remodeled kitchen.
>
> SALESPERSON: All right. We'll put that down.
>
> KEVIN: I like all the big trees on the property.
>
> SALESPERSON: Okay. We'll put that down, too.
>
> KAREN: Oh! We both liked the sunken bathtub in the master bedroom.
>
> SALESPERSON: Great. Is there anything else you can think of?

Set a goal for between six and ten items on the plus side. If you haven't reached ten at this point, refer to your notes and remind your prospects of other items to add to this column. When your goal of ten reasons for the decision has been reached, continue:

> SALESPERSON: [objective, fair] Now, how many reasons can you come up with on the negative side?
>
> KEVIN: [with a heavy sigh] Well, let's see. The down payment is a concern. It's almost all we've saved.
>
> SALESPERSON: Okay, what else?
>
> KEVIN: We were really interested in finding a home that had solar heating.
>
> SALESPERSON: Those are both valid points, Kevin. Can you come up with any others?

After a pause, it's obvious that Karen and Kevin aren't coming up with any more concerns. They've just told the salesperson, bottom line, exactly what will keep them from owning this particular home. She doesn't even have to answer those objections at this point, because what she's looking for is a clear desire on the part of Kevin and Karen to own this particular property. When that decision is made, she'll work on the financial details of how they can own this home, so she says:

> **SALESPERSON:** All right. Why don't we just add these up?

She shows them the list and together they count aloud. Afterward, she announces the results: 10 yeas, 2 nays.

> **SALESPERSON:** Karen, Kevin, don't you think the answer is rather obvious?

Expect to wait through a long silence after you pose this question. The key here is to shut your mouth and not do or say anything that takes away from your request for a decision. Your prospects will do one of three things:

- ✔ They will try to stall, put off making the decision by asking for more time or asking a question to change the subject.
- ✔ They will decide to go ahead.
- ✔ They will give you an objection.

In this situation, a silence pervades the room for some time while Kevin and Karen think this over. Finally, Kevin replies with a stall:

> **KEVIN:** I'll tell you something. We're the kind of people who really need to think it over.

When you're faced with a stall like this, consider using the story in the next section to move past it.

Getting past a vague stall to a concrete final objection

So how do you handle a situation in which the prospect absolutely insists on thinking it over? Continuing the story from the preceding section, where Kevin and Karen are thinking about investing in a home, here's how the salesperson proceeds:

SALESPERSON: That's fine, Kevin. Obviously, you wouldn't take the time to think it over unless you were seriously interested, would you?

KEVIN: *[reassuring, but committed to the stall]* Oh, we're interested. We just really need to think about this before we decide.

SALESPERSON: Because you're interested, may I assume that you will give it very careful consideration?

KAREN: Of course we will.

SALESPERSON: You're not telling me this just to get rid of me, are you?

KEVIN: *[polite, but committed to the stall]* No. I'm not trying to get rid of you. We like the house, but we have to think it over.

SALESPERSON: *[trying to keep communication open]* Just to clarify my thinking, what is it about the house that you want to think over? Is it the value of the home? The neighborhood?

Ask about the benefits of the home that you know your prospects liked. Every time they say no, they're that much closer to yes, aren't they? Kevin and Karen have answered no to every benefit, so what do they want to think over? In most cases, the decision comes down to money. Either the home is too expensive, they won't be comfortable with the large initial investment, or they may be worried about their credit and getting qualified for the loan.

SALESPERSON: Well, could it be the financing or even the initial investment that you want to think over?

KAREN: *[as though offered a life raft]* Yes. We may have another baby and I'm not sure if we should make a financial commitment like this right now.

Now the salesperson has a concrete idea of what specifically is the hurdle between herself and the close. This is how all selling situations should be handled: in a relaxed, friendly, gentle, and professional manner. It's not only what you say but how you say it that creates a successful sales environment.

Sometimes even the warmest presentation, delivered with genuine care for the customer's needs, can be met with "We're the kind of people who really need to think it over." And always remember that the "I want to think it over" line is a stall. You use it yourself when you're on the customer side of a selling situation, so why shouldn't you expect to hear it from others when you're on the persuading side of things?

Responding to "It costs too much"

When you isolate a money objection as the obstacle to final agreement, this technique is ideal. It helps both you and the customer see the big dollars they're afraid of in much smaller, easier-to-handle numbers.

To show you this technique at work, here are Karen and Kevin in the real estate office again:

> KAREN: I just feel that this home costs too much.
>
> SALESPERSON: [ever in search of specific obstacles to "yes"] Today most things seem to. Can you tell me about how much too much you feel it is?

Salespeople tend to look at the total investment when they hear "It costs too much," but this tendency usually spells trouble. Instead of addressing the total cost, go for the *difference*. If your prospect plans to spend $20,000 for a car, and the car he's looking at is $22,000, the problem isn't $22,000, it's $2,000.

> KAREN: We really wanted to spend around $110,000, and I don't feel that we can go as high as $115,000.
>
> SALESPERSON: So, Karen and Kevin, what we're really talking about is $5,000, aren't we?
>
> KEVIN: $5,000. Right. That's exactly what I'm concerned about.

Now the salesperson has gotten Kevin and Karen to admit that the real problem they're having is over $5,000. And she's ready to move to the story in the following section, where she shows them just how little money that really is.

Reducing an expense to the ridiculous

When you know exactly what amount of money your prospects are concerned about, you can work with them to help them see how they can handle the amount and have what they really want — the product or service — at the same time. Start by handing them your calculator. Giving them a calculator is a good way to get them involved as you work out the finances. Here are Kevin and Karen again, in the real estate office:

> SALESPERSON: *[asking what Karen already knows]* Karen, do you think it would be safe to assume that this would be your dream home and you could be happy here for a long time, assuming everything else was right?
>
> KAREN: Probably. I think it would be a great place to raise the kids.
>
> SALESPERSON: Okay, so let's just say that you're going to live in this beautiful home for 20 years. Would you say that's about right?
>
> KEVIN AND KAREN: Twenty years . . . yeah, that'd be about right.
>
> SALESPERSON: Let's divide that $5,000 by 20 years, okay? We get $250 per year, don't we?
>
> KEVIN: Yes.
>
> SALESPERSON: And would you say that you would actually be in the home 50 weeks a year, allowing for 2 weeks of vacation each year, of course?
>
> KEVIN: That sounds about right.
>
> SALESPERSON: Dividing our $250 per year by 50 weeks. That makes the difference in the investment $5 per week. So now we have 7 days in each of those weeks, and when we divide $5 by 7, what do we get?
>
> KAREN: *[catching an early glimpse of the ridiculous]* Seventy-one cents.

The salesperson has gotten Kevin and Karen to see that they're really upset over just 71 cents per day. Pretty ridiculous, isn't it?

Making the indirect comparison

When you make an indirect comparison, you help your prospects rationalize having the product, service, or idea you're offering simply by sacrificing, for now, some small luxury that they would certainly give up in order to have a much larger gain. Here's how the salesperson in the previous example uses this strategy with Kevin and Karen:

SALESPERSON: *[giving them something to compare it to]* Kevin, do you and your family drink much soda?

KEVIN: Sure. You know how kids are. We probably go through at least one six-pack a day.

SALESPERSON: How much are sodas these days?

KAREN: Around $2 a six-pack.

SALESPERSON: Karen, Kevin, wouldn't you agree that the benefits and the enjoyment you will get out of this wonderful home are worth 71 cents a day? Do you think that we should let 71 cents stand in the way of all the family memories you will make there, for less than it costs your family to have three sodas per day?

KEVIN: When you look at it that way, I guess it doesn't seem to be such a significant amount.

SALESPERSON: Then we've agreed, haven't we? Now, let's get to work to get you out of your existing house and into this *beautiful home by the holidays* so you and your family can begin *building memories* right away. By the way, would the 10th or the 12th be the better closing date for both of you?

Notice the words that I italicized? These keywords will create pleasant pictures in the prospects' minds. For the sake of this example, assume that Kevin and Karen said they wanted to be in the home by November 1. That gives the salesperson the license to address the upcoming holidays, a time of year that almost always creates warm feelings in buyers.

Citing a similar situation

What better way to ease your prospects' fears than a story of another couple who had all the same concerns and indecisions, but who still decided to buy and now are glad they did? Here's an example of a story you can relate to your clients, based on their fears and hesitations:

John, Beth, I know you're hesitant about the financial commitment of buying a home when you have your first baby on the way. You know, I had another family looking for the perfect home just about a year ago. We searched and searched and they just couldn't decide on a home.

One day we looked at a beautiful home and they got very excited about it. I asked them if they thought that this was the home for them, and they agreed that it was a great house. I also asked if they wanted to begin the process of owning that great home. Bob thought we should go ahead, but Jill was afraid that the home might be a bit larger than they really needed. She thought they could get by in a smaller home, and she wasn't sure that she wanted to move before their baby came.

Well, they decided to go ahead and were amazed at how much space the baby things took up. After they moved in, Bob and Jill were so glad that they decided to invest in the bigger home when they did.

Now, you'd like to be all settled in at your new home before your baby comes, wouldn't you?

Make notes about the stories you have to tell about your other satisfied clients, and then use these stories when new prospects experience the same situation, as will inevitably happen.

Noting a competitive edge

If you're faced with a prospect who doesn't want to make a decision about your product, service, or idea, you can tell a competitive-edge story to help them along. These stories don't need to be elaborate, and they're not meant to talk your prospects into anything they don't want or need. The stories just remind prospects (mainly ones who are in business, as opposed to individuals) that they have competitors. So if you're not telling them anything they don't already know, what's the appeal in competitive edge stories? In a word, *survival*.

Crunch numbers when you crunch numbers

Champion salespeople always do their selling math with a calculator. No matter how confident you are in your mathematical abilities, always use a calculator. Know your formulas and figures so that you can quickly provide any numerical information that your prospect may request.

A prospect who sees you punch numbers into your calculator — or one who runs the figures himself — probably won't question the figures. But if you start furiously scratching numbers on paper with a pencil, the prospect gets uncomfortable sitting and watching you have all the fun with numbers. Even worse, if you rattle figures off the top of your head, your prospect may

doubt you. Instead of paying attention to your presentation, he'll be looking over your shoulder to double-check your math.

Not using a calculator will raise doubts about your mathematical abilities. Plus, your prospect may wonder, "If he's this careless with figures, where else will he be careless?" You don't want to do anything at this stage of the relationship to make your prospect start wondering if he should be working with you at all. You want him entirely focused on the math at hand as you show him how he really can afford the product he wants so badly.

A little competitive-edge story like this, for example, works well:

> Mr. Ramirez, remember that many of your competitors are facing the same challenges today that you are. Isn't it interesting that, when an entire industry is fighting the same forces, some companies do a better job of meeting those challenges than others? My entire objective here today has been to help provide you with a competitive edge. Gaining a competitive edge, no matter how large or small, makes good business sense, doesn't it?

Prospects are just like anyone else: They need help making decisions. Think about it. How many things have you been talked into owning that you really didn't want? Probably not very many. Few people get talked into buying something they don't really want. If it's a major purchase, you usually will have a hard time selling your prospects on it even if they *do* want it.

Problems arise when unscrupulous salespeople lie about what a product is and what it will do. Through deceit, these salespeople violate the buyer's trust and the buyer ends up owning something other than what she thought she was getting. The jails are full of salespeople who have done things like this. They let greed get in the way of their service to customers. Such an approach to selling is the direct opposite of the kind of selling I advocate. If you put customer service ahead of money, you will *always* come out on top.

Is closing good for your customer?

Are closing questions, assumptive statements, and sales-time stories in the best interest of your customers? Based on my experience, the answer is an unequivocal "yes." I've done a lot of selling, and I always take my customers' interests to heart. I know that they'll get the truth from me, as well as great service. But I can't guarantee them truth in selling and excellent service if they go someplace else.

All along, from my early days in selling to today, I've tried to help every consumer have a positive image of the sales industry. I knew that positive image would be there if I gave my customers professional service, and I've always been one to provide it. That's why I worked harder than many of my associates to consummate sales that I knew were in the best interest of my customers. This obviously would not include selling them anything they didn't want. However, if all things were right, I would do everything I could to help my customers get over the hills of fear and procrastination.

Remember: If you properly qualify people, you'll know whether they truly have a need or desire for your product or service. If their lives will be better because they own your offering, you should do your best to persuade them into having it.

Think about it: Drawing on your own experience, have you appreciated the professionals who have helped you make buying decisions? Have you been happy enough to recommend those people to others? Of course you have! We all have. To become a champion salesperson, you should set a goal to become someone people will not hesitate to recommend. Become someone people seek out as an expert in your field. And then everyone — you and your customers — wins.

Chapter 13

Getting Referrals from Your Present Clients

For many seasoned salespeople, referrals are a major source of new business. Clients who contact you on an existing client's recommendation are usually more inclined than cold-call clients to own your product, service, or idea. Why? Because they already have a positive feeling about you and your offering — and the source of their positive feeling is someone they already know and trust. This is what we refer to as a *prequalified* lead. Prequalified, referred leads are usually slam dunks: They've already been sold on you because the person who referred you to them thinks you're a true pro. So with referrals, you enjoy tremendous credibility right from the start.

In fact, when it comes to qualified referrals, studies show a 60 percent closing rate. Compare that impressive figure to a closing rate of 10 percent with non-qualified non-referrals, and you can see just how much harder you have to work on cold calls. Don't get left out in the cold. When you can figure out how to be successful at getting referral business, giving all those choice customers to your competitors just doesn't make sense.

Salespeople universally agree that referrals are easier to convince than non-referrals. But some salespeople think controlling referral business is impossible, so they refuse to give referral methods much attention. Such salespeople take the attitude that attaining referrals is just a haphazard, sometimes-it-happens-and-sometimes-it-doesn't way to prospect. Don't buy into such thinking for a second. Professional salespeople consistently benefit from referral business — so consistently, in fact, that they shoot holes in this theory every day.

Effective ways to benefit from referral business are what this chapter is all about. Here I provide you with a proven, highly effective referral system that will help you produce a much greater number of leads. The system may not work 100 percent of the time, but even if it works only 50 percent of the time, it will generate many more selling situations with clients who look forward to finding out about you and your offering.

Never take a referral for granted. As with any other sales technique, method is not the only factor to consider when you try to get referrals. Salespeople must show referrals the same positive attitude, the same high energy level, the same respectful manner, and the same quality presentation that they show to cold calls. Referrals are only *partially* sold on you or your product. The important thing is that they're willing to give you the chance to convince them of how they'll benefit from your offering.

If you're successful, referrals just keep on coming. Before you know it, you'll create an endless chain of happily involved clients who want to do whatever they can to contribute to your success. Customers love to think that they're partially responsible for your success, and encouraging their continued participation and interest in promoting your career certainly doesn't hurt.

Where and When Referrals Arise

With qualified referrals providing you a closing ratio of a whopping 60 percent, you can't afford not to know how to identify and obtain such a substantial increase in your sales. But what if getting referrals isn't all that important to your specific selling situation? You can give those referrals to your clients or other people in related industries who thrive on referral business, which will help solidify your working relationship with them.

One way or the other, then, whether as a source of prospects for your own business or as general public relations, referrals play a key part in your success in sales. That's why it's surprising that so many people take part in referral-building activities without recognizing — and taking advantage of — the opportunities.

If only they had read a good overview that would help them recognize referrals when they see them — an overview just like the one you're on the verge of reading right now, for example.

Where you get referrals

Referrals are like flies: They're always buzzing around you. But unless they land in your soup, you don't always notice them. The key to success in getting referrals is to become like flypaper and catch all referrals that fly by.

From family and friends

Perhaps the easiest and most accessible referrals are those that your family and friends give you. If you're of the mind-set that you don't want to "burden" those close to you by asking for their help, you'd better rethink just what it is you're selling. After all, if you really believe in your product, service, or idea, don't you want the people close to you to enjoy its benefits, too? By assuming that your offering will burden others, you may be cheating them out of all the enjoyment that your offering can give them.

Through networking

Networking at business conferences, clubs, professional organizations, and religious gatherings is a way to increase your number of referrals. But the gatherings don't have to be formal affairs. Getting referrals can be as simple as mentioning to others what you do or something exciting that has happened during your busy week of selling. When you're excited, other people will be, too. People are attracted to energetic conversation and happy dispositions — so be a people magnet.

If you're having a particularly great week, share it with the world. Let them enjoy your success! Don't brag. Just allow yourself to be exuberant about your accomplishments. It will be contagious. If your week has been particularly trying or difficult, ask for the advice of the people you respect. You can use this as a way of getting others interested in your business offerings, too. The next time they see you, they'll want to hear your appreciation of the positive effects their advice had for you.

So what have you done? Through your willingness to share your concerns and victories, you have involved others in your career: Other people now have a vested interest in your future success.

From happy customers

Make sure that your sales and service are beyond reproach, because negative news spreads like fire through dried country meadows. Slip up just once, even just a little bit, and where visiting your clients and their associates was once comfortable, it becomes awkward — maybe so much so that you avoid old clients altogether, if a bad reputation precedes you. Honesty and integrity must be first and foremost in your mind if you intend to succeed in business and in life.

Satisfied customers tell at least three people about their experience with you. Dissatisfied customers tell at least 11 people. Negative stories generate more sympathy than positive stories do. So don't fan the flames of discontent.

Avoid promising the moon and the stars within a two-day delivery period unless you can also twitch your nose like Samantha on *Bewitched* or point your finger like Sabrina the Teenage Witch and make it happen. It's so easy to get carried away and tell your client what he wants to hear even when you know your information is inaccurate. In the long run, not only will you lose the disillusioned client, but you can also kiss goodbye all the wonderful referral opportunities he could have steered your way.

If you leave your customer's office with a sale but no referrals, you have unfinished business to attend to — kind of like having a great dinner, but leaving before dessert.

It's never too late to get referrals, but when you leave empty-handed, you also deprive your customers. It's true! What's the first thing you want to do when you shop nonstop for days and then eventually, finally, find a great bargain? You want to tell people about it! What's the first thing you want to do when you own a beautiful new car? Show people! What's the first thing you want to do when someone comments on what a terrific new whatchamacallit you have? Let him know where he can get one just like it for a great price! Don't cheat your customers out of all their fun by not giving them the referral tools they need to help others help you.

From other salespeople in your field

Thinking of other salespeople in the same or related fields as your enemies is neither necessary nor productive. Believe it or not, thinking of them as a possible source for referral business is much more profitable. For instance, if you are in the healthcare field and you meet a sales representative who is extremely successful selling surgical supply equipment and you are selling diagnostic testing equipment, that sales person may be able to provide referrals or at least be willing to swap referrals with you.

If your relationship with other salespeople is based on mutual respect, you'll find other salespeople sending clients your way whether you have a formal arrangement to do so or not. Perhaps another salesperson's company is smaller than yours and unequipped to handle clients beyond such-and-such magnitude. Bingo! He sends the Big Clients to you. Or maybe a contact insists on having a feature that your competitor's product doesn't have — and another prospective client trundles down the turnpike headed right your way.

Of course, returning the favor is only common courtesy. It's not unusual for salespeople at car dealerships or insurance agencies to recommend another salesperson who is better suited to meet a particular customer's needs. These people are professionals who have the needs of the client at heart and know they would do them a disservice by handling them ineffectively. They also know the value of giving good "customer" service to their fellow salespeople.

Through public-speaking engagements or teaching appointments

Public-speaking engagements and teaching appointments are great opportunities for referral business, especially if you're the professional chosen to give the presentation or to teach. When this happens, you're automatically considered the expert in your field. But to earn the reputation you've been awarded, you'd better be prepared and handle your presentation well. Compare it to giving your best sales presentation to an audience of 50 or more potential clients all at once. Pretty important, isn't it? I recommend participating in these situations only for those who can carry it off effectively. Too many people get carried away with the moment of stardom and forget that they're there to build their business, not to audition as a replacement for David Letterman. (If you're scheduled to give a presentation before a large crowd, check out *Public Speaking For Dummies,* either in print form or on audiotape, by Malcolm Kushner [published by Hungry Minds, Inc.]. I also recommend the video *How to Master the Art of Speaking,* available from my company, Tom Hopkins International.)

I once went to a conference where the speaker provided cards on which participants wrote their names and others to contact who would also benefit from attending the conference. Each referral was put on a different card along with comments on why the participants believed that their referrals would enjoy and learn from the conference. The speaker encouraged us to fill out as many cards as we liked. We then put the cards into a large barrel. Each day of the conference, a member of the speaker's entourage pulled a card from the barrel to see who would win weekend getaways, free admission to advanced seminars, audio– or videocassettes, or books that were being sold at the conference. At the end of the conference, the speaker had the makings of another conference. What a system!

When you get referrals

Knowing when you get referrals is simple! You get referrals when you ask for them. You'd be surprised how many salespeople feel awkward asking for referrals. How do such salespeople "solve" the problem of their awkwardness? They avoid the referral part of the selling situation altogether — and in the process cost themselves and their companies big bucks.

Or some salespeople try to get referrals by asking their clients, "Can you think of anyone else who might be interested?" And, the clients can think of no one who may benefit from the salesperson's offering. Such a salesperson concludes that asking for referral business didn't really work for him.

In reality, it wasn't that it was impossible for these two groups of salespeople to get referrals. Instead, it was impossible to get referrals using the methods they were using. Instead of analyzing their methods and trying something different, they stopped asking for referrals altogether.

So, specifically now, when *do* you get referrals? You prepare to get referrals the moment you make contact with someone. From the first words they utter, you should look for areas in which you can help the client isolate names and faces that she can give you later (the names, that is, not the faces). Always listen carefully, not just to what will help the present client, but also to what will help the present client's referrals — your future clients — who may also need your services.

Good referral business comes from customers with whom you have a good relationship. This doesn't necessarily mean that they own your offering. For example, you may have built a good relationship with a past or potential customer who for some reason is unable to own your product at this time. If you've kept in close contact and done a good job in building rapport with the customer, though, he more than likely would be willing to steer you toward a business associate who can benefit from your product or service. All you have to do is ask.

Although any time is a good time to get referrals, there is one specific time when your chances of getting referrals are better than most: Just after you have successfully closed a sale and the customer is excited about owning your offering. At that moment, the client is usually more than happy to give you referrals — names of other people who need what the client now owns. Just after the sale is a time when enthusiasm is high and resistance is low.

But don't just plunge in and say, "Do you know anyone else who might want my whatchamacallit?" If you ask in this way, your client probably won't be able to come up with a name. She's too distracted by her new purchase. You have to *prepare* her in the art of giving good referrals. I cover this important topic in the next section.

Seven Steps to Getting Referrals

This easy, seven-step process to obtaining referrals will give you so much more success in developing your referral business that you will make it an automatic part of every selling situation. Begin by setting a goal for how many referrals you want from each contact. Start with a goal of just one referral, and work your way up to a place where you know the steps so well and they flow so naturally that you'll get at least three referrals with every contact you make.

Get to know these seven steps to getting referrals. The better you know them, the better you'll mine the rich lode of referrals that's just waiting for you in your current clientele.

1. **Help your client think of specific people he knows.**

2. **Write the referrals' names on cards.**

3. **Ask qualifying questions about the referrals.**

4. **Ask for the referrals' addresses.**

5. **Get the referrals' addresses from the phone book (if the client doesn't know the addresses).**

6. **Ask the client to call and set your appointment with the referrals.**

7. **If the client shows nervousness or refuses to call, ask if you can use the client's name when you contact the referral.**

I cover each step in more detail in the following sections, examining this referral system so you can make it an integral part of your successful selling plan.

Step #1: Help your client think of specific people he knows

When you ask for referrals, you have to give your client a group of faces to focus on. Centering on one or two faces is impossible when his thoughts are bouncing off the wall with his new offering — which means your job is to get him focused again.

Refocus your customers by using a method like the one shown in the following hypothetical situation:

SALESPERSON: Bill, I can see you're excited with your new car, aren't you?

CLIENT: Oh, it's sweet. I can't wait to drive it off the lot!

SALESPERSON: You were a tough negotiator, Bill. I guess it feels good to know that you received significant savings on the car, too, doesn't it?

CLIENT: Yeah! I didn't expect to be able to afford a car this nice!

SALESPERSON: So tell me, Bill, where do you plan to drive your new car this first week?

CLIENT: Well, I'll be going back and forth to work, of course. And I play baseball in a city league every Thursday night. I can't wait to drive up in my new car.

SALESPERSON: I wish I could be there to see your face, as well as the faces of your co-workers and teammates. Bill, is there anyone at your workplace or on your baseball team who is in the market for a new car?

By mentioning work and baseball, the client focuses in on those people he is closest to and with whom he'll be in contact that very week . . . while his excitement over his car is still fresh. And the salesperson has helped him do that.

Step #2: Write the referrals' names on cards

When Bill has thought of several people at work and on the baseball team who are in the market for a car, take out a few 3-x-5 index cards or a small notepad and write down the names of those referrals. (Be sure to ask Bill how to spell the names.) Keep the cards out so you can jot down the information Bill gives you. Plus, you'll need those notes to qualify the referrals.

Step #3: Ask qualifying questions

While Bill is busy answering questions about the referrals, you should jot down notes to help you remember specific things about them. Here's some information you may want to know when you contact the referrals from this specific example:

- What kind of car does she drive now?
- Would she be the primary driver of the car?
- How many are in her family? (You need to know what size car she may need.)
- What did she say when you told her you were looking for a new car?

When you get in touch with the referral, you'll be able to begin a conversation with her based on Bill's answers to your questions. When you've taken a few notes, move on to the next step.

Step #4: Ask for addresses and phone numbers

Asking for the addresses and phone numbers of the referrals is more difficult because your client may not know this information offhand. But don't let that deter you. You can't just settle for the name, because there may be several people with the same name in the phone book when you try to look it up later. And knowing how to contact the referral is critical.

Step #5: Use the phone book to get the information you need

If your client is willing to give you a referral's address but doesn't know the address offhand, reach for the phone book and politely ask the client if he would be kind enough to help you out and look up the address.

Your request can be as natural as the one in the following conversation:

SALESPERSON: I don't know about you, Bill, but this has been thirsty work. What would you like to drink, a soda? Or would you prefer coffee?

BILL: Coke's fine with me.

SALESPERSON: Tell you what. While I run to get us some Cokes, would you mind looking up in the phone book the addresses of the names you gave me so we can get this done?

Ask this last question while you hand the customer the phone book, and then leave the room to get the Cokes. At this point, you've all but "closed" on how to contact the referral.

Step #6: Ask your customer to call the referral and set up the appointment

This step is where most novice salespeople balk. They won't even try it. But keep in mind that this question is simply setting the stage for the final step. Few clients will be comfortable calling to set an appointment for you. But they'll be so relieved that you offer them Step #7 that they'll jump on it. If you had gone directly from Step #5 to Step #7, you may not have gotten the same response. There is a method to my madness here. Here's how it works:

SALESPERSON: Thanks so much for the referrals, Bill. You know, since I won't get to see your excitement when you show off your new car, would you mind calling Jane and sharing your good news with her? Then we can work on arranging a time for me to meet with her.

If your customer is fine with that, then good: Start dialing. But if he hesitates and acts uncomfortable, take the pressure off immediately by moving on to the next step.

Step #7: Ask to use the client's name when you make contact with the referral

Your client may not know the referral all that well, or he may feel uncomfortable making the call. If this is the case, let him know you understand his hesitation, but ask if you can bother him for one more favor. Ask for his permission to use his name when you contact the people he referred you to. He'll probably be relieved to be let off the hot seat and be more than happy to give you permission to use his name.

How to Set Appointments with Referrals

When you call someone and you already have an "in" with a close personal friend or respected business associate, you have common ground. You also have the benefit of knowing some pertinent information that may be relevant to getting the appointment.

Before you call such a referral, review the information you wrote in your notes (see the previous section) and decide how you will set the stage for this selling situation. If you properly qualified the referral, you know enough about the prospective customer to ask just a few additional questions to get her involved and interested in your offering.

Through testimonials from your mutual business associate or friend, you can tell the referred client what your client (and their friend) thought was most attractive or appealing about your offering. Chances are good that your referral will be just as interested in those same special features as her friend or associate was. If she's not interested, keep asking questions until you discover what about your offering does interest her. Here's an example:

SALESPERSON: Hello, Jane, my name is Allen and I work at B & B Motors. I just helped Bill Robinson get his dream car, a new 300Z, and I promised him I would call you and let you know about the special offerings we're having on our Nissans this week. He just bought a beauty and told me you two had been talking together about needing a new car. Tell me, Jane, what are you looking for in a new car?

REFERRAL: Well, I'm not really ready to buy yet. I've just been looking around.

SALESPERSON: What have you seen so far that you like the best?

REFERRAL: Well, what I like and what I can afford are two different things.

SALESPERSON: I hear you. Bill said the same thing. That's why he wanted me to call you and let you know about our special promotion that's going on now. You know, you aren't too far from our dealership. I work late tonight, so I'm available around 6:00 this evening. I know Bill said you shared his love for fast sports cars. Is that right?

REFERRAL: Yes. But the ones I've seen are so expensive. I think I'm just going to wait a while.

SALESPERSON: I'll tell you what. Why don't you come on over after work and we'll sit down and you can explain to me your situation. Because of the success of the promotion, our dealership is serving munchies in our lobby in appreciation of our loyal customers. So don't eat first. You can munch out here while we talk. Is 6:00 good for you, or would 6:30 be more convenient?

REFERRAL: Actually, 6:00 is better for me.

SALESPERSON: Great, I'll see you then. Just come to the front desk and ask for Allen Brice.

Will you get referral appointments every time?

Just like you won't get a sale every time, you won't get a referral appointment every time. But you should always try to get referrals, even when you don't persuade or convince the prospect to get involved with your product or service. Now may not be the right time for that prospect, but that doesn't mean that she doesn't know anyone else who may be ripe for getting involved with the product, service, or idea you represent.

Many times you may be able to get an appointment with someone referred to you, but an appointment with the referral requires more time and persistent follow-up. **Remember:** People who are referred to you don't have a relationship with you. So you need to build that relationship by keeping your face and name in their minds and in front of their faces all the time.

I'll grant you that staying on top of those referrals isn't the easiest thing to do when you're busy trying to service old clients and contact leads you've received from other sources. Often, the ability to get the referral appointment depends on the success of your follow-up program — if, of course, you use one at all. It's disheartening to go through all the work to get referrals, only to lose them because you lack an organized follow-up system.

In Chapter 14, I show you how getting referrals and making appointments are closely linked with practicing proper and creative follow-up methods. When you follow up on those who offered the referrals, they're happy to refer you again when the situation arises. When you follow up on the referrals themselves, you give yourself greater opportunities to increase your profitability. How? By improving your closing rates through cultivating an effective referral business.

You may not get an appointment with every referral. But then you don't need to in order for referrals to become a highly productive way for you to find new business. **Remember:** Selling is a numbers game. Everyone you meet is likely to know someone else who may benefit from your product or service.

Not only did this salesperson use the qualifying questions from his referral notes, but he further qualified Jane by asking more questions. He was more likely to get the appointment because Jane knew that Bill had purchased a similar car and perhaps had similar financial concerns — and she knew that the salesperson was able to work out a way for Bill to own his dream car. The salesperson's ability to help Jane's friend Bill encouraged Jane to find out if the same would be possible for her.

What do you think the chances were of getting the appointment if the salesperson had been making a random cold call? You're right — they fall in the slim-to-none category.

Part IV
Growing Your Business

The 5th Wave   By Rich Tennant

"They've been that way for over 10 minutes. Larry's either having a staring contest with the customer, or he's afraid to ask for the sale again."

In this part . . .

When you've gotten comfortable with the selling cycle, you can turn your attention to expanding your business so you can help even more clients with your product or service. In this part, you'll find information on staying in touch with your clients so you can best serve their needs. You'll also discover how to put the Internet to work for you to generate even more sales. Finally, you'll get some great tips on managing your time, so you're available to do what really matters — keep balance in your life.

Chapter 14

Following Up and Keeping in Touch

*P*racticing consistent and persistent follow-up has been proven to be one of the most important factors in successful selling. That's why developing an organized, systematic approach to follow-up, while individualizing your chosen methods with your own creative flair, works to your advantage.

In today's market, more and more professional salespeople are practicing aggressive, thorough follow-up methods that even a few years ago would have been considered unnecessary. They're following up with people who are considered *marginal inquiries* — that is, people who don't represent a sale. If you want to compete with the big boys and girls, you must make follow-up an important part of your regular selling routine. In this chapter, I let you know with whom you should follow up and when. I also fill you in on the importance of sending thank-you notes and let you know how to get the best results from your follow-ups.

So how well do prospects respond to follow-up?

The way that your prospects respond to your follow-up depends entirely on the effectiveness and efficiency of the method of follow-up you use. If you use follow-up with flair, you can expect higher percentages of response from your prospects. Of course, the respose you get will also depend on whether you've chosen prospects who can benefit from owning your product or service.

Don't get discouraged if some prospects don't respond at all. Sometimes, no matter how good your follow-up, you get zip, zero, zilch for your efforts. If you take the goose egg more times than not, you may benefit from evaluating your methods of follow-up and putting another kind of zip into your messages.

Knowing which methods work best for you and which types of clients respond to one method of follow-up as opposed to another takes time. So be patient. Don't give up if, after your first few attempts at follow-up you get disappointing results. Instead, keep seeking ways to improve your follow-up program. Contact other professional salespeople who are willing to listen, look at your follow-up, and offer advice. Good follow-up techniques can sometimes take as long to master as good selling techniques. It doesn't happen overnight.

Knowing When (and with Whom) to Follow Up

The kind of follow-up you do depends on the kind of person you're following up with. The following five groups of people are the foundation of your business, and keeping in touch with them will build your future:

- **Referral contacts.** There's no point in asking for referrals if you don't follow up with the referrals you get. Referrals are a great source of business. Studies show that experienced salespeople spend half of the time selling a referred, qualified lead that they spend selling a non-referred, non-qualified lead — with a much higher closing rate. *Remember:* A referral is not a guaranteed sale. But contacting a referral is definitely easier than starting from scratch.

- **Current clients who are happily involved with your product or service.** You need to contact these people as part of the professional service you provide to them in appreciation of their continued loyalty — to you, your company, and your product or service.

- **Current clients who would benefit from new and improved versions of your product or service.** Reminding clients when it's time to consider updating the product you sold them is part of good customer service — and it's often a good source of sales.

✔ **Difficult-to-reach prospective clients.** Some prospects are hard to reach, so you'll need to follow up with them several times in order to finally get an appointment. *Remember:* Those salespeople who are persistent are rewarded.

✔ **Loyal clients.** Be sure to thank those clients who have been with you for years and stuck with you through thick and thin. They've been instrumental in helping you to develop your sales career through their long-term patronage, and they appreciate being thanked for it. A good time to follow up with loyal clients is when one of their referrals has become a client. Sending a thank-you note will likely result in even more referrals.

REMEMBER

Even the briefest contact or smallest sale can lead to a whole new list of potential referrals for new business.

Paying attention to what your customers want

To adopt effective methods of follow-up, you need to know the concerns that customers have about service and follow-up. After all, you'll only be able to serve your clients well when you know what they want.

Here's a list of customers' most pressing concerns about the selling and servicing of their accounts:

✔ Receiving a call that a salesperson promised to make

✔ Knowing contact numbers and the best available times to keep in touch with the sales and service people

✔ Having the ability to talk to somebody in authority

✔ Knowing that the salesperson and the salesperson's company appreciate their business

✔ Spending minimal time on hold in order to speak to a real person

✔ Being kept informed of ways to keep costs down and productivity up

✔ Being informed promptly of potential challenges and getting any problems resolved quickly

✔ Receiving acknowledgment of recognized challenges and accepting responsibility for errors

✔ Being addressed politely and receiving personal attention

✔ Being given realistic and honest information as it applies to delivery or problem-solving issues

By making follow-up and service a regular part of your day, you can efficiently address all these customer concerns and maintain an edge over your competitor, who may not be as determined to follow up as you are. When you provide excellent service and follow-up with your customers and prospects, you earn the reward of serving the lion's share of all the clients who need your offering.

Recognizing How to Follow Up

If you want your customers to remember you and your offering, you must offer them a memorable experience. If you see follow-up as boring, tedious repetition, you can expect your clients to feel the same way: bored and tired of your constant contacts.

You must *create* a need in your customers or prospects. And the need you create in your customers is directly proportionate to the enthusiasm and creativity you put into your follow-up program. So make sure that your methods of follow-up — and the messages you give through them — add up to a rewarding and memorable experience for your customers.

Phone

Telephone follow-up is perhaps the most common, least expensive, and most difficult method of follow-up to turn into a memorable experience. Why? Just look at all the ways your customers can miss you. People can avoid your calls by using screening devices such as answering machines, secretaries, or voice mail. If your phone calls are being screened, you have to get creative to instill enough curiosity in the people you're trying to reach to make them want to talk with you. Even if the people you're calling aren't trying to avoid you, they may just be very busy and what you're offering may not be the most important thing in their day — even though it is to you.

Reaching someone by telephone can be difficult if you aren't creative in your efforts. For example, when you try to reach that high-powered executive on the phone, you probably have to go through a company receptionist, a private secretary, and sometimes even a business partner before you get to the decision-maker. But the real frustration comes only when, at the end of this gauntlet, you discover that you've gone through it all just so the decision-maker can advise you to leave a message on her voice mail or pager! If you aren't prepared with a creative and tempting message, how often do you think the important decision-makers will return your call as it lines up with the dozens of other sales calls they receive on a daily basis? If you said, "Not often," you're right. Now do you see the value in giving your follow-up your own little flair?

To make your phone calls memorable, prepare a message that will get the person's attention and pique her curiosity. The people at the top are always looking for ways to improve profitability and productivity to carve out a greater percentage of market share. If you believe that your offering will help the person you're trying to reach, give her a teaser in the message that will make her want to put your name at the top of her callback list. A message such as this one, for example, will help you cut through the clutter and connect you with the people in charge:

> I'm sorry you missed my call, but you may still have an opportunity to find out how to increase quality production while decreasing company expenditures in labor and stored inventory. Look for the informational packet that I'll send to you on May 22. Expect a call back from me, Eric Post, to discuss how you and your company will benefit from our new offer. Or, for immediate information, call me tomorrow morning before 11:00 at 555-0000.

One short phone message such as this one accomplishes several objectives:

- ✔ **It peaks (to say nothing of piques) the customer's interest by teasing her with possibilities of how to do her job more efficiently.**

- ✔ **It tells the executive that you can provide individual as well as company benefits.** Mentioning the benefits to the individual is a good habit to get into, whether your offer of individual benefits occurs during follow-up or you incorporate it right into the fabric of your presentation. Stroke the ego of a high-powered executive and show her how she'll look good to the corporate elite, and she'll be that much more willing to own your offering.

- ✔ **It gives the customer a specific time to call if she wants to hear more.** By being specific, you can schedule your time to remain in your office to receive returned calls. This follow-up technique helps you avoid playing the annoying game of telephone tag with people you really need to reach. If the customer is too busy (or has not been tempted enough) to return your call at the suggested time, you've at least given yourself the opportunity to contact her via direct mail or e-mail. And guess what follows the mailing? You guessed it — another phone call!

Direct mail

Direct mail is a common method of follow-up, but your mailings don't have to be ordinary. Personalize your follow-up to make it memorable for the person you're contacting.

Network to find more ways to follow up

Top-producing salespeople have found ways to follow up that are both effective and creative. It may not be too effective to ask your competitors for their methods of follow-up. But other salespeople in your company may be doing creative things that they would be more than willing to share with you.

At your next sales meeting, make a point of discussing different methods of follow-up. This is called *networking,* even though you're doing it right at home within your own ranks of salespeople. And don't forget to follow up your discussion on follow-up by taking some follow-up action!

Before you toss all those collected business cards from all those business meetings into the circular file or tuck them away in a file you'll never see again, take the time to go through the cards and write a note about how much you enjoyed the person's input or conversation at the business meeting. If you've been thorough enough to jot down a word or two on the back of each card to remind you of your conversation, you'll have something specific to address when you do your networking follow-up.

You'd be surprised how many people have such a positive response to this type of follow-up. Many even go out of their way to contact you with future needs! If you follow up shortly after you attend the business breakfast or networking event, you'll more easily recall what everybody said. Keep a copy of your correspondence attached to the prospect's card so you can remember her when she calls.

For example, you may want to include premiums with your mailings. *Premiums* are offerings that benefit customers when they respond to a mailing. They may include a special promotional discount on your offering or a coupon to use the services included in your mailed package. Sometimes a mailing includes nothing but a premium. When the premium is the only thing in a mailing, the follow-up's only purpose is to build goodwill with your customers. If you use this method of follow-up, let the customer know that you will call him in a few days for his feedback. Your notice about the upcoming call gives you *another* opening to contact him with effective follow-up — it's a win-win situation. Your customer feels valued and you can expect a warm welcome when you contact him in hopes of keeping or receiving his business.

Another personal touch you can give to direct mailings is to include *For Your Information* (FYI) materials with a message of how your customers can benefit from them. FYI materials may not have anything to do with your personal offering, but they will let your clients know that you're thinking of them. So what qualifies as FYI material? Maybe you recently came across a press release relating to your client's field of expertise. If you did, let your client know about it. Sending the release may be of no direct, immediate benefit to you. But it will inform your customers of events that may profit him.

The more spontaneous your FYIs are, the more effective they will be. Instead of having your secretary type a formal cover letter for your FYIs, just jot a little handwritten note and attach it to the mailed material. Your note can be as simple as a few lines to let him know that you were thinking about him. Don't forget to include your business card with the note and maybe a little teaser about what's new with your product or service to get him to call.

E-mail

E-mail is a wonderful tool to use for follow up if your client uses it regularly. For those clients who do, you can send a note with an attached URL (Web site address) of an article or piece of information that the client may find useful in her business, or at the very least, interesting about her hobby. If the article is a long one, summarize in your message why you thought she'd find it interesting.

Whenever there's a new development in your industry or within your company that may impact this particular client, drop her an e-mail about it. If the new development has nothing to do with the client's needs, don't waste her time with it. I believe the general populace of the world feels guilty in some way that they're not reading as much as they should. There's an abundance of knowledge available and too many people berate themselves if they haven't read the ten best-selling business books and the latest edition of at least three newspapers in order to feel they're on top of things. So keep your e-mail messages to clients brief and to the point, and they'll be much appreciated.

By the way, it never hurts to include in the e-mail an offer to serve the client's needs should a question arise. Always, always keep yourself open to hearing from your clients.

Remembering the Importance of Thank-You Notes

Everybody likes to be appreciated, and I think you'll agree that there's precious little positive stroking in this world. So use your follow-up system to let your customers know that you appreciate their business and all the referrals they've sent your way. I call this *warm-and-fuzzy follow-up,* and it comes in a form that should become a permanent part of your sales repertoire as soon as possible — as in sometime *yesterday.* So what form should this take? The deceptively modest thank-you note.

In the following list, I've made it easy for you to get started with the thank-you note habit. Here are ten instances in which thank you notes are appropriate, followed by the exact words you can use for the occasion:

- **For telephone contact:** "Thank you for talking with me on the telephone. In today's business world, time is precious. You can rest assured that I will always respect the time you invest as we discuss the possibility of a mutually beneficial business opportunity."

- **For in-person contact:** "Thank you for taking time to meet with me. It was a pleasure meeting you, and I'm thankful for the time we shared. We have been fortunate to serve many happy clients, and I hope to some-day be able to serve you. If you have any questions, please don't hesitate to call."

- **After a demonstration or presentation:** "Thank you for giving me the opportunity to discuss with you our potential association for the mutual benefit of our firms. We believe that quality, blended with excellent service, is the foundation for a successful business."

- **After a purchase:** "Thank you for giving me the opportunity to offer you our finest service. We are confident that you will be happy with this investment toward future growth. My goal now is to offer excellent follow-up service so that you will have no reservation about referring to me others who have needs similar to yours."

- **For a referral:** "Thank you for your kind referral. You can rest assured that anyone you refer to me will receive the highest degree of professional service possible."

- **After a final refusal:** "Thank you for taking the time to consider letting me serve you. I sincerely regret that your immediate plans do not include making the investment at this time. However, if you need further information or have any questions, please feel free to call. I will keep you posted on new developments and changes that may benefit you in the future."

- **After a prospect buys from someone else:** "Thank you for taking the time to analyze my services. I regret being unable at this time to help you appreciate the benefits that we can provide you. We keep constantly informed of new developments and changes in our industry, though, so I will keep in touch with you in the hope that, in the years ahead, we will be able to do business together."

- **After a prospect buys from someone else but offers you referrals:** "Thank you for your gracious offer to give me referrals. As we discussed, I am enclosing three of my business cards, and I thank you in advance for placing them in the hands of three of your friends, acquaintances, or relatives whom I might serve. I will keep in touch and be willing to render my services as needed."

✔ **To anyone who gives you service:** "Thank you for your continued and professional service. It is gratifying to meet someone dedicated to doing a good job. I sincerely appreciate your efforts. If my company or I can serve you in any way, please do not hesitate to call."

✔ **On an anniversary:** "With warm regards, I send this note to say hello and, again, thanks for your patronage. We are continually changing and improving our products and service. If you would like an update on our latest advancements, please give me a call."

As you can see, you have many reasons to say, "Thank you." A thank-you note or two to the right person at the right time can go a long way toward building your success. How? Suppose receptionists or assistants who think they don't get enough recognition *do* get recognition from you. Will they remember? Of course, they will. Will they feel good about you? Yes. Will they be more receptive to your calls and questions? Probably. *Remember:* You can never go wrong by thanking someone.

Mother knows best

I learned the value and power of thank-you notes early in life. When we Hopkins kids were young, our parents occasionally went out with friends for dinner. As most kids do, I often tried to stay awake until my parents came home. On those times when I did manage to stay awake, invariably I saw my mother sit down at her little desk in the hallway as soon as she got home and begin to write.

One time I got up and asked her what she was doing. Her answer could have come straight out of Emily Post: "We had such a wonderful time with our dear friends this evening that I want to jot them a note to thank them for their friendship and the wonderful dinner."

My mother's simple act of gratitude — expressed to people who already knew that she and my father appreciated and enjoyed their friendship — helped to keep my parents' friendships strong for their entire lives.

Because I understood that building relationships is what selling is all about, I began early in my career to send thank-you notes to people. I set a goal to send ten thank-you notes every day. That goal meant that I had to meet and get the names of at least ten people every day. I sent thank-you notes to people I met briefly, people I showed properties to, people I talked with on the telephone, and people I actually helped to own new homes. I became a thank-you note fool.

To this day, on a plane on the way home after a seminar I write thank-you notes to students, to my staff, and to the wonderful people I meet at hotels and in taxicabs. And do you know what happens when I go back to those cities? They remember me. They remember that I cared enough to thank them for a job well done or for sharing their time with me.

I believe so strongly in the power of thank-you notes that you can find one in the back of every seminar workbook I print. And you won't have to look too hard to find my thank-you note to you somewhere in the pages of this very book.

Thank you

PROFILE OF A CHAMPION

TOM Hopkins PROFILE OF A CHAMPION INTERNATIONAL™

Dear Reader,

Thank you for giving me the opportunity to share with you our finest tactics and strategies for selling. I'm confident you'll be happy with the results you achieve as you begin to apply the material to your daily encounters.

Tom Hopkins

TOM Hopkins PROFILE OF A CHAMPION INTERNATIONAL™

Do you say "thank you" or send a gift?

If someone has gone *way* out of his way to help you, and if you think he deserves a little gift or an extra-special thank you, and if a thank you is appropriate, then by all means send that person a thank-you note right away. You don't send a thank-you note *every* time someone does something for you — you do it at those times when you know someone has put a lot of his effort, time, and energy into something for you, gone above and beyond the call of duty for you.

If a customer likes classical music, consider sending him a set of tickets to a symphony performance. You may want to send movie tickets to a secretary or assistant. You can thank clients with a round of golf at their favorite course, or give the secretary and her guest a gift certificate for lunch to show your gratitude for her extra effort to arrange the appointment that you worked on for a month.

If you don't know whether a certain thank-you gift is appropriate, ask someone else her opinion, even if you have to consult Miss Manners, Emily Post, or Dear Abby.

Many gifts to customers are tax-deductible to your business. Ask your accountant about this. Your thank you gift could be even *more* beneficial for you.

Maximizing Results from Your Follow-Ups

Maximizing results is a great goal to have in handling any contact, not just a follow-up. To do so requires efficiency, a well-laid plan, and good records. In this section, I cover just those aspects of follow-up so you can get the best results from your effort.

Imposing order

Follow-up sounds so simple when somebody advises you to send a letter or to just pick up the phone and make a call, but establishing an effective follow-up system involves much more than that. An effective follow-up plan requires you to master and implement the Rule of Six, a rule of selling that can increase your sales volume many times over:

In order to make the sale, you should contact prospects 6 times within a 12-month period.

Think of all the contacts and prospects you have — and multiply that number by six. When you look at follow-up that way, you can easily see how some salespeople get overwhelmed with follow-up. In fact, many champion salespeople hire assistants whose main function is to do prompt and effective follow-up.

Especially if you're new to sales, you probably won't be able to hire someone to take care of your follow-ups. So you need to work extra-hard to provide prompt follow-up to referrals, prospective clients, loyal customers who now own your offering, networking possibilities, and just about everybody you come into contact with during a normal business day (as if there is such a thing as a normal business day!).

In order for your follow-up to be effective, and because follow-up is a constant in the selling process, you must organize your follow-up time and program to ensure that your business stays productive. You can set up your follow-up system in several different ways — choose the method that works best for you. For example, you can use something as simple as 3-x-5 index cards to keep track of your follow-ups. Or you may want or need to use a more sophisticated filing program. In today's world of high-tech equipment, keeping all your follow-up on a sales force automation software program designed to store the maximum amount of information in the minimum amount of space may be the most efficient system of all. By setting up a database specially designed for follow-up, you can save time and energy that you can then devote to face-to-face selling. Those software programs include, ACT! and GoldMine. Other methods are Internet-driven services, such as salesforce.com. If you already use one, invest some time in learning how to maximize the "tickler" or "reminder" features. If you don't have one, be certain these features are easy to manage in any program you decide to use. (Check out Chapter 6 for more information on putting technology to work for you.)

Whichever way you choose to organize your time and the follow-up information you collect, your method should enable you to systematically and periodically keep in touch with all your contacts.

As you schedule your follow-up time, keep your customers informed of the best times to contact you. Be sure that you are accessible at the times you tell them to call. Just by being there, you eliminate telephone tag or the nagging fear that the call you've waited for all week will come when you're out on an appointment.

Let your customers know your work schedule (as much as possible), and they'll appreciate being able to reach you when you say you'll be available. Keeping your announced office hours is just another way to let your clients see how efficiently you run your business and, likewise, how efficiently you would (or do) service their needs.

Gauging your nuisance quotient

Whether you receive a *yes* or a *no* from people to whom you present your product, you should include them all in your follow-up program. With those who become clients, service is key and you can't serve them if they don't make a connection with you. Surprise, surprise — not many of them will reach out to make that connection. The job is up to you. For those people who choose to purchase from someone else or to not make any purchase at all at this time, you need to get their permission to stay in touch with new developments that may apply to their situation.

With your clients, you want to stay in touch fairly often, depending upon the product or service they acquired. If they are purchasing office supplies from you, you may need to be in touch weekly. If the purchase was a Lear Jet, you may only need to be in touch once every month or so.

Your clients may need a comfort scratch every now and then to feel you're really there for them. Your non-clients may feel you're scratching your nails on their blackboard if you call too often. You'll master the gauging of this with time and experience. If you're a beginner, ask each person how often he would like to hear from you. Don't say, "How often shall I contact you," though. He may answer with, "Don't call us. We'll call you." Instead, suggest it this way, "With your permission, I'd like to follow up with you in about 30 days just to see how well the product is meeting your needs and find out if you have any questions. Would that be all right with you?" He may suggest you call sooner or that he'll be fine for at least 30 days. You can gauge your nuisance factor based on his response.

One of the most important tidbits of sales wisdom is this: Avoid harassing your customer. Sometimes knowing when keeping in touch with your client has crossed the line to downright bothering him is difficult. But you defeat the entire purpose of follow-up if you fail to recognize the signs of annoyance a customer may be sending your way. If a customer hangs up on you, that's a pretty good sign that you've failed to recognize his annoyance. How many hang-ups do you get on a given day?

Be sensitive to your clients' needs. Don't call them on a Friday before a holiday and try to sell them your new offering over the phone. This kind of call is not follow-up; it's irritation. Similarly, don't call at lunchtime or at the very end of the day and expect a long, drawn-out conversation with your client's undivided attention. Her mind is set on beating a path to the door, not on listening to your offering.

Keep your follow-up short and sweet and do it at times most convenient for your prospects' schedules. Interruptions are sometimes unavoidable, but when too many interruptions occur, give your customers the opportunity to get back with you at a time better suited to their busy schedules.

If, after all the follow-up, you still get a *no* from a client, leave the contact or meeting on a positive note. If you know that his answer was not based on your poor performance, you may still be able to get a referral from him or do future business with him when his situation changes.

Be polite! Find out when he expects his situation to change and ask his permission to call back again. He may be receptive to hearing what you have to say a few short months down the road when he *is* ready to own your offering. If you leave him with a positive feeling and continue to build rapport through constant and persistent follow-up, the only thing stopping him from owning your offering is time — and that, too, shall pass.

If your customer admits that he has bought from your competitor, don't you think you need to discover why he chose your competitor over you? If this situation arises, don't get angry with your prospective customer. Instead, make him feel important by asking him if you can take up just a few more moments of his time to get his advice on how you can improve your sales skills or your product or service.

If you've invested a lot of time in a customer who has decided not to take you up on your offering and has instead gone with someone else, he may even feel obligated to meet with you. These meetings can be the best learning experiences you have. Not only will you find out what you may need to improve, but you will gain new insight into your competitor's offering or into what your competitor says about you and your company. Think of these times as invaluable opportunities to become a better salesperson. And don't forget to take this opportunity to follow up with a thank-you note to the customer for his advice.

If you're diligent in following up with customers who choose not to own your offering, you may just sneak them away from your competitor the next time they get the itch to own. By keeping in touch with them even better than the salesperson with whom they chose to do business, you will make the customer wish that he had done business with you. Let him see your organization and care for his well-being through your effective follow-up — and when he needs a new-and-improved version of what he now owns, he'll probably think of you first.

Being disappointed and letting your clients know you're sorry not to have the opportunity to do business with them is okay. Let them know that you're not giving up and that you still hope to win their trust. And for the customers you obtained because of your effective follow-up, remain just as consistent and persistent in the service you provide. Make sure they know that you're concerned about meeting their needs and that you put their needs before your own.

Keeping track of your successes

Be sure to keep thorough notes on all your follow-ups and the success you have with your current follow-up methods. When you do something great that gets excellent response, write it down in a *success journal* (a place where you can keep track of everything that has worked for you, follow-up or otherwise). Be specific and detailed, and describe the selling situation in which you implemented the successful follow-up method. The more information you record, the more likely you are to repeat the experience in the future.

When customers tell you what you need to work on, put those comments into your success journals, too. *Remember:* If you take all this time to write down what you do well, in addition to what you need to improve on, you should take the time to review your journal periodically and evaluate whatever changes you make.

You may need to solicit the help of another professional salesperson in your office to hold you accountable for making the changes you know you need to make and to help you implement such changes. When your colleague sees you kicking back and relaxing, she should have your permission to give you a gentle wake-up call, a reminder of what you said you wanted to do to improve your sales results.

Be a fanatic in follow-up! Even if you haven't found the most creative or memorable way to follow up, practicing follow-up with zeal is better than doing nothing at all. Allow yourself a few mistakes and plenty of time to organize and maintain your chosen follow-up schedule. Expect *gradual* increases in the number of *yes*es you get. Be diligent about follow-up with your prospects, your customers, and yourself. And above all, think of follow-up as your way to travel the path of sales success.

Chapter 15

Using the Internet to Make More Sales

. . . .

In This Chapter

▶ Researching your client's business online

▶ Presenting to your clients across the country with webcasting

▶ Being there for your clients, no matter what technologies you use

. . . .

The Internet is a fantastic tool for you to use in preparing and making sales. When used properly, it's an excellent resource that allows you to take advantage of technology that may otherwise be beyond your means. Think about the time, effort, and financial means it would require for you to have access to the most up-to-date information on any potential client if it weren't for the Internet. I strongly suggest that you quickly adopt the Internet as your new best friend — second only to the pen with which your client approves the paperwork that closes the sale.

The Internet's Positive Impact on the Selling Profession

According to *The Wall Street Journal,* 73 percent of sales professionals use the Internet at least once per day — and that number is expected to increase to about 80 percent by December 2001. Never before has accessing information, educating, and communicating — all at the same time — been easier.

The Internet is an empowering tool. It allows you to stay one step ahead of your competition and find out about a client's potential need sooner than ever. Having access to the Internet is like having a reference library at your fingertips. You can look up nearly every topic, company, or product you can think of. And the best part is that you'll usually find more than one source of information, so you can make sure that what you're getting is accurate.

Always consider the source and date of information you see online. If the information was posted by a corporation or reputable organization, it's likely valid and current. But if you're not familiar with the source of the information, be aware that it may not be the most reliable. Wise businesses and organizations post prominently the date the site was last revised, so you know how current it is.

Better than the newspaper

On the Internet, you can read all the latest news releases for your industry on Web sites such as Business Wire (www.businesswire.com) or PR Newswire (www.prnewswire.com). U.S. Newswire (www.usnewswire.com) transmits public policy press releases for the White House, government agencies, Congress, interest groups, and political parties. If the information is important to your selling career, take advantage of the latest news.

For information specific to client companies, visit their Web sites instead of waiting for the newspapers or trade magazines to pick up their news releases and print them. You'll also find news releases linked to the stock page for publicly held companies, because they want their latest good news to boost the public's confidence in their stock.

Many of the most popular newspapers and magazines have online content that is searchable, so you don't even have to flip pages to find what you're looking for. All you need do is type in a word or phrase related to your area of interest in their Search box and let it take you directly to that article.

Better than word of mouth

You can experience for yourself how your competition handles client concerns by submitting a request for information on your competitor's Web site. Look for something under the heading "Customer Service," "Technical Support," or "Contact Us." (Do the same with your own site every now and then to be sure your service is better than your competition's.)

You can also review Web sites to find out how your product ranks compared to the competition. Then you can pass that information on to your prospects. Showing your prospects that you're on top of things helps them to recognize your high level of competence, thus inspiring trust in your advice.

Better than guesswork

The Internet allows you and your company to capture very specific information on customer needs and respond to them effectively. It can allow your clients to receive answers to their concerns faster than ever before, which increases their confidence in you and your company's ability to serve.

As an example, if you purchase a particular book at Amazon.com, you'll find a list of other books purchased by the people who purchased the one you just did. In other words, Amazon is pointing you to other sources of similar information. If you want, they'll even send you e-mail updates when new books are scheduled for release by the same author or in the same genre. In other words, they understand the old qualifier that, based on your past purchases, you're likely to make a similar choice again in the future.

If your business is Internet-ready, take advantage of this excellent example and implement as many of these tools as possible to grow it. If your company collects such in-depth information, gain access to it as much as possible. The more you know about all your clients, the better you'll handle each one's individual needs. If your clients don't make purchases online, this technology may not be for you, but it's still a good lesson on the power of today's marketing strategies.

WARNING!

Never assume that your clients have only one area of needs. If your company offers a range of products, always try to get your clients happily involved with as wide a range as possible.

Avoiding personal burnout

With today's technology, you could easily be available to your clients 24 hours a day, 7 days a week, 365 days a year. Isn't that great? You can live your life entirely for your clients. Unfortunately, many salespeople try to do this — and they lose in the long run. Why? Because they lose their personal relationships and, even worse, they often lose their health.

Top people in the field of selling manage their lives to stay in balance with both business and personal issues. In order to do this, yet maintain a high level of service to your clients, you have to put in place systems to ensure that everything goes as smoothly as possible all the time.

Always remember that your family and friends or support systems come first. A quick but effective strategy for keeping them involved requires only the slightest effort on your part. Every time you get someone involved in your product or close an opportunity, or if you have had a bad day or even a bad sales presentation, make sure you share that with the people who are closest to you. Call them immediately and then call your manager. This takes no more than a few seconds of your time and will let the people in your life know that you are thinking about them in your triumphs and your failures.

Using the Internet to Your Advantage

Selling is all about servicing your clients' needs, and the Internet doesn't change that. But the Internet *does* allow you to help your clients in new and exciting ways, whether your clients are right next door or across the continent. In this section, I offer some suggestions for ways to put the Internet to work for you in your daily selling life.

Prospecting online

The Internet can be a great source for finding potential clients. If you sell products in a particular company or industry, conduct searches on those industry sites and you'll find whom to contact and maybe even find a photo and profile of Mr. or Ms. Decision-Maker.

You can also find people through online phone and e-mail directories. Some good ones are YellowPages.com (www.yellowpages.com), Yahoo! (yp.yahoo.com), or WorldPages.com (www.worldpages.com).

Many list-management companies, such as Dun & Bradstreet (www.dnb.com) and infoUSA (www.infousa.com), have also metamorphosed into Web-based businesses, allowing you to search and order lists of potential clients directly from their sites and download their contact information into your computer.

You can also use the Internet to get back in touch with former classmates, who may be potential prospects for you today. You can visit sites like Classmates Online (www.classmates.com), for example, where old high school and college friends can list their current contact information by the name of the school and year of graduation. If you attended a school but didn't graduate from it, you can still enter the year you would have graduated to find your former classmates. You may also be able to locate them via a class listing on your college or university's Web site.

If you belong to an organization related to your industry, it may have a Web site listing the other members and how to contact them. Other members may be a big help in reaching decision-makers who may be excellent prospects.

Offering to give to the other person first (before asking for something from him) makes for good networking. Sometimes, all you need do is ask, "What can I do for you?" The other person will often feel obliged to make the same offer — and you get what you wanted in the first place.

The Internet cannot replace a warm-blooded sales professional for creating long-term, caring relationships. So even if you gain most of your clients via the Web, if you really want to *keep* their business, you need to provide them with a warm body to contact if they have questions or concerns.

Presenting and selling online

Ideally, your company's Web site will effectively present your message to create enough trust that potential clients will view or read about your product or service and choose to get happily involved — maybe even placing an online order. Selling online is how hundreds of small companies have become very, very profitable.

Not only does your online presence need to put forth the image and message that you desire, but the living, breathing people who actually fulfill the orders need to do what your site promises. Keep in mind the old selling adage to "under-promise and over-deliver" in order to please your clients.

Be careful of how much dazzle and showmanship you put into your Web presentations. Not everyone has a computer connection at the maximum speed, so your presentation should be developed to dazzle the low-end connections — or you'll lose them to frustration.

When your prospect will be doing the reading, keep your words to a minimum, use contrasting colors and easy-to-read fonts, and don't clutter the screen with images. For more information on the look and feel of your Web site, pick up a copy of *Selling Online For Dummies,* by Leslie Heeter Lundquist (published by Hungry Minds, Inc.).

Presenting from afar

If you can't be with your prospect, but she needs information right away, you can use your Web site to get her the information she needs. Knowing your company's Web site inside and out is definitely a necessity if you want to succeed in using it to your advantage. So start by locating the exact URL (Web address) for each piece of information your prospect needs to see. Then send those URLs to the prospect in the order in which you recommend she views those pages, and explain that in your e-mail. For example, your instructions to your client may be as follows:

> Start with our home page at www.mycompanyhomepage.com. Then go to www.mycompany.com/theparticularproductyoureinterestedin. Here, you can see a photo of the item and read a description of what it will do for you. Next go to www.mycompany.com/testimonialfortheparticularproductyoureinterestedin. Here, you'll see how much others have enjoyed and benefited from owning the product. You may want to follow that by going to www.mycompany.com/howtoordertheparticularproductyoureinterestedin. Here you can place an order and receive a confirmation-of-delivery date.

If you have to work with clients this way *always* follow up your instructions with a personal phone call to answer any questions they may have about ownership, delivery, installation, and so on. Your clients may have questions that can't be answered by your Web site — and that's what you're there for.

For more sophisticated products or services, or when a more in-depth online presentation is needed, you can also take advantage of an online service such as WebEx (www.webex.com), which allows you to take customers through your own customized PowerPoint presentation or slide show from afar.

In addition to giving a PowerPoint presentation over the Internet, you can take advantage of *webcasting* in your sales as well. Webcasting is not unlike telecasting, which is what your local news station does several times each day. Instead, webcasting is done over the Internet. If your company uses webcasting, you can attend your national sales meeting from your desk. Your client can view the latest news on products and services if they are webcast. And webcasting is a wonderful method for getting consistent, firsthand, high-quality video or slide messages to your clients. You can also use webcasting for real-time communication. A chat session can be included with the webcast so you can interact with and answer questions from the audience, even if you're not in the room with them.

To see a demonstration of how webcasting works — and to determine whether it's a tool you can benefit from — visit WebCasting, Inc., at www.webcasting.com and check out its demos. Not only does webcasting save money and time, but WebCasting's reporting facility can account for each viewer of the material, which helps in production of future projects. Other sources for webcasting include www.webex.com and www.placeware.com. Visit a few different sites and see if what they offer is right for you.

Telemarketing with the best of them

If you do a lot of long-distance selling or if you're in telephone sales (where you rarely meet your client in person), you can use your Web site to enhance the prospective client's satisfaction. How? By directing him through the site while you're on the phone with him. Walking through the site together is the next best thing to sitting at a table with your prospect and demonstrating your product or brochures. You may use the same links discussed in the preceding section, or you can follow an entirely different path, dictated by the client's questions and concerns. The key here is to absolutely, positively know what's on your site and what may be missing. You don't want to get caught off guard by a client's question.

Never direct a client to an area of the site that you haven't been to recently. It may have changed and you could end up with egg on your face, not looking too competent.

Staying in touch with your clients

Another great use of the Internet is in staying connected with your clients, building those long-term relationships, and inspiring loyalty. Sounds like a lot of reward from just a few keystrokes, doesn't it?

If John BigBoss is your largest client and his interests involve fishing, use some of your 30 minutes a day to seek out new Web sites on fishing and pass those URLs along to old John — just to let him know you're thinking about him and want him to enjoy his hobbies. Why? When John enjoys his hobbies, he's happy. And if he's happy because of something you did for him, he'll want to stay connected to you.

If you find an article online about a client's particular industry or a client's competition, you may want to print it out and send it to her along with a short "I'm thinking of you" note. Or just drop her an e-mail with the link attached.

If your client's company stock has a great day, send a congratulatory note. How will you know about that great day? Check the company's listing on the stock exchange. It's as simple as visiting the Web sites of the New York Stock Exchange (`www.nyse.com`) or Nasdaq (`www.nasdaq.com`) and entering the company's symbols to see today's activities and news releases.

Avoiding techno-burnout

Do you know what the best thing is about having all this technology to help you take care of business? It all has an "off" setting — and you should take advantage of that in order to rest and recreate. If you don't take care of yourself, you won't be able to do a good job of taking care of anyone else. Champion salespeople know when to forward everything to someone else and let that person take care of it.

Although most salespeople like to think of themselves as being indispensable — and they actually may be the only people in the world who can serve their clients best — everyone requires balance. In order to achieve and maintain balance, you need to determine how many

of the 86,400 seconds of your day you'll devote to clients, how many to your personal development, how many to your loved ones, and so on.

Don't become so much of a Techno-Joe that you lose sight of what's really important — the service you provide to your clients and the personal relationships that fulfill your life. I'm sure you've heard the saying that no one on his deathbed ever said, "I wish I'd spent more time at work" (or, in this case, "more time learning that software"). Your computer, mobile phone, and PalmPilot won't show up at your funeral, so don't allow them to take over your life. *Remember:* They're just tools for you to master — in order to live your life to the fullest.

Chapter 16

Planning Your Time Efficiently

- -

In This Chapter

▶ Paying attention to how you use your time

▶ Setting aside time every day to plan

▶ Keeping interruptions to a minimum

▶ Removing the clutter from your workspace

▶ Jumping over the common pitfalls of time management

- -

*T*ime is your most valuable resource, and until you realize that, you'll always be wondering where all your time goes. Don't worry, though. You're not alone. Everyone is searching for more time. The value of time has increased dramatically in recent years. So why has time's stock risen so high? Because of an adaptation of the law of supply and demand: The busier you become, the more time you need. Ask a dozen people to name one thing that would make their lives easier, and the overwhelming response will be more time. When you have more time to do the things you *need* to do, you can usually generate more income to do the things you *want* to do. As my dear friend and fellow trainer Zig Ziglar says, "When you do what you need to do when you need to do it, you will soon have the time to do what you want to do when you want to do it."

In this chapter, I give you some great tips for staying on top of your time, so that you have more time to do the things you *want* to do instead of only being able to do the things you *need* to do.

For more great tips on managing time, turn to *Time Management For Dummies,* 2nd Edition, by Jeffrey J. Mayer (published by Hungry Minds, Inc.).

Investing Your Time, Instead of Spending It

Average salespeople often spend their time foolishly doing unproductive busywork — and then they wonder where their day went, why they accomplished so little, and why they never seem to have time for the fun stuff they'd really like to do. The key word there is *spend:* They *spent* their time instead of *investing* it. And that makes all the difference.

Managing yourself to get a handle on your time

Time-management is really all about managing your self. Don't believe me? Stop and think about it for a minute. When did you last control time? Can you stop time or even slow it down? No way. Can you negotiate with time? If you've figured out how, then you should be writing a book instead of reading one. No one has more time to invest than you do and you don't have any more time than anyone else, yet some people succeed more often than others, and they do it without controlling time. They do it by disciplining themselves to make the most of every minute.

For example, if you have a healthy dose of road time in your selling life, you can choose to use that time to listen to motivational or educational tapes or CDs. In doing so, you turn your required expenditures of time into investments in your professional education.

Another way to manage yourself when you have to spend time traveling is to cluster your appointments. By organizing your presentations or customer service appointments by geographical area, you can save a lot of travel time — and if you live in a rather large metropolitan area,

you're saving time sitting in traffic as well. If your travel time is primarily within major cities, you may want to schedule it so that you don't get stuck in rush-hour traffic. Besides, taking side streets and back roads may lead you to new opportunities if you keep your eyes open and remain aware of your surroundings

If you can't put your fingers on the contact information for all your clients within a matter of minutes, consider investing some time in good contact management software. With today's technology, the only reason a client or prospective client's information won't be at your fingertips is because you didn't invest the time to input it correctly as soon as you received it. Entering the information only takes a few minutes, and then it's there forever.

If you think that people who practice time-management strategies are fanatical workaholics who leave no time for personal relaxation, you're mistaken. Just the opposite is the case. In operating more efficiently, they create *more* time for personal endeavors. Invest time in planning your time, and you'll think of dozens of ways to manage yourself more efficiently.

The words *spending* and *investing* connote very different ideas. When you spend money, you probably think of the loss of that money rather than the benefits you'll enjoy from whatever it was you spent your money on. On the other hand, the word *invest* signifies a payment from which you will derive a return; you don't focus on the momentary loss of money, but rather on the gain of the product or service that you will receive. Similarly, when you spend your time instead of investing it, you focus on lost time rather than on personal gain.

If you've never put a dollar value on your time before, do it now. To determine what your time is worth, take your hourly rate and follow this simple equation:

$$\frac{\text{Gross Income}}{\text{Total Annual Working Hours}} = \text{Hourly Rate}$$

To see the value of this equation, suppose that your annual income is $30,000 and you work 40 hours a week for 50 weeks a year (allowing 2 weeks off for vacation). That means that the value of each hour in your workweek is $15. In straight-commission sales, if you spend just one hour each day of each workweek on unproductive activity, you spend about $3,750 a year on nothing. And that's exactly what you have to show for your wasted time, too — nothing. When you choose not to manage your time, you may end up wasting 12 percent of your annual income or more. And this amount doesn't even account for all the future business you lost because you spent time instead of investing it. If you're a regular, full-time employee, that $3,750 is money your employer may as well drop off the roof for all the productivity she gets for it.

In sales or persuasion situations, you often don't see immediate financial payoff from the time you invest. When I was selling real estate, for example, I invested my time in prospecting, demonstrating property, and getting agreements approved, but I saw no return until the transaction was completed and my broker had the check. The final transaction commonly occurred weeks, and in some cases months, after my actual investment of time. During the period between my invested time and my financial reward, I sometimes lost sight of my goals — but that's normal in selling. The longer the period between selling and payoff, the harder it is to stay focused on investing your time wisely. When you invest time in the people you're trying to persuade, thinking of the returns on your investment is normal. I don't know of any new salesperson who doesn't take out her calculator and figure the percentage she gets on a sale as soon as she's out of sight of the client. After all, helping others is a career choice that pays very well when done correctly.

Making Time to Plan Time

People who don't practice effective time management often complain that they don't have time to plan their time. But if you don't make time for planning and self-improvement, you may as well plan to earn the same income that you earn today for the rest of your life. It's a fact: By taking the time to plan, you will save as much as 20 to 30 times the amount of time that you expend in the planning process.

When you plan your time, divide the things on which you choose to invest time into four categories:

- **Immediate activities:** These are the tasks you must complete today.

- **Secondary activities**: These tasks are ones that are close to immediate, but not quite. You probably need to complete them this week instead of today, for example.

- **Relatively unimportant activities:** These tasks don't need to be completed by a specific deadline. You can work them in when you have a spare moment.

- **Emergencies:** Although they're rare, you need to build time into your schedule to handle emergencies, so you're not left hanging when they happen.

In the following sections, I go into more depth on each of these four categories.

Immediate activities

Immediate activities are *only* those activities that you must complete today. If you clutter your mind with things that should be secondary activities (the things you don't have to do today), you can end up neglecting your immediate activities or not giving them the full, focused attention they require.

Ask yourself these questions to determine the immediacy of your activities and prioritize them by either the amount of relief you'll feel in getting them done or the amount of goodwill or income they'll generate:

- If I can achieve only three or four activities today, which ones should they be? What if I can only accomplish one?

- Which activities will yield the largest rewards?

- Which activities will complicate my day tomorrow if I do not accomplish them today?

> ✔ Which of these activities can I delegate to someone else in order to leave myself more time to generate more business or enhance my personal relationships?
>
> ✔ Which activities, if I postpone them, will damage my relationships with others?

Have your immediate activities in front of you at all times. If you can't see what you need to accomplish today because you've buried your immediate activities under other less-important work, those activities can get lost in the shuffle — and you can lose sight of your goals.

Enter your immediate activities into your computer or handheld planner and set them so that you're reminded about them automatically. If the task is a large one, break it down into smaller pieces so you can accomplish those pieces and get them off that screen. Accomplishing those smaller pieces of the project leaves you with a very satisfying feeling — and when you're feeling good, you're more productive.

Secondary activities

Identifying your secondary group of activities is usually easier than identifying immediate ones. Some secondary activities may be almost-but-not-quite immediate, so put them at the top of your secondary activity list. As you do for immediate activities, prioritize your secondary list so you finish what's most important first.

Put any paperwork related to those secondary activities in a desk drawer or a letter tray that you can move to your desk or even put on the floor if necessary. Don't let yourself get preoccupied with piles of paperwork. Paperwork overload causes stress and confuses you about what really needs immediate attention.

Stay on top of your paperwork

If you dread doing paperwork, don't leave it for the end of the day if you can help it. By paperwork, I also include computer-generated reports or online reports that your company may require. If something unexpected comes up, you won't get to your reports, and the next day you'll just have twice as much to do. This buildup, in turn, causes you even more anxiety because now you *really* have a big task ahead of you.

Do your paperwork in the first hour of each day, if at all possible, when you're fresh. When it's done, you're free to concentrate on the more productive parts of your day.

Pick up paperwork only once. Decide its importance and deal with it by passing it on or filing it. Don't read it and put it in a pile to be looked at again later.

Relatively unimportant activities

Identifying which tasks fall into the "relatively unimportant" category is difficult: You may think everything needs your attention (if it didn't, it wouldn't come your way, right?). But such thinking simply isn't true. Other people pass many unimportant activities to you to take care of — activities that have a funny habit of working themselves out if you just give them a little time. By putting those activities in your "relatively unimportant" category, you may be able to avoid spending time on these chores when you should be investing time on your immediate activities.

So what do I mean by *relatively unimportant activities?* Think about the number of times an associate has come to you for help with a problem, only to reveal that it wasn't your assistance she wanted after all? She just wanted you to take on the problem as yours. What begins as a favor thus ends up being a real chore. Her worries become your worries — and she's off having a relaxed two-hour lunch, knowing you'll take care of it.

I'm not suggesting that you never help an associate, but I *am* cautioning you about taking on work that should be someone else's responsibility. If you help an associate, make sure that you get compensated, either financially or by an exchange of help on one of your projects. And always get *your* work done first. Establish reasonable rules with your peers about work-related assistance. Doing so helps prevent hard feelings later.

Emergencies

Planning your time efficiently can prevent some emergencies from happening in the first place, but you should always have an alternate approach to your most important activities just in case an emergency arises. Planning ahead and being prepared like good little Boy and Girl Scouts will keep you from panicking and completely trashing your schedule, and that of others, when emergencies do arise.

If you have children, you know that, from time to time, they get sick or hurt, or they forget to tell you about vital events you need to attend. If you have a whole day of report writing to get done and you get one of those "Mrs. Slack, Mary Beth has just thrown up at school. How soon can you pick her up?" calls, do you have a backup person, such as a grandparent, who would be willing to care for your daughter at least until you can get there yourself? If not, see what you can do about getting that backup in place. Then notify the people at work that you're leaving in 15 minutes so they can get what they absolutely need from you. Save all your report data onto a disk, grab your laptop and your daily planner, and head for the door. Or, if you use e-mail, send the file to yourself at home so it's waiting for you when you arrive.

Technology being what it is, don't count on every e-mail being *where* it should be *when* it should be 100 percent of the time. Transferring your files to a disk is still a good idea.

Have backup plans in place for transportation as well. Is there someone else at work who lives near you whom you can hitch a ride with on those mornings when your car won't start? Or if there's a bus route close by, do you have a schedule handy? Is there a taxicab number in your address book? Better yet, do you have a wireless phone to call for help if you have a flat tire out in the middle of nowhere? If not, you'd better keep a pair of tennies in the car for that long walk to the pay phone.

Having the convenience of a mobile phone has saved many a sale. If you don't already have a mobile phone, get one so you can be more accessible to your loved ones, your clients, and your boss. *Remember:* You can always turn the phone off when you're doing something really important or when proper etiquette requires.

Time-Surfing the Wave of the Future

A couple decades ago, I discovered a lot about a strategy called *time-surfing* with Alan Lakein, and in the following sections, I tell you how to use it to become a champion in sales.

Just as you separate work tasks into three categories, you need to separate your personal life into three areas in order to effectively organize your time. You need to

✔ Investigate your yesterday.

✔ Analyze your today.

✔ Discover your tomorrow.

In other words, you time-surf. In the following sections, I show you how to do it.

Investigating your past

Start by taking some time to write down what you do with each of the 168 hours in your typical week. If you're like many self-management beginners, you probably have habits that are serious time wasters — but you can easily eliminate those habits when you become aware of them. Try to be as honest and thorough as possible.

Keep a daily log of your typical routine — and do this for seven days. The log will help you establish an accurate record of the habits you may need to change. The best way to keep such a log is to jot down the time you spend moving through your daily routine: three hours running errands, five minutes looking for a purchase agreement, half a day scouring around for a misplaced phone message, ten minutes trying to get refocused after an interruption, and so on. After completing this time log for seven days, you'll be amazed at how much time you cannot account for and how much time you waste on relatively unimportant activities. Few people know how they spend their time — in this way, time is just like money. You know you start the week with $50 in your wallet. On Wednesday, you only have $7. So where did that $43 go? Remembering where your spent your money is difficult, and the same is true with time. Unless you account for it daily, it's gone with the wind.

Get tough with yourself. Do this audit for seven days. After you complete each daily sheet, be sure to tally your total hours spent on each kind of activity. Keep all your sheets and evaluate them at the end of the week. Above all, be honest when you record the time you spend on each activity. If you cheat, you're cheating yourself.

Analyzing your today

If you use the word *productivity* when you refer to time planning, time planning won't be such a mystery to you. People frequently come up to me or write to me and say, "Tom, I just can't plan my time," or, "I just can't seem to keep up with everything I need to do." Invariably, I give such people a saying that someone gave me when I first started out in sales, a saying that made a huge impact on my career and my success. It also made a lot of further discussion on the subject of time management unnecessary for me. It goes like this:

I must do the most productive thing possible at every given moment.

I have been teaching that saying for over 20 years, but it's so simple that many people don't understand it. Here's how to think of it: No matter what you're doing, ask yourself, "Is this the most productive thing I can do at this time?" You need to do a few simple things to answer that question:

- ✔ Keep a list of important tasks.
- ✔ Keep an appointment calendar.
- ✔ Know what your time is worth.

To increase your productivity, you must figure out, by doing the most productive thing at each moment, how to increase the value of each hour. If that sounds simple, it's because it *is*. You increase the value of each hour by constantly asking yourself that same question: "Is what I'm doing right now the most productive thing I can do?"

Some salespeople spend all their time getting organized and getting ready for persuasion situations that never come about. To them, getting organized itself has become the game. Sometimes people overvalue the organizing stage because they're afraid of facing rejection or failure, so they hide from seeing the public. In most cases, though, salespeople who make organizing the end rather than the means just don't appreciate the difference between productivity and organization. To many salespeople, time planning revolves around just buying a time-planning device, program, or binder and filling in the squares. Of course, those tasks are necessary. But they're just a small part of a very big picture. Time planning actually starts with goals. Why? Because setting goals is the only way you can tell what the most productive tasks are at any given moment.

When you're planning for the upcoming day, ask yourself the following questions:

- ✔ Did I accomplish all my high-priority items today?
- ✔ Did I reach or surpass my goals for today?
- ✔ Did I invest as much time in persuading others as I planned?
- ✔ Did I contact every prospect that I put on my list for today? If not, why not? What prevented me from getting to that prospect?
- ✔ How much time did I spend prospecting for new clients?
- ✔ How much time did I waste chatting with co-workers or clients?
- ✔ What is the most productive thing I did today?
- ✔ What is the least productive thing I did today?
- ✔ Of the things I consider a waste of time, could I have avoided or eliminated any of them?

- ✔ How much time did I spend doing something that will profit me? Can I devote more time to that activity tomorrow?

- ✔ Was today a productive day for me? Was it productive for my company?

- ✔ Did I take care of all the paperwork I needed to take care of today?

- ✔ How many of today's activities have helped me achieve my goals?

- ✔ How much time today did I allot to my family? Did I spend this time with them? Was it quality time, or was I just at the same place they were, at the same time?

- ✔ What can I do to improve the quality of time I devote to my family?

- ✔ Did I plan for, and take some time to work on, my emotional or physical health?

- ✔ If I could live today over, what would I change?

- ✔ What did I do today that I feel really good about?

- ✔ Did I send thank-you notes to the people I dealt with today?

- ✔ What or who wasted the greatest amount of my time?

The answers to these questions will help you see what you're doing right and let you know what you can improve upon tomorrow.

Discovering your tomorrow

Assume that your goals and priorities are in line (and turn to Chapter 18 if they're not). You know what you want and how you want to get there. Your goals are all in writing and your priorities are set. Your daily time planning should start at night before you go to bed. Go through your time planner and lay out the day to come. Get a handle on your top six priorities, as well as who you will see or call, for the next day. Then add any personal areas you need to cover the next day. Writing down or entering the next day's top six priorities shouldn't take more than 10 to 15 minutes if you do it in a nice, quiet spot. When you've mapped out the next day, forget it and go to bed.

At the beginning of the day you've just mapped out, the most productive thing possible may be a 20-minute workout at 6:00 a.m., or breakfast with the family, or working in the garden, or any of a thousand other things that may be important to you and part of your goals and priorities. You have many choices throughout your day. Only *you* know if what you're doing is the most productive thing in relation to the goals and aspirations you want to achieve.

People grow up being told what to do for as much as the first 20 years of their lives — at home, at school, and sometimes even at a job. So the fact that some people lack a certain amount of self-discipline when they go into a career such as selling, which leaves people almost entirely to their own resources, isn't surprising. I'd like to have a dollar for every time I've heard a salesperson say, "I went into sales so I could be my own boss," or, "I went into sales so no one would tell me what to do," or, "I went into sales for more free time." All those reasons are great. But the people who hold those reasons had better develop a strong degree of self-discipline for doing what needs to be done. If they don't, they'll soon be back at a job where someone's telling them what to do.

To get started with an effective time-management method, don't try to plan for every minute of the day. Being inaccurate is too easy when you forecast time for task completion. Instead, start by planning just 75 percent of your total work time. That way, you allow for interruptions, delays, and unexpected emergencies. As your workday planning improves, you can increase to planning 90 percent of your day. But never plan for 100 percent — if you do, you won't leave room for the unexpected, and you'll just frustrate yourself when you can't accomplish your designated goals.

Remain flexible. Not much is black and white in the world of selling; there are many areas of gray. By staying flexible, you can maintain your equilibrium and move on to greater things. Don't lock yourself into a time-management program so rigid that you don't have time for anything else.

Achieving balance

Take a look at five areas of your life: family, health, finances, hobbies, and your spirit. Why focus on so many areas outside of your career? Because when you're turned on, motivated, and feeling good, you persuade better. If you let yourself become just a sales machine with no time for anything else, you'll burn out. You'll also probably create problems in your personal relationships. And your health most likely will suffer. Besides all that, you'll have no fun, you'll start feeling sorry for yourself, and your career will go down the drain.

Sometimes the most productive thing you can do may be to meet your spouse for lunch and thank him for supporting your goals and putting up with your long hours. Or to go see your child in a school event and enjoy her childhood. Or to take a physical workout to help ensure your good health and high energy. Or to plant roses if planting roses invigorates you.

To be successful, you need to be a finely tuned machine that can function over the long haul and face deadlines, rejection, the public, and your competition. You also must be able to meet your company's expectations and all the other demands put on you as a professional salesperson and problem solver. Keep yourself tuned and in balance — physically and psychologically. And remember that balance starts with goals and productivity.

Winners always plan their time. To increase your productivity and your income, you must plan your time like a professional. Professional salespeople are very conscious of the value of their customers' time, as well as their own. All sales professionals must make daily decisions on priorities. Some are major, some are minor — but all are factors in the management of time. Every professional salesperson needs a systematic approach to setting priorities.

Over the years, I've noticed that successful people who run large companies and build fortunes don't spend much more time working than anyone else. The difference with them is that they get more productivity out of each hour of every day. They don't try to do too much at once and, because they don't, they are more productive at accomplishing the day's most important goals.

Knowing When and Where to Plan

If you want to manage your time wisely, you'll need a planning device of some sort. Whether you prefer the pen-and-paper route or the high-tech one, find an option that works well for you. Also, look for contact management software that includes a calendar section so you'll have both your contact information and meeting schedule all in one place. Many of these programs will even flag you if you try to enter a meeting that conflicts with another event you already have scheduled, which can help you save face with clients instead of having to call them to reschedule. Some contact management software is even available online so you don't have to be concerned about your laptop crashing and losing all your valuable information. Others are customized to the specific needs of salespeople — with forms for travel itineraries, charting activity and productivity, meeting notes, expense reports, and so on. Take some time to find one you think you'll be comfortable using. If you're not comfortable, you won't use it and you'll be defeating your purpose of planning. (Turn to Chapter 6 for more information on contact management software.)

On the first day of every month, set aside 15 minutes at your desk or with your briefcase or laptop (wherever you keep all your pertinent information) to do your planning. Take a few moments to review all unfinished business and plan how and when you'll get it done. Write down everything you want to accomplish that month. Be realistic and be very specific.

Include any family or social events that you're committed to attend. Then add any important dates: family, friend, and client birthdays; your wedding anniversary, if it's this month; your child's school play; your spouse's company picnic. Then note all the company meetings you must attend for the month. Add any projects you're working on, their estimated completion dates, and reminders to follow up on them. If you're working on a large project, break it down into smaller pieces that you can accomplish each week. Taking large projects a week at a time helps you see your progress, and the one big project won't seem so oppressive.

In daily time planning, keep track of all activities as you go. Don't wait until 4:00 p.m. to try to remember what you did at 9:30 a.m. Be truthful. Don't play around with numbers or fake anything just so you can check it off. And don't overwhelm yourself with writing down every detail of your workday. You're not trying to write a book. Just note the key events and any information you simply wouldn't want to forget.

I strongly recommend that you do your planning where you conduct your business. If you wait until you get home, you won't have that phone number or other detail you need to record and you'll only half plan. If that means you sit in your car to plan, so be it. You may need triggers to remember everything you need to plan and those triggers will be most available to you at your place of business.

Organizing Your Workspace

One of the main causes of wasted time and lost income is disorganized office space. Believe it or not, clearing your desk also helps to clear your mind. When your mind is clear, you're more able to focus on one task at a time. And all you can accomplish is one thing at a time, anyway, so why try to do more.

So where do you start? Try the tips in the following sections.

Keep only immediate activities on your desk

Keep everything but your most pressing tasks out of sight. And keep everything you need for accomplishing the immediate tasks somewhere nearby (in a place you'll remember), so you don't waste time running hither and yon looking for what you need.

Take charge of your time

If you suffer innumerable interruptions, close your door. If you don't have a door, try earplugs or a headset attached to a cassette player to isolate yourself. Maybe your company will allow you to post a sign on your door saying something like this: "Unless you are a client with a large need, or have a fantastic lead for me, please let me do what I need to find those people." As a last resort, consider posting a snarling Doberman near your desk!

Develop your ability to focus on your work. Let your co-workers or family know that sometimes they simply cannot interrupt you. Don't answer your telephone — let voice mail be your receptionist for a while.

Make yourself less accessible. If you need to, set up a specific time of day for your associates to freely walk into your office; make all other times off-limits. If an associate drops by at a bad time, don't be afraid to look at your watch and say, "I'd love to catch up with you, but let's do it at 3:00." If what he has to tell you is important enough, he'll be happy to schedule the time. If it's not that important, he'll beg off, and you will have saved yourself from spending time listening to him.

Handle phone calls wisely

If the phone is not a necessary tool of your immediate business, remove it from your desk. Put it on a table behind you or even on the floor if you must — but get it out of your sight.

Not every phone call is an emergency. When the other party gets off the subject, or when the other party stays on the subject but is long-winded, try these techniques:

- ✔ **If you initiate the call, tell the person, "I have three things to cover with you."** If he starts to get sidetracked, you have the right to bring him back to one of your three topics.

- ✔ **If the other party initiates the call and you don't have a lot of time to give him, let him know his call is important, but that you were just heading out the door.** He doesn't need to know it was to get a glass of water. Get the basic information he needs to tell you and make an appointment to call him back. Unless it's an irate customer who has a total stoppage of an assembly line because of your equipment, most people will be willing to accept a callback. If they can't wait, it's an emergency and you'll have to handle it on the spot.

- ✔ **Call a long-winded person just before lunchtime or just before he goes home for the day.** If that's not possible, start your call by saying, "I'm really pressed for time, but I just wanted to let you know something," or, "I'm on my way to an appointment, but I wanted to touch base with you."

If you don't take control in these situations, you'll forever be at the mercy of others. And they will hardly ever have your best interest in mind.

Avoiding the Most Common Time Traps

You probably know some people who have raised time wasting to an art form. They have mastered the ability to fall into every time trap they encounter. Not surprisingly, these folks aren't the people who get things done, help the most people, or earn the biggest incomes in selling. If you want to get more *yes*es in your life, knowing — and avoiding — the following common time traps is a great place to start.

Desperately seeking what shouldn't be lost

A sure way to waste valuable time is to keep looking for something you desperately need because you were careless when you "put it away." Looking for lost items is the single biggest time waster for everyone. How many hours have you wasted looking for the scrap of paper you wrote an important phone number on or for the folder with all the referrals that your new client gave you? How about your sunglasses or your car keys? Ring any bells? Those few minutes here and there can really add up, so designate a specific place for every item you use regularly, and then make sure you always use it. If you always hang your keys on a hook by the door, you won't spend precious time searching for them.

Failing to do the job right the first time

Because of the demands salespeople place on themselves, they tend to rush through their paperwork and their planning of presentations without carefully checking or rechecking details. Get out of that habit right away. An old saying goes, "If you don't have time to do it right the first time, how will you find time to do it again?" Consider how much less time you need to do something right the first time than you need if you have to go back and do it over. Don't risk angering others with costly delays or mistakes caused by carelessly written paperwork. Champions double-check everything for accuracy and clarity.

Procrastinating

Procrastination can kill your career. Don't feel alone on this one; everyone procrastinates. Most people procrastinate because of fear. They fear making a mistake, so instead they do nothing. The trouble with doing nothing, though, is this: Doing nothing can only *produce* nothing. Mistakes can and will happen. Champions accept their mistakes and learn from their experiences.

If a client phones to report a problem with the product or service she acquired from a salesperson, what do most salespeople do? They put off the challenge until tomorrow. By then, though, when they do call to apologize and solve the problem, the client may be furious and vow never to do business with the salesperson's company again. So the salesperson has to work doubly hard and spend even more time with the client, just to diffuse her anger.

Always call an angry client immediately. The longer you wait, the more the situation worsens. Perhaps you've heard the saying that "a professional is someone who does things even when he doesn't want to." How true.

Making unnecessary or unnecessarily long phone calls

The telephone can be your greatest ally or your greatest enemy, especially when it comes to time management. Here are some ideas to help you deal with wasted time on the phone:

- ✔ **Set aside specific time each day to take and make phone calls.**

- ✔ **Set a time limit for your calls.**

- ✔ **Write down your objective for the phone call and focus on it.**

- ✔ **Have all your materials and information within reach before you pick up the phone.**

- ✔ **Put a specific time limit on all calls.**

- ✔ **Find polite but effective exit lines to help you get off the phone without interrupting the other person or abruptly ending the conversation.** For example, try saying, "Barbara, just one more thing before I hang up. . . ." Such a statement lets the person know that you're coming to the end of the call.

- ✔ **Let all your customers know exactly when you're available for them to call you.** This information should be printed on your business card and become a part of your e-mail signature information.

- ✔ **If you do business with someone who chatters and won't let you off the phone, whenever he calls, tell him you're in the middle of something extremely urgent and that you will call him back.** Then, call him just before the time when he leaves for the day. You'll be surprised how brief conversations with such people can become.

- ✔ **If you spend great amounts of time on the phone, or if you're in telemarketing, invest in a high-quality headset so you can use both hands to attend to other things while you're on the phone.**

If you think of the phone as a business tool, not unlike your computer, mobile phone, and calculator, you'll be able to form new habits for using it that should keep you out of that common time trap.

Holding unnecessary or unnecessarily long meetings

Attending too many nonproductive meetings can be a major time waster. If you're in management and you think you waste a great deal of your time in meetings, maybe you should reevaluate how often you need to meet with your people and what you need to accomplish when you do get together. Is a daily or weekly meeting really necessary? Or can more effective communications within the company eliminate the need for such meetings? Don't hold a $1,000 meeting to solve a $50 problem.

Many people have found that holding meetings standing up is highly productive. When people don't settle into comfortable chairs for the duration, they finish their business much more quickly. I once attended a meeting to determine when the best time for another meeting would be. See what I mean?

Attending client lunches that last for two or more hours

As with the phone, when you're out for lunch with clients, you need to develop ways to let them know that you've finished your business for today and that you must move on. For example, when you sit down for lunch at noon with a notorious "friendly afternoon waster," you can say something to the effect of "This works out great. I don't have another commitment until 1:30, so I have plenty of time to talk." Or, you *could* say, "Pound it down, Frank, I'm outta here in 30 minutes!" But somehow I just don't think those words would be quite as effective.

Engaging in negative thinking

Negative thoughts that produce negative talk are another big waste of time for salespeople. If you dwell on life's negatives, what do you think you can accomplish? I'm positive (ahem) that you will accomplish very little. Push negative thoughts from your mind. No one who was a negative thinker ever became a success in selling.

Instead of focusing on things you don't like, think about the positive things you can do. And by all means surround yourself with positive thinkers — their positive energy will rub off on you.

Not using driving time wisely

Most people in professional selling spend a lot of time in their cars driving from appointment to appointment. The average salesperson drives 25,000 miles a year for her job. That works out to about 500 hours a year, or about 16 weeks — your basic college semester.

So how can you make the best use of this time? Hundreds of educational programs are available on cassette. Publishing companies record books on cassette because people don't always have time to read a book. You can use this driving time to listen to programs on sales training, motivation, self-esteem, financial planning, small business strategies, foreign languages, classic literature, history, as well as a growing number of how-to programs and the latest popular novels. That way you're getting where you need to go, both literally and figuratively.

Not confirming appointments

I'm always amazed at how many people do not confirm appointments before they leave the office or their previous customer. Why do salespeople fail to confirm appointments? The old standby: fear. Some salespeople fear that, if they call, the person may say, "Never mind." Such salespeople would rather drive all the way to a customer's office and have the receptionist tell them that the customer got called out of town for the day.

A quick phone call before you leave not only can save you valuable selling time; it also tells the prospect that you're a professional with something valuable to say. If you handle it properly, your brief call to confirm may keep your appointment from being the one that gets canceled if your customer needs to change his decision-making schedule. When you call to confirm an appointment, do it this way:

> Hi, Jim. I've spent a lot of time preparing for our meeting, and I just thought I'd call to let you know that I'll be there right at 2:00. I think you'll be excited about what I have to show you.

Never say, "I'm just calling to confirm." When you let the decision-maker know how much time and effort you've put into preparing for this meeting, he'll feel guilty about canceling and be more likely to find a way to keep the appointment. And another benefit: Even if the decision-maker does have to cancel, you have him on the phone to immediately schedule another appointment. If for some reason you can't get to the person you have the appointment with, tell the person taking the message that you're on your way and you'll be on time. Ask the message taker to convey your message to the customer you're meeting with.

Always take the time to confirm your appointments. The time you save will be well worth the time you invest. The time you save frees up your time to prospect for new business or to take care of something else on your list.

Television

My experience with high achievers says that they do not waste time watching television. TV watching is probably the single least-productive activity in the American lifestyle. I'm not going to preach to you about the mindlessness of most of what's on TV these days, but I will say this: TV should be used properly. Some examples of how to use your TV are

- ✔ As a shelf on which to display your sales trophies and books and tapes related to selling.
- ✔ For watching selling-skills videos.
- ✔ For winding down from a productive day by enjoying a quality program with your loved ones.

What part of the word *no* can't you say?

Many of us just can't say no when people want a chunk of our time. But it's better that you say no to someone, and get the job done, than it is to say yes and not get the job done. Sometimes you're not even the most capable person to do the job. Professionals recognize their limitations. And when they bump into their limitations, they delegate requests for work that's outside their scope to colleagues who are more capable and more likely to complete the job efficiently. If you explain, with warmth and care, the fact that others are better suited to getting the job done properly, the people who ask you for favors will appreciate your honesty and your ability to refer them to someone trustworthy to do the job. As you become more successful, your time becomes more valuable, making it all the more important for you to learn when (and how) to say no.

Short of these reasons, I can't think of many others that are worth spending your valuable time watching TV. Only you know how much you really watch, so the next time an hour in front of the TV turns into three, stop and ask yourself what else you could've been doing with your time instead.

Handling Interruptions

You should always allow part of your day to work with people, support your co-workers, or help the company problem solve. But you also need to allow yourself some solo time, both at work and in your personal life. *Solo time* is time for whatever you need to do. It can be your time for emotional and physical health in your private life, as well as your most productive work time.

During your solo work time, if someone asks, "Do you have a minute?" just answer, "Not right now. Can it wait until 11:00?" By that time, most people who were looking for your help will have solved the problem themselves, or they will have realized that their problem wasn't all that important anyway.

Here are some tips for handling interruptions to your solo time:

- ✔ **Rearrange your office so that your desk is out of the line of sight from people who walk down the hallway.** If people don't see you as they're walking down the hall, they're less likely to stop in to chat.

- ✔ **Remove extra chairs from your office.** Position any necessary chairs as far away from your desk as possible. This way, people won't be tempted to sit down for long periods of time.

- ✔ **Place a large clock where you and any visitors can see it clearly.** A clock will help you — and your visitors — keep track of how much of your time they're taking up.

- ✔ **Don't look up when someone walks into your office.** This habit is hard to get into, but if you appear to be extremely busy and the potential interruption is nothing serious, most people will simply walk away. This advice may sound cold, but if you can't get your work done, your inefficiency will cause your customers to receive less service, and it will cause you to earn a lower income.

To get started on minimizing interruptions, keep an interruption log just for one day. In it, record the following:

- ✔ Who interrupted you
- ✔ What time he came and left

- ✔ How much time you wasted
- ✔ What you can do about it

If the same person is interrupting you all the time or the same type of challenge is continually presenting itself, taking a bit of time to train that person or to institute a new procedure can save you a lot of time in the long run.

When an occasional crisis comes up, deal with it quickly, and then go right back to your original schedule. You don't have to become antisocial around the office, but you may be surprised at how much more efficient you can be when you start taking back stray minutes here and there. Time flies . . . and you never hear the rustle of its gossamer wings.

Staying in touch with customers without losing time

In the past few years, many new timesaving products have enabled salespeople to become more and more efficient. Back in my selling days, I had to write down and keep track of an incredible amount of information. Who could have imagined back then that in 30 years we would have laptop computers, wireless phones, and the Internet! The high-tech revolution has accelerated the pace of all aspects of our lives. And, especially for salespeople, those changes are for the better.

If you invest in nothing else for your success, get a mobile phone. I can't imagine anyone in outside sales who wouldn't benefit greatly from this important timesaver. A mobile phone more than pays for itself in the greater income you will earn because of the improved service you can give your customers. With a mobile phone, your office can always reach you if a customer has a challenge or if a prospect you've been working with calls to say that she's ready to do business with you.

One thing to remember about mobile phones is to use proper business etiquette. Never take a mobile phone that's turned on into a presentation unless both you and the customer are waiting for an important call about that particular meeting. If your phone rings in the middle of the presentation and you stop to take the call, you in effect tell that person that he isn't as important as whoever is calling. And that's not the message you want to communicate. The same advice is true for pagers as well; set them on vibrate or turn them off when you're with a prospect.

Part V
You Can't Win 'Em All

The 5th Wave   By Rich Tennant

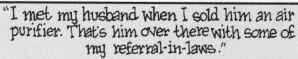

"I met my husband when I sold him an air purifier. That's him over there with some of my referral-in-laws."

In this part . . .

Rejection is a part of life, and it's certainly a part of selling. So in this part I help you handle the rejections you're bound to face and show you how each rejection actually means more success for you. I also help you focus on your long-term goals so that the daily setbacks of selling won't get you down.

Chapter 17

Handling Failure and Rejection

- -

- -

*N*o person has walked the earth who didn't experience rejection. It just hasn't happened. You're *bound* to experience rejection — it's as inevitable as death and taxes. What will separate you from all those who let themselves get sidetracked by rejection is your attitude toward it.

As you gain more experience in persuading, convincing, or selling others, you also create a protective shell that protects you from the slings and arrows of outrageous rejection. If you don't jump out there and take some of those arrows, you won't discover how to protect yourself, you'll take rejection personally, and you may end up depressing yourself right out of the persuasion business altogether.

So what's the best weapon to use when fighting those inadequate feelings created by failure and rejection? *Enthusiasm!* That one little word, a word you've heard so many times, can make the difference between being a highly successful champion in sales and an ineffective struggler. If you're just going through the motions of selling but doing so with little or no enthusiasm for the job, you'll be terribly disappointed with your results on payday. Your income in selling is in direct proportion to the amount of service you give others. Little service = little income. Lots of service = lots of income.

You won't have much success in serving others unless you're enthusiastic about what you do. As a matter of fact, if you aren't enthusiastic about every selling contact you make, you may as well save yourself and your prospects the time and trouble of showing up at all. You would have been just as productive staying home in your jammies and slippers, because clients won't want to get involved with you any more than you want to get them involved.

Dwindling enthusiasm isn't the only concern of professional persuaders, but it is the forerunner of many more difficulties that may short-circuit your career. To see what makes enthusiasm such a rare commodity in many sales situations, you need to examine where enthusiasm comes from and why it so easily gives up the ghost to depression and inactivity.

If people knew the secret of why enthusiasm wanes and depression creeps through the back door, they would easily see the enemy approach and prepare for its descent on their livelihoods. The hard part about battling the depression experienced because of failure and rejection is that it sneaks in disguised as a friend to bring you comfort, relaxation, or even fun, and you don't recognize depression for what it is: a total thief of your motivation to succeed. Instead of focusing on why depression happens, in this chapter I focus on how to overcome such feelings. Keep reading, and you'll see what motivates people and what you can do to increase your own levels of enthusiasm in your selling career and beyond.

Finding Out What Motivates You

Why do you do what you do? Philosophers, psychologists, and psychiatrists have had a field day with that question for hundreds of years. And they've come up with a short list of the most common reasons people give for doing whatever it is they do. Review the following sections so you can determine what *your* primary motivator is and then use that knowledge to spur yourself on to even greater success.

Money

Many professional salespeople admit to being motivated to sell because they enjoy lighting up the faces of the people they help to benefit from their offering. Few but the candid and outspoken, however, say that money motivates them to sell.

Give yourself permission right now to admit that money is a big motivator. Being money conscious is okay — as long as the money you make is in direct proportion to the service you give your clients. If that's not the case with you (if you're raking in the dough but providing poor service), your money will soon disappear — as will your motivation to strive toward greater achievements in sales.

Money can be one of your motivators, or even your primary motivator, but it cannot be the be-all and end-all of all your sales transactions. Many top producers look at the amount of money they make as a reflection of the excellent service and high sales standards they develop over the years in their industries. When champion salespeople notice a decline in income, they look to improve service and product knowledge instead of wasting time being depressed about how a drop in income could have happened to them.

Security

Many people say they work to have security. But what exactly does that mean? Security is a false motivator, because there are no guarantees in life, much less in sales. So when it comes right down to it, there is no such thing as security. In fact, you are only as secure as your ability to handle insecurity.

That statement is so important that it bears repeating:

RED FLAG

You are only as secure as your ability to handle insecurity.

No matter who you are, you've never been totally secure. I don't care how successful you are — you've experienced fear and want somewhere along the way. Fear and want can even motivate you to achieve. So it isn't the state of being free of these feelings that contributes to security, but rather how you deal with the insecurities that confront you.

The key to getting what you want may be the ability to give up what you have. If you're bound and determined that you will never take a chance to further your career, then you may as well get out of sales right now, because taking risks is what selling is all about. If you can't give up what you have, then keep it; but resign yourself to the knowledge that you will never go much farther up the ladder of success.

REMEMBER

Most famous and powerful people who have acquired a great deal of security or money have also lost as much (if not more) than they have made. What sets these people apart from the average worker is that they were willing to take the chance in order to become all that they could be, whereas the average worker is not willing to take the necessary risks.

RED FLAG

Great salespeople follow the same pattern. Be willing to give up what you have for what you can attain. Be a risk taker. You may wonder how you ever find security if you're constantly taking risks. With whatever semblance of security you ever find will come the knowledge that you create your own destiny. Your success and security are determined primarily by your ability to overcome the setbacks that your career in sales hands you. And, believe me, in sales you'll have plenty of time to test your ability to be a risk taker.

Achievement

Everyone wants to achieve something. Some people strive only for modest goals, while others shoot for the moon — but all are in gear to achieve. In fact, few people are born who wander aimlessly through life without, at the very least, the desire to achieve the basic needs of food and shelter.

All people believe that they should get what they deserve, and unfortunately, many of them feel they're deserving of greatness, whether they work for it or not. In those moments when you're brutally honest with yourself, you probably realize that you usually get what you deserve.

Achievement isn't always measured monetarily. Instead, you can measure it by the influence and power you wield or by the humanitarian efforts you give to those in need. Achievement means different things to different people — but it's usually a great motivator.

Recognition

For most people, the need for recognition begins in childhood. Think about it: When you were 5 or 6 years old, you probably stood on your head, played dress-up, or did other clever little-kid things that adults thought were adorable, just so that you would get attention. Some children have even been known to eat bugs or destroy things, all for the sake of recognition.

Not only do people have a need for recognition, but they also like to be the ones to do the recognizing. Look at much of the media today. Whether the recognition is negative or positive, the results are similar. Think about how most people recognize the evil but well-publicized face of Charles Manson more quickly than they do the face of someone who has *positively* changed history, someone like Neil Armstrong, for example.

Recognition is a tricky business — but it's a motivator nonetheless!

Acceptance from others

Relying on acceptance from others as motivation can be a dangerous thing. The day you rise above the masses as a top producer is the same day that others stop trying to climb up to your level. So what do they do instead? They try to pull you down. The old adage "It's lonely at the top" is true.

When was the last time you heard people say or do things to bring a person down who is already down in the dumps? It just doesn't happen that way. You can always find someone to tell you, "Oh that won't work!" or to say, "Well, that may have worked for them, but do you really believe that you can carry it off?"

Try to surround yourself with positive people who support you in your efforts toward a successful career. Why not make it your philosophy to keep company with people who have similar goals and desires as yours? Try to get the acceptance of the people whom you know are good for you — and try to get the dismissal of the people who are not. When you think about it, how many people in your lifetime have you accepted advice from who are more messed up than you? Stay away from the negative people: They only pull your opportunities down the tubes with them.

Self-acceptance

When you accept yourself and you're happy with the person you are, you experience a freedom you never thought possible. You are free to do things your own way or not to do them at all. You are free to enjoy life and all the wonders it has to offer. You are free of the damaging effects of rejection and failure. Just remember that many of these motivators work together.

- ✔ You cannot get recognition if you have achieved nothing.
- ✔ You cannot attempt the things you want to achieve without first having a sense of security in your ability to do so.
- ✔ You cannot earn money without giving service. In fact, in sales, money is a scoreboard reflection of the amount of service you give.

Most people measure their success by how much money they have, so self-acceptance runs neck and neck with the amount of money they accumulate. When you truly accept yourself, you can do what you *want* to do and not what you think you *should* do. Life is much sweeter when you accept yourself — and wonderful things and people seem to gravitate toward you.

Like people, all motivators are interrelated. You're not in this alone, so what you do or don't do may profoundly affect many others in your sphere of influence. Keep that in mind the next time you're tempted to do something you instinctively know is not the best thing for you to do. Whichever way you look at it, you are not alone in this universe and the ripple effect is alive and well, especially in the sales industry.

Knowing What Discourages You

If motivators are what make people move forward toward successful sales careers and de-motivators cause them to stop dead in their tracks or even go backward, why doesn't everyone just do the things that motivate them? Believe it or not, it's because the average human being is more de-motivated than motivated. Negativity is kind of like gravity — a powerful force that can hold you back and requires tremendous effort to overcome.

Just as you need to know what motivates you to succeed, you also need to recognize the danger signals that will bring your career to a halt. Here are four of the most powerful de-motivators that stop people from achieving.

The eternal conflict between motivators and de-motivators

Motivators and de-motivators are powerful opposing forces that work to contradict themselves in your selling situations. If you're unable to maintain a high level of enthusiasm, you de-motivate and enter your danger zone. When you are in this place, one of two things happens: Either you become withdrawn or you become hostile. Not a pretty picture, is it?

On the other hand, when you're motivated, happily striving for security, recognition, and the other motivators, you're more likely to be in your comfort zone and encouraged to keep performing, reaching ever higher levels of achievement.

Of course, discomfort can be a catalyst to get you moving, because your main goal in life (if you're like most people) is being comfortable. But when the momentum builds, your enthusiasm will carry you to a new comfortable level of performance.

Turning negative situations into positive ones is what makes selling so exciting. Entering the office of a hostile or withdrawn executive and leaving him an hour later with a smile on his face and a positive attitude with which to face the rest of the day is really a kick. What an experience!

Loss of security

A big de-motivator for many people is the fear of losing their security — financially or otherwise. But when you begin a career in sales, or when you take your career up a notch, you often have to spend money to make money. So instead of thinking of this as a loss of security, think of it as a business investment, an investment in your future. Even large corporations spend money on training their sales force and creating goodwill with prospective clients, and you're not any different. To build your business, you need to invest time and money — and you have to rid yourself of the fear of losing security. Only then will you truly succeed.

Self-doubt

Self-doubt is a big de-motivator in selling. I can hear what some of your family members probably said the day you told them you were going into sales: "What? Are you crazy?" or, "Selling . . . it's feast or famine!" or, "Can you get me stuff wholesale?" They have yet to discover what you and I already know: Selling is one of the few careers left that offers great security — when you overcome self-doubts and learn the strategies of selling, that is.

Most beginners in sales busy themselves with the unnecessary question of "What did I do wrong?" when they do not succeed in their selling attempts. The difference between champions and novices is that champions ask themselves a different question: "What did I do *right?*" When the champion examines what was right about the sale, she can easily keep doing what was right over and over again. The champion in sales has learned this important lesson:

> The only way you ever learn what to do right in selling is by doing it wrong, keeping your enthusiasm, figuring out what to do, and overcoming that pain. Just keep on keeping on!

The only way to overcome self-doubts is to face them, look them in the eye, and stare them down by doing the exact opposite of what they make you feel like doing. Don't give in to your self-doubts. Develop strong habits such as well-honed sales skills, post-sales analyses, and keeping good notes for yourself.

Fear of failure

A great many people are so afraid of failing that they just quit trying. Now there's a surefire way never to experience failure — never attempt anything in the first place! Of course, you won't experience any successes, either, so you throw out the baby with the bathwater if you let this de-motivator get the better of you. You will never *not* close the sale if you never meet the client.

I recommend that you live by this principle:

Do what you fear the most — and you control your fear.

If you're afraid of one of the required aspects of selling, such as phoning for appointments, you're going to need to face it down if you truly want to succeed in sales. Almost anything you do that you once feared doing turns out to be much easier to do than you thought. The process gets easier each time you make yourself do what you fear until, one day, you forget how badly you feared what you feared so much only a few months before. (Did you follow that?)

Control your fears, and you will receive such gratification that soon you will burn with anticipation to do what you once dreaded. Bungee jumping, anyone?

Change

Change is a fierce opponent of progress. You've probably often heard statements such as these: "We've always done it this way," "You'll get used to it — it's just my way of doing things," or "We prefer to stay with the standard procedure." Workers really don't favor the old ways, though. Instead, what they really favor is resisting the pain in change. If they only knew for certain that the potential benefits in making change far outweigh the pains, their resistance would quickly dissipate.

The hardest thing for most salespeople to do is to prospect. Wouldn't hanging around the lobby or the office and waiting for people to come through the doors begging for your product be wonderful? Dream on!

The champion salesperson's anti-failure formula

What's the first word your mother and father taught you when you were a baby? *No.* Ah, those were the days, now weren't they? And why do you suppose *no* was the first word you learned? Because your parents wanted to protect you from painful experiences.

But all you knew as a child was that *no* kept you from getting what you wanted. So, as you grew older and kept hearing *no,* you didn't give up quite as easily as when you were a baby. You caught on to this persuasion stuff early on when you realized that *no* doesn't necessarily mean "No! Absolutely not! Never! No way!" and you tried to cajole your parents to see things differently — even if it involved holding your breath and turning several lovely shades of blue.

The same thing happens in your selling career. When you begin in sales and you hear *no,* you think it's the end of the discussion. Some beginning salespeople even relate stories of how they never got completely through their prepared presentation because the moment the client said *no* the salespeople slid out the door quicker than a pat of butter on hot pancakes.

As they matured in sales, though, their stories changed. *No* took on different meanings. *No* came to mean many things besides a plain-old, final, everyday *No.* These salespeople began to realize that *No* could mean, "Slow down," "Explain that part a little more," "You haven't presented the feature I'm most interested in yet," "You need to ask more questions about my likes and dislikes," or, "I don't want to part with that much money right now." These salespeople realized — as one of their first steps toward professionalism — that they could overcome *all* those things instead of having to slip out the back door with their tails tucked between their legs.

Use the following champion's anti-failure formula only when you know you have no chance to get to *Yes* during your meeting. If you follow this formula, you will be able to look at every *No* you receive as money in your pocket. Here's the formula:

Suppose that you earn $100 for the closing of a sale. So 1 sale = $100. For the sake of this formula, imagine that, for every 10 contacts you make, you receive 1 sale. So 10 contacts = 1 sale. So every contact, whether it results in a *Yes* or a *No,* is worth $10. Every rejection you get brings you that much closer to that $100.

So what does that knowledge do for you? If you concentrate on it, you will see every *No* as a moneymaker instead of getting down on yourself when the prospect gives you a *No.* Instead of getting angry or feeling as though you've wasted an hour of your day, think of a *No* as being handed $10 and moving you one step closer to your goal.

Here's another way to look at it: If you work with a client who has said *No* many times, but you persist in your attempts for a *Yes,* then you may sit through $200 to $300 dollars' worth of *No*s in that one meeting when it results in a long-term sales relationship. Just keep asking. Don't fear rejection. Welcome the admiration the client will have for you when he realizes that you hung in there 'til the end.

If you can push yourself to make your calls, get out of the office, meet with the people who need to hear about your offering, and call back the difficult clients you sometimes wish you'd never heard of, you're on the road to sales success. You don't have to depend on or blame your company when business is bad. You are responsible for your own success or failure, whatever the case may be — so take charge.

By the way, doing what you don't want to do is what you are paid the most to do. You really have to *want* to change. Being satisfied with yourself today is still crucial, but if you want more tomorrow, then you must be willing to put up with the pain of change. According to Dr. Maxwell Maltz, former plastic surgeon and developer of psycho-cybernetics, it takes 21 days to effect change. So you'll need about 21 days of concentrating and studying the material in this book for this material to become a part of you. No pain, no gain.

Overcoming Failure

As a salesperson (especially if you're new to sales) you'll experience nonsuccess (another word for failure) at least once or twice a day. How you handle that experience will determine how far and how fast you'll start seeing sales or persuasion success. In the following sections, I recommend five strategies for overcoming failure, specific attitudes to adopt to help you look at failure in a new light.

View failure as a learning experience

When you demonstrate your product to a disinterested party, when you are rejected by a prospect, or when you thought you had your offering sold and the transaction falls through, you can react in one of two ways: You can get angry and be unproductive, or you can investigate the reasons for the failure. I recommend the second of these two options, because when you discover what went wrong, you can prevent those pitfalls from happening again.

Look at the tremendous negatives Thomas Edison overcame when he invented the light bulb. Edison performed over 1,000 failed experiments before he succeeded. But because of his persistence, today we have the light bulb, an invention that has changed our quality of life. Can you imagine receiving a big fat *No* to what you want to achieve more than 1,000 times — and still persisting? What fortitude! The priceless part of the story of the light bulb, though, is Edison's comments in response to questions about how he felt after experiencing all that failure: "I did not fail a thousand times. I only learned a thousand ways that it wouldn't work." You see? It's all in the way you look at things.

Think of failure as the negative feedback you need in order to change your direction

Negative feedback is really just the information you need to get on course again. What a delightful way to look at rejection! When a client never gives you any negative feedback and loves everything presented in your offering yet still decides not to own, you have nowhere to turn. But when a client tells you what she doesn't like, you have a place to start.

Think of yourself as a torpedo being guided by a machine that feeds it negative information only to keep the torpedo on course. If it veers to the left, the machine says *No* and guides the torpedo back on path. Through a series of *No* corrections, the torpedo makes it to its proper destination.

But what if the torpedo's feelings were hurt from all this negative input and it entered its danger zone? What are the two things that occur when you enter into *your* danger zone? Withdrawal or hostility. So what would happen if the torpedo decided it couldn't take any more rejection and returned home? *Bam* to the mother ship. Or what if the torpedo took the rejection personally and decided to take it out on the closest target? An innocent victim gets hurt.

If you take negatives personally, not only will you not reach your destination, but others around you will share in your untimely explosions. That's why some salespeople lose it right in the midst of their colleagues and why some just stop showing up at the office and stay in bed all day feeling sorry for themselves. When the torpedoes hit the wrong target, everybody loses!

See failure as an opportunity to develop your sense of humor

Can you remember having an absolutely disastrous meeting with a prospect? At the time, you wanted to crawl in a hole and never see daylight again. But what did you find yourself doing about two weeks down the road? Sure enough, after a little time to heal, you told the story to your peers, embellishing it to provide special effects, and everyone — including you — got a good laugh.

When you're dealing with failure, you have to learn to laugh sooner. Laughter is a powerful tool in healing hurt feelings and wounded pride. As a matter of fact, when you share your humorous stories with other salespeople, you find out that similar things have happened to them. Misery loves company, you know!

The Champion's Creed

To keep your attitude up when things are down, follow what I call my Champion's Creed. I dubbed my students as champions many years ago because they were striving to reach that status in their selling careers by attending my seminars and learning the techniques I used to become successful in sales. This creed was created for them, and because you're striving to improve your selling skills, it'll work for you, too. Here it is:

I'm not judged by the number of times I fail but by the number of times I succeed. And the number of times I succeed is in direct proportion to the number of times I fail and keep trying.

This advice is so true. If you focus on your successes through your success journal and sales records, you'll have an easier time recovering every nonsuccess you encounter.

Look at failure as an opportunity to practice your techniques and perfect your performance

What happens when you do everything you were supposed to do and the client *still* doesn't decide to own your offering? What has she given you? That's right! She's given you an opportunity to practice and perfect your selling skills.

View failure as the game you must play to win

Selling is a percentage game — a game of numbers. The person who sees more people and faces more rejection also makes more money. So, even if you haven't gambled before, you begin to do just that when you get into the game of sales. With every *No* you hear, you're one step closer to hearing a *Yes*.

In life, it is not the number of times you fail that count, but the number of times you succeed. And selling is no different.

Chapter 18

Setting Goals to Stay Focused

. . . .

In This Chapter

▶ Achieving balance in the goals you set

▶ Following through with your goals

▶ Starting all over by setting new goals after you've achieved others

. . . .

Success should be something you don't just kinda-sorta want to reach, but something you *must* reach. Those who achieve the most, burn with a *have to* not a *want to*.

If you have no concrete goals and you've been succeeding in spite of yourself, just think of how much *more* success you would enjoy if you set your sights on a definite path and had a specific time frame in which you expected to reach your destination. If you're a newcomer to sales, and you think you don't need to set goals — think again. The sooner you map a course of success, the more likely you are to reach what you want.

Even though you don't need to set goals in order to reach some level of selling success, most professionals who fail to set goals reach a peak in their selling skills and lack either the motivation or the direction to go beyond it. They never move upward to a higher selling status. What they don't know — and what you *should* know — is that goals give you three distinct benefits that help you succeed:

✔ They keep you on track.

✔ They let you know when and what to celebrate.

✔ They give you a focused plan to sell by.

And, if nothing else, goals let others know what they have to shoot for to keep up with your standards of selling. In this chapter, I give you the information you need to make goal setting a part of your daily life.

Setting Realistic and Effective Goals

When you first considered a career in sales, you probably had some vague notions of success in mind. Now you need to turn those notions into specific, vivid pictures. Those pictures will entice you when you feel like packing it all in and running away to a deserted isle somewhere in the South Pacific to lie on the beach watching your toenails grow.

When you're setting goals, give yourself the time and privacy you need in order to think about what would make you happy, what would motivate you to sell with the big boys and girls. Goal setting should be fun, so don't make it so difficult that you end up setting no goals at all, out of fear that the goals you set will be wrong. So what if they are? Are the goals police going to come to your front door and ask to do an audit of your goals? Probably not. Goals are maps — and sometimes maps change. They include unfinished roads or roads that you need to detour around while improvement is underway. The road map you create for yourself is no different.

When you're in the beginning stages of goal setting, you need to remember two things:

- ✔ **The goal must be better than your best — but believable.** Don't set a goal that you don't think you can reach. The trick to setting goals is to make them high enough to push you to strong levels of performance, yet reasonable enough that you can envision reaching them. If you set goals you don't think you can reach, then you most likely won't pay the price to reach them when the going gets tough.

- ✔ **Set goals based on productivity, not on production.** If you set goals based on the money you want to make, you're setting yourself up for failure. It's better to set productivity goals; they'll give you a guideline for how many people you must contact in a week or how many calls you must make. Productivity precedes production anyway, so if you set production goals you're jumping the gun. Actively pursue your productivity goals and increased production will result. For example, you are productive if you make 20 phone calls today. Even if you only spoke with three people, you've been productive. You are productive if you mailed information and thank-you notes to those three people, even if you didn't generate a sale from those contacts — yet.

Keeping these two rules of goal setting in mind will help you form and stay committed to what is important in your life.

Breaking Down Your Goals into Smaller Pieces

When you're setting goals, always begin with long-term goals and work backward to medium-range and short-term goals. Your long-term goals are probably the hardest to set anyway, so if you set those first, you accomplish the tough stuff right up front.

Long-term goals

Long-term goals should be 20-year projections. Granted, if you're 75, your 20-year goal may be just to plant both feet on the ground each morning. No matter how young or old you are, picturing what you want your life to be like 20 years from today is difficult. But set them anyway — keeping in mind that your goals may change.

Three areas you may want to consider when you set your long-term goals are personal accomplishments, status symbols, and net worth. When you set long-term goals, be specific. Instead of saying, "In 20 years, I want to live in a large house and be financially independent," say something like this:

> In 20 years, in June 2021, I want to live in a large beachfront house by the Pacific Ocean, on property that covers about 50,000 square feet, and I want to own it free and clear with $1,000,000,000 in the bank.

Get the picture? Your long-range goals don't have to be this grand, but they do need to be this *specific*.

Medium-range goals

When you finish setting your long-term goals, cut them in half and set medium-range goals for about ten years down the road. Compare your 10-year goals to your 20-year goals, and then determine the activity you need to keep to make those goals a reality. Then, divide your ten-year goals into five-year goals. Your medium-range goals will be your largest and perhaps fuzziest area, the goals you'll probably have to adjust the most frequently.

Short-term goals

Surprise, surprise: Your short-term goals will demand most of your attention. For best results with short-term goals, never set them for any longer than 90 days. Short-term goals for anything longer than 90 days aren't immediate enough to create a sense of urgency. Immediately after you set short-term goals, you need to start taking steps to reach them. That way, they take root as real, not-to-be-denied entities in your mind — not tomorrow, not next week, but as soon as you make them. Your 90-day goals should then be broken down into 60-day goals, 30-day goals, and eventually, the steps you can put in your planner to take today to achieve them.

Set a well-balanced diet of goals with the help of your family

Setting personal as well as career goals is important in order to keep your life well balanced. If all your goals are business goals, you'll have trouble taking time out for family and friends because you'll always be pushing toward the next career goal.

Although I encourage you to pursue your business goals with fervor, I also encourage you *not* to pursue them at the expense of family, friends, or time out for yourself. If you do, you risk becoming so single-minded that you eliminate the human qualities you need in order to succeed in sales. Nobody wants to do business with someone who is too busy to understand and care about his needs. Setting personal goals gives you life both in and after business.

As a way to make sure that your goals are well balanced, let your family help you set them. If you do, they'll more likely understand when, say, you have to spend a late night working or invest in a two-day training seminar. Your family will be more willing to share in your sacrifices if you let them share in the celebration of achieving your goals as well.

Another benefit from involving the entire family is that they hold you accountable for your part of the goal and will do what it takes to motivate you. Have you ever thought that sleeping an extra few hours is just what you needed, only to have your spouse encourage you to get up and get busy earning your share of that trip that you both set as a mutual short-term goal? You knew you should get up, but your immediate desire for sleep clouded your judgment. How do you think you'd feel, and what message would you send to your spouse, by showing him that sleeping is more important to you than working to achieve shared goals?

Remember that your family and friends are your true support system. Share your goals, your successes, and even your failures with them. When you have made a sale, scheduled a big appointment, or just had a presentation go sour, give someone you care about a call and share the moment. She will know that you are thinking of her throughout your day, and you'll feel a whole lot better.

For example, if one of your short-term goals is to buy a Cadillac, then go down and order one that you can pick up in 90 days. That will light a fire under you, don't you think? Talk about making it a reality! If you feel too pressured to reach a goal right after you set it, then you're not sure you can reach your goals. You see, if your belief were real, ordering the car would just excite you to get actively involved in its achievement.

Putting Your Goals in Writing

When you've set your goals, you need to make your final commitment to your goals by putting them in writing. This step is the single, most vital one in goal setting. Writing down your goals makes them something you can grab onto. The day you write down your goals is the day you commit yourself to reaching them. Until they're in writing, they're merely wishes and dreams. After you write them down, your mind will start seeking out whatever it takes to make those goals a reality.

Writing down your goals helps you do what I call *in-your-face goals viewing*. For maximum effect, put your list of goals where you can look at them often. When you'd rather nap, remind yourself of the importance of getting your behind out of bed and doing what you know you have to do to succeed. Each time you accomplish a step toward achievement, visibly scratch a line through that step. That's the basic formula for proper in-your-face goals viewing (and you thought this book didn't come with any extras, didn't you?). In-your-face goals viewing is great if you need a tangible reminder of how far you've come toward your goals. What's better, it you to complete the effort. No matter how tough the going gets, you don't want to put your foot on a banana peel when you're right at the brink of reaching your goals.

The harder you work toward a goal, the sweeter the taste of success. Don't think for a second that your road to success won't be painful at times. If you don't experience at least a little bit of stretching to achieve your goals, you probably haven't set them high enough to challenge you. And if your goals *aren't* high enough, then they may be holding you back, making you content to reach levels that are no big deal for you. So when the road gets rocky, dig in your heels and let nothing distract you from your goals. The people who persevere today produce tomorrow. Giving up immediate gratification or postponing what would satisfy you for today just for a promise of greater things down the road isn't natural. In today's instant-gratification society, long-term gains are almost unheard of. But don't sell yourself short by settling for what you know will bring you only temporary satisfaction. If you settle for less than your goals, that's exactly what you end up with — less.

If you're determined and enthusiastic about your goals, you won't settle or waver. Your resolve helps you keep a vivid picture in your mind of what you want to happen and how you will make it happen. If your imagination isn't vivid enough, cut out pictures or write detailed descriptions of your goals so that you can refer to them when you get distracted. The more reminders you force yourself to bump into, the more determined you are — and the more determined you are, the more goals you will achieve.

Take all of your goals extremely seriously, no matter how small each goal. Reward yourself and congratulate yourself for starting the habit of planning your life. You will reap unbelievable rewards.

If you want your life to change, then *you* have to change it — or you'll stay pretty much the same as you are. So set some goals that turn you on and get your life into gear. All you have to do is make the effort to do it. You can change and become or do anything you want. Just want!

Follow these four steps in goal achieving, and you'll be on the straight-and-narrow road to reaching your goals:

- ✔ Put your goals in writing.
- ✔ Vividly imagine your goals and create a clear picture of them in your mind.
- ✔ Set goals that you want more than anything.
- ✔ Commit to your goals sincerely and completely.

If you do all four of these things, and if you review your goals daily, you will soon find yourself making great headway toward achieving them. You will be focused both consciously and subconsciously on seeking out the means to your chosen end.

Figuring Out What to Do When You Achieve Your Goals

The funny thing about achieving your goals is that, as you get close to achieving them and you look back, the struggle to achieve them doesn't seem as difficult as you had originally thought. Time has a way of blurring the gory details of the daily grind. For example, think back now to what you were doing five years ago. Now think forward five years. Which seems longer? If you're like most people, the future always seems to loom out there longer because you don't know everything that will happen and how your life will take shape.

Signing a contract with yourself

An effective tool to help you reach your goals is a binding contract in which you commit to reaching your goals. Such contracts are hard to recognize in the wild, but if you see something that looks like this, you're probably face to face with a bona fide self-contract. Feel free to use this one to make a deal with yourself — and be sure to hold yourself to it.

Date: _____ 20_____

Name: _____

The undersigned proposes to furnish all materials and perform all labor necessary to complete the following goal:

_____
_____
_____
_____
_____
_____
_____
_____
_____
_____
_____

I hereby swear to start today to reach out and do more with my life and achieve the greatness that I know lies within me, which is waiting to be brought out.

From this day forward, I will not deny myself any longer. Today is the day when I finally get the guts to do what I know I must do and quit taking the easy way out. I will pay the price that is necessary to reach this goal because I know the pain of not fulfilling myself is greater than the pain of doing any job, no matter how hard the job may be.

I understand that I will reach my life's plan by reaching one goal at a time, each smaller goal putting me one step closer to my greater future. I understand that each contract I fulfill always puts me one step closer to what I want out of life, and I will not have to settle for what others give me or for just earning a living. I have the power to change my life.

_____
Signature

As I endorse this contract, I understand that my future is in my hands only and I can look to no one else for its fulfillment.

(continued)

(continued)

Acceptance

Upon the completion of this goal, I congratulate you for proving that you can do anything that you want and be anything that you want. You also can get anything you want as long as you know what it is.

You have taken one more step toward being the person you dream of. You may take pride in knowing that you have the backbone to plan and reach a goal.

You are now one step closer to your major goal. As you know, major goals are just a string of successful small goals that lead you to the top.

_____

Signature

Date Fulfilled: _____ 20_____

Terms and Conditions

1. Any goal you ever include in this contract, no matter how small, must be treated with great respect, because the achievement of goals builds your character and self-image.

2. This contract must be filled out in full and dated with starting and completion dates.

3. Your goal must be precise and explicit. It must paint a very clear picture of what you want and when you want it.

4. In front of the mirror every day, you must read all of your contracts that you have not completed, and you must read them with great conviction so as to embed your goals into your subconscious mind.

5. When you reach a goal, you must sign the contract and then write, in large red letters on the face of the contract, "This contract fulfilled." You must save all fulfilled contracts and keep them in order by date completed, so that you may see a pattern of growth.

6. You must remember that you can be as great as anyone, but you also must remember that you have a plan. Each goal in your plan, no matter how small, must become part of your larger plan; when it does, it may then help you to turn your beautiful dreams into a fantastic, rewarding life.

7. Do not make conflicting goals, such as "I will spend more time at home" and "I will double my sales," because they may not work together and may cause frustration in your life.

8. Your goals must entice you so intensely that they ignite your soul and make you burn with enthusiasm.

9. You cannot reach a destination if you do not know how to get there. Each goal becomes a stopping point or starting point on the road map of your life, which in turn becomes the blueprint for your every success. If you don't have a blueprint, how are you going to build your life?

But when you get in the habit of setting goals, you'll find yourself looking toward the next set of goals before you close on those you're about to achieve — and that's a good thing to do. ***Remember:*** Success is in the journey, not the arrival. You don't want to wait to set new goals until you're done with the ones you have today. Keeping your eyes on the future and the opportunities it can bring your way brings with it many advantages. Soon you get so caught up in the goal-setting process that achieving your goals becomes reward enough.

When you achieve your goals, one of the first things you want to do is celebrate your success. When you celebrate, keep these suggestions in mind:

- ✔ **Include in your celebration everyone you involved in the setting and accomplishing of your goals.** They were there with you in the beginning, and they'll be eager to rejoice with you in your successes.

- ✔ **Celebrate in proportion to your achievement.** For example, don't give yourself a trip to Hawaii for calling a hundred people in one month. A hundred calls in a month is part of your job, and you know it. A good reward for this accomplishment may be a dinner at a special restaurant or a new shirt and tie (for the gents) or a dress (for the ladies).

- ✔ **Ready yourself for a letdown after you achieve a difficult goal.** Indulging the natural tendency for a letdown is okay, but don't allow the letdown to run too long. The longer you remain inactive, the harder it is to get revved up again. Play a while, but then head back to work. After all, if you sell something that you enjoy, your work is just an extension of your hobbies anyway.

After you celebrate, start working on the new goals you set for yourself. Keep records of all your successes. When they start piling up, you'll want to do whatever it takes to add to that file. Remember the difficulties you overcame while you accomplished each preceding goal; mentally reward yourself for your successes. When you do set the next goal, push yourself just a tad more. Always stretch yourself; that's what keeps you growing in sales. If everything's too easy, you get bored — and selling stops being a hobby and looks more and more like a job.

The harder the goal is to achieve, the more value you find in its achievement. Don't wait until you close on one goal before you set your next one. Have your new goal already in place so that you're ready to work the necessary steps to make you succeed again.

The Law of Expectation

Most people have experienced the phenomenon of fulfilled expectations, but they tend to shrug off fulfilled expectations as coincidences instead of planned, envisioned events.

The Law of Expectation states otherwise:

> **When you think something will happen, and you feel strongly about it, you will bring about its happening.**

I think this is where the phrase "Mind over matter" came from. The Law of Expectation works with simple things, as well as with matters as complicated as achieving your 20-year goals.

For example, one evening a friend of mine left home to take a walk. All she took with her were the keys to her apartment (and, of course, the clothes on her back and the shoes on her feet). She had been out for about an hour and was returning home right around dark when she felt a grate beneath her feet. No sooner did she feel the grate than the thought crossed her mind that if she dropped her keys into the grate she would not be able to get back into her apartment because her husband was away on a three-day business trip. What do you suppose happened? You got it! The keys fell into the grate and left my friend with the dilemma of finding the best way to break into her own apartment.

Now because my friend learns from every situation, even the negative ones, after the whole ordeal she sat down to record what her experience had taught her. One of the things she learned was the power of her thoughts. But she learned something else just as important. When she finally broke into her apartment, she realized just how easy the task really was. The next day she went to the hardware store and bought various goodies that, after she installed them, made breaking in difficult if not impossible. She avoided a dangerous situation (a possible burglary) by being open to learning from what began as a negative experience.

So be your own fortune-teller. Predict your own success by making your goals happen. The more you believe in your own success, the more you will do to turn your goals into realities. Success is no accident! You plan it, you work on it, you monitor it, and you adjust it to enable yourself to enjoy a productive and prosperous life. People may look at the success you've spent years accomplishing and see you as an overnight wonder. They may even try to tell you how lucky you are to have the things you have. Well, I say you create your own luck. You control your own destiny. Lady Luck has little to do with your success, and she shouldn't get the credit for your achievements.

Part VI
The Part of Tens

The 5th Wave   By Rich Tennant

"I don't take 'no' for an answer. Nor do I take 'whatever', 'as if', or 'duh'."

In this part . . .

These short chapters are packed with quick ideas about selling and persuading that can be read any time you have a few minutes. Here you'll find information on the most common sales mistakes (so you can be sure to avoid them), the characteristics of professional persuaders, and ways to master the art of selling. I also give you some fantastic Web sites to turn to for even more information. Champion salespeople know how to make the most of every minute, so if you find yourself waiting to meet with a prospect, use the time to read a chapter from this part and you're sure to gain useful information in the process.

Chapter 19

The Ten Biggest Sales Mistakes

*E*veryone makes mistakes in life. And you should *expect* to make some when you're trying something new. In this chapter, I share with you the ten most common mistakes others who have gone before you have made, so the start of your journey may be a bit more successful.

Not Understanding Selling

In most cases, the only contact a business has with the outside world is through its salespeople — and the only reason to have salespeople is for them to sell the product or service. Selling is done through the gathering and sharing of information via professional skills. Those skills help the prospective client make decisions that move them to making the final ownership decision.

This observation may seem elementary, but if you walk into most small businesses in the world today you may find it difficult to find someone who can tell you the company's current style of selling and how they are analyzing it for improvement. They may even have trouble describing their ideal customer to you. You can't know too much about why customers do and don't buy your product or service — and gaining that knowledge is a function of selling.

Professional sales training doesn't involve tips for becoming pushy or aggressive. Any sales trainer who would teach persuaders to become pushy and aggressive would have to be classified as incompetent. Professional salespeople or persuaders are low-key, service-oriented, and relationship-builders.

Expecting Things to Improve by Themselves

Having incompetent or untrained people serving customers is bad business. You may as well toss your advertising dollars to the wind if your people aren't prepared to sell and service prospects when they contact your business. The same goes for individuals. If you aren't satisfied with your personal rate of persuasion or volume of sales, you *can* improve. To admit that you can improve and then *not* take any steps to correct the situation is simply foolish.

Sales skills are not a gift of birth. They are learned skills that anyone can master with a little study and work. Start watching others in persuasion situations wherever you go. Ask yourself why some persuaders are good and why some are bad. You will find that identifying why they are bad is much easier — when persuaders are bad, you can usually tell that they're incompetent, that they don't know what they're talking about, or that they're just making mistakes in general. But when salespeople are well trained and highly skilled, things seem to move forward so smoothly that spotting the sale happening is almost impossible. That's why you tend to think of these people as naturals. Even though they may be naturally comfortable talking with others, the actual skill of persuading must be learned just as the ins and outs of the product or service must be learned in order to succeed.

Talking Too Much and Not Listening Enough

Most people think that in order to persuade you have to be a good talker. A typical good talker thinks that he can tell the customer enough about the product that she will automatically buy. But the truth is just the opposite.

A good salesperson is just like a great detective: He asks questions, takes notes, and listens intently to the customer's spoken words, as well as to her body language.

In most cases, people who want to talk too much want to control the conversation and are more likely to be aggressive and pushy. Professional sales training involves more questioning techniques and intent listening techniques that it does speaking skills. It's not talking, but knowing the proper questions to ask, that leads to closing a sale. A salesperson who has been trained to ask questions *leads* the buyer down the path to the sale. He doesn't *push* her down that path.

When you're talking, you're only finding out what you already know.

Using Words That Kill Sales

In any presentation you make, your words paint a picture. And a few wrong word pictures can ruin the entire portrait you're trying to paint.

How many presentations do you suppose are made daily throughout the world in an effort to win approval but don't succeed just because of the sales-killing pictures that the presenter's words paint? For example, a salesperson may create an image of ownership of a used home to a young couple, then raise doubts and concerns by saying something about how home ownership helps develop do-it-yourself skills. The young couple may have no do-it-yourself skills and now fear expenses of upkeep for the property. Or, it may be as simple as referring to the "contract" they'll have to "sign" in order to have the product installed. Both of those terms can bring to mind negative images. *Contracts* are legally binding and should be avoided by the average person unless they have the advice of their attorney. Mom and Dad always warned you not to *sign* anything without thoroughly reading and understanding it. By using the wrong words, salespeople create negative pictures in the minds of the people they strive to serve — giving them more reasons not to go ahead than to get involved.

Not Knowing When to Close the Sale

Most customers who leave a place of business without owning a product or service are shrugged off by untrained salespeople as being "just lookers" or "be-backs" or any number of other euphemisms that hide the basic fact that the salesperson did not sell the customers. A professional salesperson, however, prefers to see such customers as what they really are: lost sales.

Ask for your prospect's decision when you recognize his *buying signs,* such as asking more questions or using language that shows an attitude of ownership, such as, "Yessir, that Van Gogh original certainly will enhance our living room." A key word to look for from the customer is the word *will* — as opposed to something more hesitant such as *might* or *would.* Buying signs also include asking for more details, wanting to see the instructions for how to operate your product, and asking financing questions. He may ask questions that refer to delivery, such as "Is it in stock?" or "Is there a delivery charge?" When you see such signs, *yes* is right around the corner.

Not Knowing How to Close the Sale

In many cases, all you have to do to close the sale is ask.

If a customer asks, "Do you have it in red?" and you say, "I believe I do have a red one," what do you gain? Nothing.

Why not ask this instead:

> If I have the red one, do you want to take it with you today, or shall I ship it?

Or this:

> Let me check on our color selection. By the way, would you like it gift-wrapped?

In other words, ask a question that moves the prospect into a position of having to make an ownership decision.

Lack of Sincerity

If you're trying to persuade someone else to adopt your point of view, to own your product, or to start an account with your service, you must first get him to see that you're talking with him for his benefit, not yours.

You have to get the dollar signs out of your eyes. Never let greed get in your way of doing what's right. If you don't sincerely believe that what you have to offer is good for the other party, yet you still try to convince him to own, one of two things will happen:

- ✔ He'll recognize your insincerity, not get involved with you, and tell at least 11 other people how terrible his experience with you was, thus ruining your reputation.

- ✔ If you do persuade him, and if what you're selling is *not* good for him, you are nothing more than a con artist and he'll take every measure possible to see that you are punished as one.

First and foremost when you're professionally selling or persuading others must be your sincere desire to serve others and help them get involved in something that's truly beneficial for them. Honesty and integrity are the key elements to every successful selling career.

Not Paying Enough Attention to Details

When you wing it on your presentation, skim over details, and ignore important cues from others, you also skim over big potential wins for yourself. Lost or misplaced orders, letters with typographical errors, and missed appointments or delivery dates all ruin your credibility with your prospects. They take away from the high level of competence professionals strive so hard to display. If your clients don't have the impression that you're doing your best for them, they'll find someone who will — maybe even someone else in your own office. Ooh, that would hurt, wouldn't it?

Letting Yourself Slump

If you could chart your daily activities, productivity, and winning presentations on a graph, what would it look like? Are you a bull in the first week of every month and a bear in the last? Most people have patterns to their selling cycles and efforts. If you watch your cycles carefully, you'll see a slump coming long before it hits and be able to correct the errors of your ways to even out your successes. Getting out of a slump takes a lot out of you, both mentally and physically. Why put yourself through hard times when you can keep on an even keel instead?

Not Keeping in Touch

Most people who switch from your product, service, or idea to another do so because you're being apathetic and someone else is paying them more attention. Someone else is keeping in contact on a regular basis. Someone else is making them feel important.

When all it takes is a few contacts by phone or mail to keep people doing business with you, why would you ever get so lazy as to let them go?

All you need to do is schedule two or three quick phone calls to say, "Diane, this is Tom from ABC Company. I'm just calling to see if you're still enjoying the increased productivity and cost savings with your new fax machine. If all is well, I won't keep you. I just wanted to touch base with you and thank you once again for your business." These words take about 12 seconds to say. And isn't a 12-second investment worth it if it keeps a customer?

Chapter 20

Ten Ways to Improve Your Selling

In This Chapter

▶ Recognizing the little things you can do to make a big difference in your sales

▶ Putting your clients first

*W*hen you attain a certain level of professionalism, you'll find that you're selling more. This increase in sales is a culmination of a lot of things: You're finding out how to find the best people to sell to, you're qualifying those people quickly and smoothly, you're recognizing buying signs, and, most importantly, you're enjoying all of it. Here's how you get started on your rise to that fun level of professionalism.

Prepare Yourself

Prepare yourself both mentally and physically for the challenge of persuading others. Dress appropriately. Give yourself an attitude check. Clear your mind of everything except what you need to think about for the presentation. Review any notes or information that may be vital within a few hours of meeting with your prospects. Doing your homework will help you pass the test every time.

Make a Good First Impression

You won't hear too many winning stories about people who overcame bad first impressions to go on to land a major account or persuade an important person to their way of thinking. Going in confident and handling the initial rapport-setting stage properly goes a long way toward winning.

Determine Quickly Whether You Can Help Your Prospect

By asking a few simple questions, you can determine quickly if the person you're meeting with is right for your offering. By doing this, you maximize your efforts by continuing presentations only with someone who can make a decision. Making a quick determination also shows the other person the courtesy of not wanting to waste her time with detailed information that's of no benefit to her.

Give Every Presentation 110 Percent

Never sell a prospect short. In doing so, you show a lack of respect toward him, which will eventually become clear — and when it does, you'll probably lose whatever you just gained. Don't take shortcuts — drop a step and you may lose a sale.

By making every presentation as though it's the most important thing in your life at that moment, you show the decision-makers that you're sincere about their needs and that they're important to you. Generally, people will *be* whatever you expect them to be, so expect your prospects to be vital to your overall success in life, and treat them with the proper amount of respect.

Address Concerns Completely

If and when your prospect voices a concern about something, don't ever glide over it. Let it stop you momentarily. Think about what was said and what you may have said or done to trigger the comment. Then carefully and thoughtfully address the concern: "What I understand from your comment, Mr. Friedman, is that you're concerned about the size of the trunk in your new vehicle, is that correct?" If it is, you'd better find out what Mr. Friedman expects to put into it. And if it's a critical point, find the right vehicle for him based on the trunk size.

Confirm Everything

Miscommunication costs people loads of money, time, and effort every year. Missed appointments, flights, or phone calls can destroy in minutes what may have taken months to build. Inattention to details, wrong orders, and wrong people handling important tasks takes its toll as well. Taking just a few seconds to confirm (and reconfirm) everything will bring you more success.

Ask for the Decision

You have nothing to lose by asking a prospect for a decision. If she's not ready to make a decision and that's what you find out by asking, great. But if she is ready and you don't ask, you lose everything. If you truly believe in the good of what you're doing, you should have no challenge asking the other party to commit her time, effort, or money to your cause or for your product or service.

Hesitation is an indication of doubt — and you should never be the one having doubts when you're in the persuader's seat.

Tell Your Prospects about Others

Few people want to be guinea pigs. They don't want to be the first to try something — they want to know that others have preceded them. By sharing experiences you've had with others just like them — others who bought your product, use your service, or are committed to the same project — you give your prospects permission to be like those others and invest in what you're selling. They'll recognize the landscape and understand that they're not going into uncharted waters. Overcoming their fears will take you far in convincing or persuading people, especially if you can use examples of people they know.

Work At It Constantly

The most successful people in the world rarely take time off from what they do that makes them successful. I'm not suggesting that you become a workaholic, but you can certainly think about new strategies, new ideas, and new people to contact even when you're lying on a beach in the Bahamas for a well-deserved rest. By living and breathing what you believe in the most, the best new ideas will be drawn to you. You'll constantly have your success antenna up and tuning in to the best information for you.

Be a Product of the Product

If you believe in what you're doing, you must *personally* be a part of it. If you're selling Fords, you don't want to be seen driving a Chevy. If you sell home-security systems, you'd better have one in your home. If you market freelance graphic design, your business cards had better be creative.

If you can talk personally about your own experiences with your product, service, or idea, you'll win over a lot more people than if you can't.

Chapter 21

Ten Ways to Master the Art of Selling

*I*f all you want to do is discover how the masters of sales accomplish what they accomplish, or to admire the top professionals for their incredible achievements, you would be able to do that by reading this book. But if you want to achieve that master's status in sales yourself, then you have to do more than a one-time read-through. *Selling For Dummies* is a reference tool for people like you — people who want to discover the basic techniques of sales and establish a strong foundation of good habits on which to build great careers. So don't save *Selling For Dummies* a space on the top shelf of your bookcase with all the other dust collectors. Keep it within easy reach so that when you need to refer back to one of its pearls of wisdom for encouragement, you won't have far to go.

In this chapter, you have ten choice bits of selling wisdom to return to over the years. Use this chapter as your road map to mastering the art of selling, as your ten easy steps to becoming a champion in all your future selling situations.

Adopt an Attitude of Discovery

Before you enter into any new experience, make sure you bring an attitude of positive anticipation and enthusiasm. What you discover in this book will be directly proportionate to the time you spend studying and practicing the techniques and suggestions offered in its pages. As a result of what you discover, your income will grow right along with the maturity of your knowledge in sales.

If you want to be a master of persuasion and selling, keep in mind that all masters were excellent students first. In addition to that general advice, I can give you three specific hints to make your experience more productive:

- **Discover your best learning environment.** Figure out where and how you can most effectively focus on learning. For some, sitting in the family room with the family as they watch football may be the appropriate place, while others require silence and isolation to best comprehend what they read. Whatever your personal needs, if you plan to study, memorize, and adopt the sales techniques in this book, you need to make the most of the time you set aside for that purpose.

- **Study at a pace that fits you.** Some people learn better when they read little bits of information and give themselves a chance to internalize what they've learned. Others like to take big clumps of information at one sitting so they can see the bigger picture and understand the full concept of what is being presented.

- **Limit your interruptions.** Set up a regular time to study, and let your family and friends know that you will be unavailable during this time. This may be a good time to let your answering machine screen your calls, as well as a good time to turn off your pager. If your concentration skills are anywhere near average, you need eight to ten minutes after being interrupted to regain the concentration level you were at before the interruption. That's why staying in the study mode when people interrupt you is so hard. Getting 30 minutes of uninterrupted reading and studying is better than patching together four or five interrupted periods to equal an hour of study time. If you can't hide out for a long period of time, cut your time or break it into two sessions in order to maximize your learning.

By analyzing your optimum learning patterns and working with them, your attitude about the material being studied will be positive. You'll be more relaxed and definitely learn at a faster pace.

Have Realistic Expectations

After reading this book and continuing to study sales, you should be able to use common sales techniques in unique ways. I'm not trying to turn out uniform little sales clones by having everyone who reads this book say the same words and practice the same methods at the expense of their own individuality.

If you take from this book ideas you had not thought of before and combine them with the sales experience you already have, you will lend to the selling situation a flavor all your own. But you need to *adapt* some of this material in order to create a genuine presentation and communicate naturally with the customer.

Be patient with yourself. Don't expect to be a winner 100 percent of the time. On the other hand, be honest with yourself and recognize times when inadequate knowledge or an inaccurate application of new selling techniques has kept you from giving your best performance.

Know your limitations, but don't be bound by them. Do what you know you should do, do it the best way you know how, and stay on the lookout for ways to improve your selling skills.

Keep an Open Mind and Welcome Change

Wanting to return to your cocoon when things get tough is only natural, especially if you experienced some success through your old methods. Nobody ever said that change would be easy. Think what those poor little caterpillars have to go through to become butterflies. If you have a difficult time with change, adopting some of the techniques in this book will require a supreme effort on your part. Most of the time, changing your old selling habits is harder than trying new ones.

One thing you can do to better accommodate change is to select only a few things to change at first. No matter how much you need to work on, you'll be too distracted and fragmented if you try to change everything at once. Changing all your selling skills at once is like going on a diet, starting an exercise program, and giving up smoking, all at the same time. Not an easy thing to do. For best results, choose two things to change that would significantly increase your sales. Work on those aspects of your performance until they become normal parts of your routine. When that happens, choose two more new selling skills to learn or change.

During this period of change or improvement, you'll go through the normal feelings of anxiety and confusion. Sometimes your presentation may be awkward or rough around the edges. But think of yourself as a diamond in the rough. As soon as you get some polish and put yourself in the proper setting, you'll outshine them all.

As you become a more effective salesperson, you'll find yourself applying what you've discovered to your personal relationships and decisions. But there's lag time between the practice and the perfection, so allow yourself and others time to adjust to the new and improved version of you. For example, if your goal requires you to work many more hours than you've ever worked, share this with your family and friends and ask them to help you to be your most productive self. Recognize that they may have as much difficulty adjusting to your changes as you yourself will have.

If you stay open-minded and flexible, you'll be able to welcome the changes necessary for a successful career in sales.

Rehearse, Perform, and Critique Your New Skills

After you internalize some of your new selling techniques, you need to practice them. At first, go over them by yourself until you feel confident enough to practice them in front of your family, friends, or peers who can give you some important pointers.

If you get advice from people you respect, listen! On the other hand, if you get unsolicited advice from people you don't respect, don't let them share in your learning experience: Their responses may damage your delicate psyche.

When you've rehearsed so much that the words are permanently etched on your brain, it's time for your opening night performance. Performing new selling skills and concepts in front of strangers who may recognize your twitching eye and sweaty palms as lack of polish is scary. Give yourself permission to be a rookie, but be sure to follow the rookie rules:

- ✔ Give yourself many, many opportunities to perfect your new selling techniques.

- ✔ When you look back, feed the positive — celebrate all the things you did right.

- ✔ Hold on to your rookie enthusiasm even when you become a polished sales professional.

Honestly critique your performance of your new skills. At this point, you need to look with a critical but fair eye. You'll be able to do this only after you have performed your new skills for an extended period of time and are able to see measurable increases in your sales. You need to have a tool by which to measure your success. For example, if you've been in sales for a while but haven't been able to reach the level of success you'd hoped for, you may want to jot down your sales ratios and compare the old with the new. Seeing positive results gives you something tangible to encourage a continued pattern of improvement.

If a specific stumbling block keeps inhibiting your sales growth, ask another sales professional whom you respect for some advice. Sometimes taking such a person along on a presentation or taping a meeting and critiquing it together can be a big help. In fact, you may be surprised to review a taped presentation and discover all the things you could have done differently. Critiquing a taped presentation gives you some distance from the excitement and anxiety of the initial meeting and allows you to look at your performance more objectively. Some tapes hold great entertainment value. You'll be amazed at how many things you don't remember and how many things you'd swear you never did or said — it's a real eye-opener.

Personalize Your New Sales Skills

When you memorize concepts and specific words — and sometimes you must memorize word for word — look for ways to make the words you memorize reflect your personality. Practice how you will say them. Think about how you will carry yourself, how you will stand or sit when you utter those words. Use your sense of humor, your previous knowledge, and your natural speech and mannerisms to make your new selling skills sound spontaneous.

The worst thing you can do is memorize phrases and then shut off your personality and resort to a robot imitation whenever you get desperate. The thing to remember as you sell is to be genuine and personable. Being yourself is almost impossible to do if you haven't made the concepts you've learned uniquely yours by wrapping them in your own words and actions. The last thing you want your clients to feel is that they're being given a canned presentation.

Be Disciplined

If you crave the financial and personal freedom that a successful sales career can provide, you have to be willing to go the extra mile. If that means working on a Friday night when all your friends are at an office party, then so be it! If that means getting up hours earlier each morning until you master your new skills, then that's what you must do! If that means no more two-hour lunches or lazy afternoons for a while, then make the sacrifice!

Be a self-disciplined self-starter, and eventually you'll reap rewards.

One of the greatest pitfalls of great success in a short period of time is a failure to *continue* to hustle. People have a tendency to want to rest on their laurels when they know they're good. Slowing down after achieving success quickly is a dangerous mistake. The fact that you've tasted some success doesn't mean that you can stop hustling and fall back into the same old methods that crippled your sales career.

Stay on your feet and run the race to the finish. Don't allow yourself the luxury of self-doubts or overconfidence. They are production killers. The real trick is to remain balanced during your successes. Don't let increased sales go to your head or repeated rejection beat you down. Although it can be almost impossible at times, always strive to keep your activities and attitudes balanced.

Evaluate the Results

Accurately evaluating the results you're getting with your newfound selling skills is difficult if you don't know what your sales results were before you changed. Sure, you'll have a hunch about how things are going, but often you can't trust these feelings. For example, when you're discouraged, you tend to see your accomplishments unfavorably. During such times, your successes diminish, and you can easily feed the negative until it grows into an unconquerable monster. On the other hand, on days when you're overly optimistic, you may conveniently blame a bungled presentation or the lack of knowledge on the customer and fail to take the necessary steps for self-improvement.

When you evaluate the results of your efforts, avoid comparing your progress to someone else's. Even if the salesperson has received the same training and has read the same books as you, everyone learns differently. Some learn more quickly than others yet can't retain the information for long. Others learn slowly and give the appearance of having fallen behind, when actually they've internalized the information and will receive longer-lasting rewards for their efforts.

Keep a Success Journal

Keep what I call a *success journal* to monitor your performance. By recording specific instances and details of when you successfully used new selling techniques, you not only immediately reinforce the benefits to your career, but more important, when you need encouragement you also can review your journal and relive a positive selling experience. Do it. You'll be surprised at what a great motivational tool a success journal can be.

When you review your success journal, compare what you did right in a given situation to what you did when you did not get the sale. When you make such a comparison, the reasons for not getting the sale should become obvious to you. By comparing an unsuccessful experience to a successful one, you see what you left out or skimmed over and why you failed to convince the customer of the benefits of your offering.

When such negatives occur, you need to adjust your presentation or sales techniques. And the only way you can accurately adjust is to write down your achievements and recognize a good model for a successful sale. After you have contemplated what you need to do to improve your selling, the next step is to just do it.

If you're going to play the "if only" game, then be a finisher. It's okay to ponder what could have been (for example, "If only I had asked more questions . . ." or "If only I had been able to answer the client's objections with more skill . . ."). The trouble with playing "if only," though, is that many times you're defeated before you finish.

After you think about all the *if only*s, you must envision yourself as that master of sales and then act on your visions. "If only" is a game of recognizing areas that need improvement. After you recognize those areas, you need to take action and turn your *If only* into *Because I:*

> "If only I had asked more questions" becomes "Because I asked more questions, I closed the sale."

> "If only I had been able to answer the client's objections with more skill" becomes "Because I successfully answered the client's objections, she was able to benefit by owning my offering."

By monitoring and adjusting your new selling skills, you continue to increase your sales ratios. Be diligent and persistent in your self-evaluation, though. Don't just look at your sales once a year and make bold promises about how you'll do things differently at some unspecified future date. Be meticulous in your search for excellence and be specific in your plans for improvement.

How effective can a statement like "Next year I want to do a bigger volume of business" really be? Wouldn't the following be much clearer and more productive:

> Beginning January 1, I will spend two hours more a day prospecting and increase my face-to-face selling by 20 percent. In the process, I will increase my sales volume by 5 percent.

This revised statement gives you a more distinct monthly, weekly, and daily activity schedule to follow in order for you to improve.

Learn from Every Selling Situation

You'll be surprised at how many unexpected selling situations you notice when you keep your eyes and ears open. You'll soon see in almost every situation an opportunity for someone to sell. Not only will you be alert to the selling situation, but you'll also start to critique the selling skills used in situations that surround you on a daily basis. When you witness a good job of selling, make a note of it in your success journal. When a master sells you on something, jot down the superior job she did in selling you her offering. Make specific notes of things she did that especially impressed or influenced you.

To observe all this selling going on around you, you have to stop, listen, and take time to reflect on the situation. If you are not a party to the sale, being an observer is, of course, easier. Not being a party to the sale gives you the distance to recognize some of the familiar selling techniques being used. But that distance also enables you to observe the expressions and actions of the other party as a result of these selling methods being used.

You may see a salesperson use a common technique with a personal twist — and you realize that the strategy you previously thought would not work for you most certainly will if you give it your own personal twist. Creativity is the name of the game in many selling situations. Don't let yourself become trapped into one single mode of thinking or one way of looking at things. If you can be flexible, almost anything is possible.

And if you're one who learns by experience, isn't it better to learn from others' mistakes than from your own? Their loss becomes your gain. And the experience you observe doesn't always have to be positive in order to have a positive effect on your selling career. Sometimes the negative lessons have a stronger impact than those that look smooth and effortless.

Make a Commitment

Think of every technique you read in this book as one link in the chain of your success in sales. If you have a weak chain, then you may need to review a chapter or two to build, say, your presentation or prospecting skills. If you don't go back and make the weak link stronger, your career chain will never carry the weight it needs to carry in order to haul you up to top-producer status.

When you find yourself in the fortunate position of top dog, champion salesperson, you'll probably get asked to teach some of what you know to others. The class you teach can be a training class for newcomers to your office. It can be a back-to-the-basics program for seasoned salespeople who have allowed their focus to blur. It can be as simple as letting your children know what gets results and what doesn't.

If you don't already know it, you'll relearn one *big* lesson every time you teach: When you teach, you learn. By teaching your techniques to others, you clarify your own skills and reinforce your knowledge of what makes an effective salesperson. Teachers are students, too. If you can remain flexible — sometimes the teacher, sometimes the student — the opportunity to learn in diverse situations will constantly present itself and you'll be there to learn from the experience.

This business of getting what you want cannot be a totally selfish act, though. Your selling success increases at a significant pace when your attention to serve your clients and satisfy their needs is number one on your list. Even though you want to make more profit and more sales, remember that you're most apt to accomplish these goals only when you put your customers first.

When your clients know that you're not concerned with being the star, but that you are putting their needs before your own, they will forgive some awkwardness or lack of product knowledge. When they know your integrity and honesty, most customers go the extra mile with you to make your meetings mutually beneficial. People are the key to your sales success.

At the risk of sounding repetitious, let me say that again:

People are the key to your sales success.

Treat customers with great sensitivity and unflagging respect. Remember this fundamental principle and, before you know it, all the techniques you've mastered will naturally improve your ability to sell with the best of the best.

Chapter 22

Ten Characteristics of Professional Persuaders

*I*n analyzing people who are most successful at persuading, convincing, or selling others on their ideas, products, or services, I've found ten characteristics that appear to be common among them. Read through this list of ten and see how many apply to you now. If you don't find these characteristics in your current bag of traits, consider adopting them in order to hear more *yes*es in your life.

A Burning Desire to Prove Something to Someone

A professional persuader has a strong reason for wanting to succeed.

ANECDOTE

My reason was to prove myself to my parents. I quit college after 90 days, knowing that formal education wasn't for me. My parents had high hopes for me and were quite disappointed, resigning themselves to accepting my decision. My dad told me, "Your mother and I will always love you, even though you'll never amount to anything." That was my first motivational talk, and it kindled my desire to become the best and prove something to my parents.

An Interest in Others

Professional persuaders are truly interested in other people and in making those people's lives better. They know how to draw others out, making them feel important and getting to know their prospects well enough to determine how they can help.

Confidence and Strength

Professional persuaders radiate confidence and strength in the way they walk and talk and in their overall presence. They have good posture. They wear their clothing well. They use positive body language cues to let others read their competence level.

Empathy for the People They Serve

Professional persuaders balance their own personal egos and their need for success with warmth and sincerity. Their sincere interest in their prospects' happiness creates a bond of trust and openness that allows them to serve not only their prospects but their prospects' friends, relatives, and acquaintances.

A Focus on Goals

Professional persuaders have set their goals and put them in writing. They know exactly what they're striving for and when they expect to accomplish it. Knowing how their future will look helps them keep focused on doing what is productive today.

An Ability to Stick to Their Daily Plans

Having set goals for what they want to accomplish each day allows professional persuaders to plan their time most effectively to take steps toward achieving those goals. They rely on proven systems for planning their time and have discovered effective time-management strategies.

Enthusiasm through Difficult Situations

Professional persuaders know the past can't be changed and the future can't be controlled, so they live for today, doing the best they can to make each day a day of accomplishment and fulfillment.

A Positive Attitude

Professional persuaders keep themselves in a positive shell and avoid jealousy, gossip, anger, or negative thinking. They don't allow negativity to steal their energy or tempt them to stray from their chosen course.

An Understanding That People Come Before Money

Professional persuaders love people and use money instead of loving money and using people. They understand the old adages that you have to spend money to make money and that persuasion is a people business. And they invest wisely in things for the good of the people they serve.

An Investment in Their Minds

Professional persuaders are lifelong learners. Congratulations! I know you have this trait simply because you're reading this page. Set a goal to be a lifelong learner, and you'll never have a dull moment. Plus, you'll achieve tremendous success in whatever you set your mind to studying!

Chapter 23

Ten Advanced Closes

W hen you're ready to move ahead in your selling strategies, here are some additional closing stories that have proven successful for myself and for others in sales.

The Wish-Ida Close

When you know what you're offering is truly good for your prospective client, and your prospect has agreed but just doesn't seem to want to make a decision, the wish-ida closing story is perfect. It's lighthearted, yet it makes a valid point:

> Everyone's a member of the Wish-Ida Club. Wish Ida bought real estate in Arizona 15 years ago. Wish Ida invested in some stock 20 years ago so I'd be rich today. Wish Ida grabbed a chance to gain an exclusive advantage. Wouldn't it be great to get rid of at least one Wish Ida by saying yes to something you really want?

The Business-Productivity Close

When marketing products or services to businesses, the business's main concern is always going to be the bottom line and whether your product or service makes or saves them money. If your product does not clearly fall into one of those categories, the business productivity close helps the prospect view the decision from a different perspective — that of happier employees:

What I am offering is not just a product/service. It's a boost in employee morale. Haven't you noticed that anything new increases job interest and excitement in your employees? Excitement increases morale. Morale increases productivity, and what is productivity worth?

The Best-Things-in-Life Close

Everyone wants to have the best things in life. Everyone wants to believe that he has made some of the best decisions when considering major purchases or investments. The best-things-in-life close gets the prospect's mind off the money objection and onto the enjoyment of benefits, which is what owner-ship is really all about:

Isn't it true that the only time you have ever really benefited from anything in your life has been when you said yes instead of no? You said yes to your marriage. (*Optional:* And I can see how happy you are.) You said yes to your job, your home, your car — all the things that I'm sure you enjoy. You see, when you say yes to me, it's not really *me* you are saying yes to, but all the benefits that we offer, and those are the things you really want for your family, don't you agree?

The No Close

When you've given your best presentation and your prospect still says "No," you have little to lose by saying these words and putting your shoes on your prospect's feet. ***Note:*** You must speak these words with sincerity and empa-thy for your prospect's situation.

Mr. Johnson, there are many salespeople in the world and they all have opportunities that they're confident are good for you. And they have persuasive reasons for you to invest with them, haven't they? You, of course, can say no to any or all of them, can't you? You see, as a professional with ABC Company, my experience has taught me an overwhelming truth. No one can say no to me. All he can say no to is himself and his future _____. Tell me, how can I accept this kind of no? In fact, if you were me, would you let Mr. Johnson say no to anything so critical to his _____?

The Lost-Sale Close

If you've done everything and your prospect still doesn't go ahead, admit defeat. Pack up your visual aids and prepare to head for the door. Then, use the lost-sale close like a good little Columbo fan. More often than not, it reopens conversation enough that your prospect will give you something to grasp onto to tell you if he may say yes.

Pardon me, Mr. Johnson. Before I leave, may I apologize for not doing my job today? You see, if I had not been inept, I would have said the things necessary to convince you of the value of my product. Because I didn't, you and your company will not be enjoying the benefits of our product and service and, believe me, I am truly sorry. Mr. Johnson, I believe in my product and earn a living helping people own it. So that I don't make the same mistake again, will you please tell me what I did wrong?

The My-Dear-Old-Mother Close

I would never tell you to tell your prospects anything that's untrue, so the next time you talk to your mother or grandmother or someone else's mother, ask her if she's ever been in a situation in which silence means consent. If she has, ask her to say those words to you. Now you can honestly use that line as a close. If she hasn't heard of such a situation, simply ask if she believes it can happen.

This technique can be your salvation when you find yourself involved in a series of silences as you roll from close to close with the same prospect.

If you have a clever way to break tension, pressure turns into humor — explosive laughter sometimes. Lots of people can handle pressure, but laughter will pop them wide open. So when the pressure has been on for several seconds after your last close and it's getting heavy in the room, suddenly grin from ear to ear and say, "My dear old grandmother once said, 'Silence means consent.' Was she right?"

The Law-of-Ten Close

This close works especially well for intangibles such as financial services, insurance, or education. It's also useful for large-ticket items such as real estate or stocks — items that appreciate in value. If the person is not totally a wish-ida person (covered earlier in this chapter), something in her life has appreciated in value. Here's how to use it:

CHAMPION STRATEGY #1

> Ms. Garcia, I've found over the years that a good test of the value of something is to determine whether it will stand the test of ten-times. For example, you may have invested in a home, car, clothes, jewelry, or something that gave you great pleasure. But, after you owned it for a while, could you answer this question positively: "Would I now be willing to pay ten times more for it than I did?" In other words, has it given you that much pleasure, increased mental attitude, or income?
>
> If you paid for some advice that greatly improved your health, it was probably worth more than you paid for it. If you received some information that allowed you to have a life-changing experience or increase in income or self-image, it was worth more than you paid for it. There are a lot of things in our lives that I think you would have paid ten times more for, considering what they've done for you.
>
> Ms. Garcia, step with me into the future. Ten years from now, will today's investment be worth more or less to you than you'll be investing in it today?

The Buyer's-Remorse Close

When people are making major decisions, you can expect them to have second thoughts about things after the decision is made. That's why so many contractual agreements for large-ticket items have a 72-hour clause that allows buyers to change their minds. Champions understand this and figure out how to address the issue before they leave a new client with these words:

> John, Mary, I feel good about the decision you have made tonight to get involved with _____. I can tell you're both excited and somewhat relieved. From time to time, I have had people just like you who were positive about the decision they had made until they shared it with a friend or relative. The well-meaning friend or relative, not understanding all the facts and maybe even being a little envious, would discourage them from their decision for one reason or another. John, Mary, please don't let this happen to you. In fact, if you think you may change your mind, please tell me now.

The It's-Not-in-the-Budget Close

Business people say "it's not in the budget" as a standard line to get rid of average salespeople. Why? Because that line *works* with average salespeople. Professionals are businesspeople themselves, and they understand the value of having and managing a budget. They also know that the budget is little more than a tool and it's not carved in stone. But if the product or service you're offering has enough value, most companies will find a way to loosen up that budget or take steps to own it. These words will often cause the business owner to give you the real reason he isn't going ahead with your product or service — and then you can continue your selling cycle in the appropriate manner.

> I can understand that, Jim. That's why I contacted you in the first place. I'm fully aware of the fact that every well-managed business controls the flow of its money with a carefully planned budget. The budget is a necessary tool for every company to give direction to its goals. However, the tool itself doesn't dictate how the company is run. It must be flexible. You, as the controller of that budget, retain for yourself the right to flex that budget in the best interest of the company's financial present and competitive future, don't you? What we have been examining here today is a system that will allow your company an immediate and continuing competitive edge. Tell me, under these conditions, will your budget flex or will it dictate your actions?

The Take-It-Away Close

Some people won't want to make a decision on ownership simply because they feel they can make the decision at any time. And that may be the case, unless you're working on a special offer or limited quantity of product. No one wants to be thought of as not good enough for something. As a child, if you knew you could play ball, but someone said you may not be good enough for the team, you probably wanted to be on the team more than ever. By subtly inferring that you have to see if your prospect qualifies before she can own the product, she may try awfully hard to get it. This works especially well on products that involve financing or insurance (which may require the client to meet a certain health standard).

Chapter 24

Ten of the Best Web Sites for Sales Professionals

▶ Knowing where to turn for the latest and greatest sales information online

▶ Researching your prospective clients on the Internet

▶ Being able to converse with your clients on topics that interest them

I'm so happy you turned to this chapter. If you're new to the Internet, check these sites out early in your surfing days. If you've been online for a while, you may have already found the benefits offered by these businesses. If not, check them out and consider adding them to your Favorites list in your Web browser.

Because I'm a continual student of this ever-evolving technological resource, if you find great sites *specifically for sales professionals* that I don't list here, send them to me at info@tomhopkins.com. If I agree with your evaluation, I'll be happy to share those sites with my students as well.

Tom Hopkins International

www.tomhopkins.com

If I don't believe that my own site is helpful to salespeople, I shouldn't be writing this book. My site includes many free resources for salespeople, including an e-mail newsletter, articles on particular selling-related situations, a listing of my seminar schedule (in case you'd like to train with me live and in person), and links to other sites that offer excellent information and/or resources. My entire catalog of sales-training products is also available for your perusal. How do you learn best: through CD, audiocassette, printed book, online training, live seminar, or video? I have them all.

Hungry Minds

www.hungryminds.com

Hungry Minds is my publisher. I love these guys! This Web site is where complicated subjects become simple, where the book meets the Web, where your computer is your classroom, where learning is easier than ever. Here's especially good advice: If your biggest client is a fan of football and you're not, brush up on the subject with a copy of *Football For Dummies*. Hungry Minds offers a wide array of topics in the *For Dummies* series, simplified to quickly enable you to hold a valid conversation on any subject with your clients.

WellConnected

www.wellconn.com

The folks at WellConnected have made getting into the thank-you habit very easy for sales professionals. Thank-you notes and specialty gifts to clients can help you grow your business to a 100-percent referral business. It did mine. Now, you can use the same plan I did — online. Build one-to-one relationships stronger than ever with the great thank-you notes and gifts available from this site.

Toastmasters International

www.toastmasters.org

Whether you're a professional, student, stay-at-home parent, or retiree, Toastmasters is the best way to improve your communication skills. Toastmasters can help you lose the fear of public speaking and gain skills that will help you be more successful in whatever path you choose. You'll be a better listener. You'll easily lead teams and conduct meetings. You'll comfortably give and receive constructive evaluation. You already have some or all of these skills, but in Toastmasters, you will enhance them.

Corpedia Education

www.corpedia.com

This site is where to go if you need education that is relevant to the corporate world. Courses are available from such experts as Peter Drucker, Tom Peters, and yours truly, to name a few. Ready-made courses may be just what you need. Or your company may want to consider customizing some of the courses to your particular needs. This company is your "corporate encyclopedia" of reference on the best sales and management information available today.

infoUSA.com

www.infousa.com

Lists galore! Here you will find information on 200 million consumers and over 12 million businesses. You can search by business type. You can search for Baby Boomers with high incomes in your area. The information comes from a wide range of resources and includes details sales professionals like to know, such as contact names and numbers of employees, along with the usual address and phone information.

Hoover's Online

www.hooversonline.com

This Web site has information on more than 300 industries. Find companies not just by what they're named, but also by what they do, where they're based, or how they're structured. Find out about current and future trends, identify key players, and explore industry links. Their Career Development section includes job postings, a training center to help you update your skills, and a salary comparison to see how your earnings rank among other sales professionals. You can even book your business travel here.

Ziglar Training Systems

www.zigziglar.com

Besides being a dear friend, Zig is one of the most powerful speakers I've ever seen. Since 1970, he has traveled over five million miles across the world delivering powerful life-improvement messages, cultivating the energy of change. His sales strategies are based on sound, ethical principles of helping others. I strongly recommend that anyone serious about their selling career invest time and effort in getting to know Zig and his message. Check out Zig's book *Success For Dummies* (published by Hungry Minds, Inc.), too.

Selling Power Magazine

www.sellingpower.com

This is the Web site of the best periodical for salespeople — bar none. This publication covers the ins and outs of the real world of selling. The one you and I are in every day. Visit their site. Subscribe to the free newsletter, and consider rewarding yourself with a subscription to the monthly print magazine. You'll find fantastic ideas for strategies and tactics to help you get and keep the edge on your competition.

salesforce.com

www.salesforce.com

Salesforce.com provides online Customer Relationship Management that immediately helps your company acquire and retain customers. This is one of the finest online contact management software programs available. The program is available from any Web browser, is easy to use, and makes sharing information across your company simple. No hardware or software is required.

Appendix

Recommended Resources

- -

*I*n this appendix, I list books, videos, and audios, that I have read, listened to, or written — ones that I believe are useful to anyone wanting a balanced and successful life. I provide resources on selling careers, selling real estate, and sales management as well, in case you want more information on selling in the traditional sense. Finally, you'll also find Web sites to visit for more information. The information is divided into categories based on the realm of your life it relates to — physical, emotional, and so on.

Each area of your life affects the others. If you are physically, emotionally, or spiritually out of balance, your career and financial life will be, too.

Physical

Investing a lot of time getting wealthy through providing service to others isn't wise if you lose your health along the way. I've known a lot of unhealthy wealthy people who would give all the money they have to get their health back. Don't be like that. By taking good care of yourself, you'll have more strength and stamina for the trenches.

- ✔ *Fitness For Dummies,* **2nd Edition, by Suzanne Schlosberg and Liz Neporent (published by Hungry Minds, Inc.).** This book tells you everything you need to know about staying fit in the same easy-to-understand, no-nonsense way as the other books in the *For Dummies* series.

- ✔ *Fit for Life II: Living Health,* **by Harvey Diamond.** Harvey Diamond has a long-standing track record for helping people create healthy lifestyles, and this book is a great resource if you're looking to do that in your own life.

- ✔ *The Ultimate Fit or Fat,* **by Covert Bailey.** Talk about simplification. After you read this book, Bailey's Target Diet will stick in your mind and you'll have the knowledge of how to make healthy eating choices with you always.

- ✔ *The McDougall Program: Twelve Days to Dynamic Health,* **by John A. McDougall, M.D.** You have to start somewhere. If all you're willing to commit is 12 days, this is the book to work with. If, after those 12 days, you aren't totally committed to living healthier, I'll be quite surprised.

- ✔ *The Turning Point Library,* **by Ron Fronk.** With Ron Fronk's guidance, you'll find yourself paying closer attention to balance in your life and how powerful gentle exercise can be. Call 623-551-0153 to order these audiocassettes.

- ✔ *The Corporate Athlete: How to Achieve Maximal Performance in Business and Life,* **by Jack Groeppel.** Using this book, consider what you would do to develop a healthy business. Then use those ideas to improve your own health.

Emotional

Understanding the importance of *physical* health is easy, but too often I find that my students ignore the value of *emotional* health. Commit some of your study time to resources such as these and you'll be surprised at how strong you can become.

- ✔ *Success For Dummies,* **by Zig Ziglar (published by Hungry Minds, Inc.).** Zig is my dear friend, and he has inspired millions, including myself, to seek success through service to others. This book is an excellent read!

- ✔ *Time Management For Dummies,* **2nd Edition, by Jeffrey J. Mayer (published by Hungry Minds, Inc.).** When you understand and take action to control the time you have, you become more powerful emotionally. Use the simple strategies in this book to your benefit.

- ✔ *Creating a Lifestyle You Can Live With,* **by Ron L. Fronk.** This book includes some very simple, no-nonsense ideas for de-stressing your life and improving your overall health.

- ✔ *The Greatest Salesman in the World,* **by Og Mandino.** This book is a true classic that will help you find the true meaning of giving service to others.

- ✔ *How to Win Friends and Influence People,* **by Dale Carnegie.** This book is another classic! A must for anyone who wants to be successful in life.

- ✔ *The Official Guide to Success,* **by Tom Hopkins.** This series of books and tapes is the culmination of my very own personal development journey early in my career. The key points covered are those that made the greatest impact on my personal success.

- ✔ *Dream Power,* **by Rudy Ruettiger.** With this audiocassette, you can learn to master the power of your dreams to help you achieve the success you desire. Call 702-263-0170 to order.

- ✔ *The Art of the Fresh Start,* **by Glenna Salsbury.** It's bound to happen: At some point in your life you will find yourself in uncharted waters — at least uncharted for you. In this book, Glenna offers great wisdom in helping you find your way to personal happiness.

Spirituality/Relationships

My own spiritual journey has taken me along a Christian path. Therefore, the books I recommend here represent my own personal beliefs — but I would never force them on anyone. However, if you are a fellow seeker, the following should prove themselves excellent guides.

If you are of a different spiritual persuasion, seek out the most recommended resources in your faith and commit to further study and spiritual development.

- ✔ *The Bible.* Profound thoughts for everyone for all times.

- ✔ *Effective Prayer Life,* **by Chuck Smith.** This books is a sensible and easy-to-apply guide to a proper dynamic prayer life. Chuck is truly one of the great men of God of our time.

- ✔ *Love for a Lifetime: Building a Marriage That Will Go the Distance,* **by James C. Dobson.** Dobson is one of the most prolific authors on relationships, and this book is important for married couples or for those looking for a long-term, lasting love relationship.

- ✔ *More Than a Carpenter,* **by Josh McDowell.** This book is truly one of the most inspiring presentations of the Gospel of Jesus Christ and one of the most comprehensive presentations on how to have a personal relationship with God.

- ✔ *Promises: A Daily Guide to Supernatural Living,* **by Bill Bright.** This book boils down what every Christian needs to know that is in the *Bible* regarding promises. Bill Bright brings a very easy and understandable style to the subject.

- ✔ *Left Behind* **series, by Tim LaHaye and Jerry B. Jenkins.** This entire series will grab you from the moment you begin. It is a no-punches-pulled story that intertwines scripture and the life in which we live in a very unveiling and exciting series. Every book is a page turner.

- ✔ *Meditations for the Road Warrior,* **by Mark Sanborn and Terry L. Paulson.** This is a fun, stimulating book designed for those people who live from city to city as part of their work. A must-have for all business travelers.

- ✔ **Marriage Matters (**`www.marriagematters.com`**).** Wise advice online. This Web site is easily searchable and updated regularly.

Financial

Don't become a success and risk losing it all. As you go about investing, find out how money works and whom to trust in helping you manage it.

- *Personal Finance For Dummies,* **3rd Edition, by Eric Tyson (published by Hungry Minds, Inc.).** This book is a great resource for all matters financial. If you're looking for a book that demystifies the world of finance and puts it into terms that are easy to understand, this is the book for you.

- *The Richest Man in Babylon,* **by George S. Clason.** This book is an ever-so-simple lesson in wise money management that has made wealthy people out of many.

- *Seven Strategies for Wealth and Happiness,* **by Jim Rohn.** This book offers a philosophical approach for taking into consideration how you want to manage your financial rewards.

- *Financial Peace,* **by Dave Ramsey.** With the advice Dave offers in this book, the phrase *financial peace* will no longer be an oxymoron for you.

Selling

Early in my career, it was suggested that I work on building my own reference library of books and recordings that would help me achieve, not only in sales, but in other areas where selling skills apply. In this list, I include some wonderful reference tools for anyone in any field of selling.

My introduction to the profession of selling was in the field of real estate, so I have a soft spot in my heart for those in that profession today. For this reason, you'll see references here that are specific to the real estate industry.

- *Sales Closing For Dummies,* **by Tom Hopkins (published by Hungry Minds, Inc.).** If the closing step is ever a little rough for you, this is the reference guide you'll want to keep on your desk, in your car, or in your briefcase.

- *Sales Prospecting For Dummies,* **by Tom Hopkins (published by Hungry Minds, Inc.).** This book is filled with ideas for where to find your next clients and how to approach them most effectively.

- *How to List and Sell Real Estate in the 21st Century,* **by Danielle Kennedy.** Danielle Kennedy is my go-to person for any information regarding the current practices and strategies in the field of real estate.

- *How to Master the Art of Listing and Selling Real Estate,* **by Tom Hopkins.** From my early days of selling . . . these are the exact strategies and words I used to make real estate sales records that still stand today.

- *How to Master the Art of Selling,* **by Tom Hopkins.** Find out how to approach, qualify, present, and close sales. This reference book is full of exact words to use that are psychologically sound.

- *See You at the Top,* **by Zig Ziglar.** Zig is one of the most respected trainers of our time. His advice in this book is bound to take you to the top — if you just apply it.

- ✔ *Swim with the Sharks without Being Eaten Alive: Outsell, Outmanage, Outmotivate, and Outnegotiate Your Competition,* **by Harvey McKay.** This book provides excellent information on what you should know about your clients in order to build long-term relationships and a sound referral base.

- ✔ *Your Guide To Greatness in Sales: How to Become a Complete Salesperson,* **by Tom Hopkins.** This book is about the other side of sales — what you'll encounter when seeking a sales position, fellow salespeople, managers, and how to work most effectively in many of the most common situations.

- ✔ *Zig Ziglar's Secrets of Closing the Sale,* **by Zig Ziglar.** The fact that Zig knows how to close sales is no secret. Discover his proven-effective strategies and watch your sales soar.

Sales Management

When I moved into sales management, I found there was very little training available. It was just expected that because I was good at selling I'd be good at managing others who sold. Believe me, the transition wasn't very smooth. However, I learned some powerful lessons along the way. One was to keep my eye out for good, solid sales management training for others who may end up in the same situation in which I found myself. This list is a great starting point for anyone new to management or thinking about going into management.

- ✔ *The One Minute Manager,* **by Kenneth Blanchard and Spencer Johnson.** Long touted as the best, simple book for how to manage others.

- ✔ *Successful Strategies for Sales Managers,* **by Floyd Wickman.** In this book, Floyd tells you, from personal experience, how to best manage and pull together your team of sales professionals.

- ✔ **Corpedia Education (**www.corpedia.com**).** This Web site offers online training courses by Peter Drucker that are excellent for managers. Learn at your own pace. Watch for my sales courses there, too.

- ✔ *Management Challenges for the 21st Century,* **by Peter F. Drucker.** There is no one who can compare with Peter Drucker when it comes to understanding the evolution of business to what it has become today. An excellent read.

- ✔ *How to Gain, Train, and Maintain a Dynamic Sales Force,* **by Tom Hopkins.** Discover the simple, yet effective, strategies I employed during my days as a sales manager. This audio program covers hiring, getting your people involved in training, and handling counseling and termination situations with ease.

Index